£22.50

56D

UNEMPLOYMENT IN THE UK

UNEMPLOYMENT IN THE UK

Politics and Policies

Jeremy Moon
Department of Politics,
University of Western Australia
and
J. J. Richardson
Department of Politics,
University of Strathclyde

Gower

Published by
Gower Publishing Company Limited,
Gower House,
Croft Road,
Aldershot,
Hants GU11 3HR,
England

Gower Publishing Company,
Old Post Road,
Brookfield,
Vermont 05036,
U.S.A.

British Library Cataloguing in Publication Data

Moon, Jeremy
Unemployment in the U.K.: politics and policies.
1. Unemployment—Government policy—Great Britain
I. Title   II. Richardson, J. J.
331.13'7941   HD5765.A6

Library of Congress Cataloging in Publication Data

Moon, Jeremy, 1955–
Unemployment in the UK.
Bibliography: p.
1. Unemployment—Great Britain.
2. Unemployment—Government policy—Great Britain.
3. Great Britain—Full employment policies.
I. Richardson, J. J. (Jeremy John)   II. Title.
HD5765.A6M66 1985   331.13'7941   85-5515

ISBN 0 566 00892 0 (cased)
    0 566 00893 9 (paper)

Typeset by Action Typesetting of Gloucester,
Printed in Great Britain by Biddles Ltd, Guildford, Surrey

Contents

Tables

Figures

Preface

Our mutual interest in the political management of high unemployment began – initially independently – at the University of Keele during 1981. On moving to the University of Strathclyde in 1982 we directed more concentrated attention to various aspects of the question, with financial support from the University and from the Leverhulme Trust.

The views thus constitute the fruits of about three years' work, during which time we have presented papers on the subject to the Political Studies Association, the European Consortium for Political Research, and the ESRC panel on Employment and Unemployment, and had the benefit of useful critical comment. We are also grateful to the many who have given us the benefit of their experience working in the field, whether for central or local government, business, labour or voluntary organisations, and to Frank Kirwan and Douglas Webber (both of the University of Strathclyde) who each commented upon earlier drafts of chapters. Responsibility for the final package lies, of course, with us.

Finally, thanks are due to our secretaries who typed the manuscript: Margaret Totterdell, Janet Lace and Grace Hunter and to Philippa Moon for compiling the index.

Jeremy Moon and
J. J. Richardson
Glasgow, June 1984

Note

The economic environment in which the unemployment issue exists has inevitably changed somewhat since the completion of our manuscript. Then the international value of the pound was widely considered as high, but more recently its value has plummetted. Whether the improved export opportunities presented, or the depressive effects of higher interest rates will have the greatest impact on British industry and employment prospects remains to be seen. The political environment has also changed, notably with the ending of the miners' strike which may give greater opportunity for the Opposition to exploit the unemployment issue, focussing public attention on the inadequacies of government policies in the field. Although we do not at present know the Chancellor's mind, it seems likely that he will make some attempt to be seen to be doing something about jobs in his 1985 budget. Since we completed the manuscript some more up to date economic indicators have become available and we have done our best to include these where appropriate.

One thing has not changed however: the continued upward trend in the underlying unemployment rate.

Glasgow, March 1985

Introduction

If opinion polls are to be believed, the issue of unemployment has reigned, interrupted only by the Falklands War, as the most important issue facing the country over the last five years. Indeed, in the previous nine years it was also perceived as one of the most important issues for several considerable periods. Thus successive governments have considered it an imperative to be doing – or at least to be seen to be doing – something about the problem, and we have witnessed a succession of policy responses, with some similarities and some differences from one government to another. There is no doubt that the next election will, again, see unemployment as a central issue. Moreover, there is no doubt that the unemployment crisis is not just a problem over which the main political parties do battle. It causes untold hardship and distress to thousands of families – leading to increased crime, violence in the home and even an increased suicide rate. It may even threaten the stability of our society by creating a group of third class citizens who see no hope for themselves or their families within the present economic and political system.

If the confidence in western national governments to solve societies' problems has waned in general over the last decade, it has done so particularly in the field of unemployment. Very few OECD countries have escaped the onset of comparatively high levels of unemployment, especially since the 1973 oil crisis. Those countries which have avoided very high levels of unemployment – Austria, Japan, Norway, Sweden and Switzerland – have done so for rather special (and often different) reasons. Unemployment has become an international problem, and indeed is to some extent a function of the international monetary and energy problems.

The international dimension apart, and notwithstanding the fact that some countries have so far warded off high levels of unemployment, unemployment is a notoriously difficult problem for governments to manage in a mixed economy. This is not simply because without a state-owned economy governments are unable to give everybody 'something to do' with impunity. It is also because the unemployment issue, like inflation but unlike many other problems faced by government, is not primarily a *sectoral* one. It cuts across the whole range of key economic and social spheres which successive British governments have been trying to tackle, viz. international competitiveness, inflation, the public sector borrowing requirement, and a socially acceptable restructuring of industry.

Further, there are varying views as to what the problem of unemployment actually is. At one extreme, the problem for a government is simply that widespread publication of information regarding unemployment may be detrimental to the electorate's perceptions of that government's record. Thus, the artificial reduction of the crude numbers registered as unemployed (by a variety of means) constitutes a response consistent with a view of unemployment as a purely *political* problem. An alternative view of the problem is that the current lack of jobs in Britain is a function of over-paid labour, which reduces the competitiveness of British goods. Thus, tolerating increases in unemployment (with the attendant short-term social costs) in order to reduce relative labour costs and to increase employment in commercially viable jobs in the long-term, is a rational policy response. Another view of the issue is that 'the problem' is merely to find work for people in the short-term until there is an upturn in the world economy. A consequent policy may be that the government creates jobs irrespective of their immediate economic worth or contribution to the gross national product. In fact, the behaviour of successive governments has suggested that they have adhered to all three views: an inconsistency which is not *necessarily* to be deplored.

These three different views of the problem in question do however illustrate the difficulties involved in defining any single policy as a response to unemployment. Also an array of related motives may exist for the introduction of a particular policy having employment or unemployment implications. A response of one government to the problem may be characterised as an avoidance of the problem by its critics. Such imperspicuity is particularly acute in the case of fiscal and monetary measures, which can simultaneously be directed towards solving several problems. Even with youth job-creation policies however, the problem remains: are such innovations primarily responses to unemployment, or rather to another manifestation, such as urban unrest?

The cross-sectoral nature of the unemployment problem necessarily blurs the clear identification of policies as responses to unemployment *per se*. This is because policies genuinely do span more than one sector, and because governments may find advantage in describing a policy in one way rather than another. Policies in response to unemployment overlap most obviously with policies in the following areas: youth training, vocational preparation, industrial training, inner-cities, regional aids and other incentives by which government can stimulate industrial growth. Thus the introduction of a new youth training initiative could be described simultaneously as a response to the problems of youth unemployment, as an educational innovation, and as meeting the shortage of skills in industry. Similarly, an adult employment subsidy scheme could be described as a response to the problem of unemployment, or to the need to maintain an active and skilled workforce during a depression in order to be prepared to exploit an upturn in demand, or to a perceived need in the community, e.g. environmental improvement.

Other policy areas may be also considered to overlap with that of unemployment. It could be argued that legislation aimed at reducing industrial unrest is in fact designed to increase Britain's attractiveness to investors and thus to stimulate further employment. Equally, some might argue that reducing the real levels of unemployment benefit would have the effect of discouraging individuals from staying out of work longer than is 'necessary'. It is generally agreed though, that the voluntary unemployed constitute only a small percentage of benefit claimants. (Even Norman Tebbit, the former Secretary of State for Employment and considered to be a 'hawk' in such matters, has not persisted with his reference to getting on a bike to find work.) Finally, of course, policies in response to unemployment may be directly related to budgetary policies, as most famously illustrated by Anthony Barber's expansionary budget of 1972 which was directly linked to the escalating unemployment figures of the winter 1971 – 2.

Ultimately, of course, the unemployment policy area can be said to overlap with every sector of employment in which redundancies take place, and which comply with or benefit from some form of government intervention in response to unemployment. This is especially evident in the realm of *ad hoc* government interventions to save or maintain an industrial organisation, with the alternative consequences of a large number of redundancies very much in mind. Hence, unemployment is necessarily one of the factors involved in, for example, policy-making for British motorcar manufacturing and for the steel-making industries. The multi-dimensional nature of the unemployment problem has also led to those seeking various policy changes to utilise it for their cause. For instance, an expansion of Sunday trading in England and Wales has been justified on the grounds that it could increase jobs in the retail trade. Similarly, the insulation industry has pressed for more public subsidies for insulating houses on the grounds that this would create jobs.

What then is the purpose of this volume? It certainly is not an attempt to explain the growth of unemployment in the United Kingdom, although a brief discussion of the international economic setting and the domestic economic conditions and policies impinging most directly upon the problem is provided in the first chapter. Nor is it devised as a treatise on the best solution to the problem, although possible avenues for future policies are discussed in the concluding chapter. This book is primarily concerned with the nature of unemployment as a *political issue,* and with the ways in which successive governments have responded to it. This not only involves an assessment of the 'high' politics of the impact of the issue in general election, but also an analysis of the blend of policy responses which government have introduced, and their impact, and the manner in which the policies emerge and are implemented (which in combination we refer to as the 'policy process'). In Chapter 5 we assess the employment and political impact of the range of responses to unemployment from outside central government, and Chapter 6 provides an analysis of policy responses in other western countries, notably the USA, Sweden, France and West Germany.

1 Unemployment: Economic and Social Perspectives

The purpose of this chapter is to provide the economic and social setting for the study of the political issue of unemployment. Discussion will initially focus upon international economic factors and their contribution to the British experience of unemployment. Whilst there is agreement that international factors are very significant, questions of the precise combination of factors and the nature of their impact are hotly disputed by economists and politicians (see Chapter 2.1). It is not our purpose as political scientists to try to produce a fresh analysis of the *economic* causes of unemployment. This chapter is intended to provide some general economic background to both the growth of unemployment and government responses to it, outlining some of the salient distributional features and social aspects of the problem.

1.1 Unemployment and the international economy

For an economy so dependent upon international markets and products, it is of course a truism to say that the level of British unemployment is a function of world-wide economic changes which affect employment in all advanced mixed economies. The extent to which international, as opposed to domestic, factors are causal is less certain. UK levels of unemployment and rates of increase have at times been considerably higher than those of other western industrialised countries, but they have by no means been unique. Most liberal democratic states with mixed economies who had enjoyed 'full' or near full employment since the early 1950s have been haunted by the spectre of rising unemployment over the last decade (see Table 1.1).

Table 1.1 *Annual average unemployment rates in selected OECD countries 1971–1983*

	1971	1974	1977	1980	1983
France	2.10	2.25	4.80	6.30	8.00
Italy	3.20	2.85	7.10	7.40	9.70
Sweden	2.10	2.00	1.80	2.00	3.50
United Kingdom	3.00	2.52	5.70	2.00	13.10
USA	5.90	5.60	7.00	7.00	9.50
West Germany	0.70	2.65	4.60	3.10	8.00

SOURCE: OECD, *Economic Outlooks* (OECD standardised unemployment rates)

The table does however obscure the impact of two factors which make direct comparison difficult. First, the figures disguise differential direct responses to unemployment among the countries. Some governments have provided a greater number of job-creation, work-experience, training and labour subsidy schemes to minimise the impact of unemployment upon their workforces. Further, the prior existence of a system of national service may have helped governments to cope better with rising youth unemployment, exacerbated by recent disadvantageous demographic trends. Equally, some countries, such as France and West Germany, have operated major apprenticeship training programmes from well before the rise in unemployment over the last decade. This has enabled them to experience only a relatively small problem of youth unemployment, which is probably the most politically sensitive aspect of the issue in the UK.

In the 1983 General Election both the Labour Party and the Liberal/SDP Alliance promised to extend the term of the major Youth Training Scheme for school-leavers from one year to two. This would clearly not only cushion school-leavers against the economic, social and psychological disadvantages of unemployment, but could also reduce the official unemployment figures by around 400,000. Some governments have been able to 'export' a proportion of their unemployment problem. Between 1973 and 1978, about 730,000 guest workers in West Germany left the country, having lost their jobs and being unable to qualify for state benefits. British governments have increasingly restricted the availability of British citizenship. However, there has as yet been no suggestion from official sources that rights of immigrant British citizens to stay in the country and enjoy the full benefits commonly available should be withdrawn. The proposal made to this effect by a right wing minority at the 1983 Conservative Party Conference was firmly rejected by the Cabinet.

A problem adding to the difficulty of assessing the real impact of international factors upon individual countries is that of ascertaining the nature and magnitude of the effects of domestic economic factors and policies upon levels and rates of unemployment. Generally, government parties have tended to emphasise the impact of international factors, whereas opposition parties have pointed to the responsibility of government policies for unemployment. The Labour Party and Liberal/SDP Alliance have consistently argued that the increase in unemployment by two million since 1979 is primarily the fault of the Thatcher Government's economic policies. The government has tended to emphasise British structural economic factors and to stress that Britain's experience is part of a world-wide problem. This view, however, received untimely criticism from the Commons Treasury and Civil Service Committee chaired by the senior Conservative back bencher Edward du

Cann, whose draft report blaming an overvalued pound for high UK unemployment appeared during the 1983 General Election campaign. Whilst each country's unemployment 'profile' has obviously been characterised by indigenous economic and political conditions, by government policies, and by the role of non-governmental organisations, it is nevertheless clear that international economic factors have had a very significant impact throughout.

Although with hindsight it is easy to say that western governments should have been better prepared for it, the impact of the 1973 Middle East war has been traumatic. The control over the oil supplies to western countries was initially used by OPEC for political purposes (because of the support given by most western governments to Israel), but the realisation of the economic hold that oil-producing countries had over the West led to a series of oil-price increases. These had significant effects of lowering levels of world demand for goods and of increasing costs of production. Consequently, only the most competitive producers in the world were able to maintain their exports. British industry has in any case found it increasingly difficult to sell abroad, and in the years since 1961 (with the exception of 1971) any balance of payments surpluses have been achieved by invisible earnings and oil.

Table 1.2 shows that even though the record for UK visible trade had never been good over this period, the years immediately after the oil-price increases were little short of disastrous. This lack of competitiveness was largely due to combinations of over-manning, high unit-labour costs and inadequate new capital investments. Table 1.3 indicates that unit-labour costs in manufacturing have risen much faster in the UK than among her competitors, and, significantly, the difference is larger in 1972 – 82 (the period when competitiveness was even more imperative) than in 1962 – 72. Table 1.4 shows that among the UK's main competitors, only the USA improved its rate of production per employee at a slower rate than the UK over the period 1960 – 79, although the British record markedly improved between 1979 and 1982, relatively speaking.

Political considerations again loomed large when the oil supplies were further restricted during the particularly anti-western phase of the Iranian revolution in 1979. In combination, these various shocks to the international supply and price of oil have been major contributors to the international recession. It is ironic that in recent years the real price of oil has fallen somewhat, due to the recession leading to a fall in demand for energy, which in turn produced an oil glut (see Table 1.5).

To illustrate the importance of the American economy for the economic well-being of the international (and especially the industrialised countries), it is said that when America sneezes the rest of the world catches cold. The American economy has impacted upon the western industrialised world in two important respects over the last decade. First,

Table 1.2   Summary of UK balance of payments 1961–1983 (£million)

	Visible balance	Oil balance	Invisible balance	Total balance
1961	− 140		+ 187	+ 47
1962	− 100		+ 255	+ 155
1963	− 119		+ 244	+ 125
1964	− 543		+ 185	− 358
1965	− 260		+ 230	− 30
1966	− 108		+ 238	+ 130
1967	− 599		+ 330	− 269
1968	− 712		+ 468	− 244
1969	− 209		+ 714	+ 505
1970	− 34		+ 857	+ 823
1971	+ 190		+ 934	+1124
1972	− 748		+ 971	+ 223
1973	−2586		+1607	− 979
1974	−5351		+2073	−3278
1975	−3333		+1820	−1513
1976	−3929		+3093	− 836
1977	−2284		+2338	+ 54
1978	−1542		+2700	+1158
1979	−3449	− 731	+2796	− 653
1980	+1361	+ 315	+2216	+3477
1981	+3360	+3112	+3570	+6930
1982	+2055	+4605	+2826	+4881
1983	−1105	—	+3399	+2294

SOURCE: CSO (various)

Table 1.3   Unit labour costs in manufacturing 1962–1982

	Real % increases	
	1962–1972	1972–1982
USA	1.8	7.4
Japan	3.2	4.1
West Germany	3.6	5.2
France	3.0	11.0
UK	4.3	14.9

SOURCE: OECD, *Economic Outlook* **34**, December 1984, p.52.

if the USA had not been so oil-dependent the effects of the changes in oil price and supply would not have been so marked: the knock-on effects of the fall in demand within the USA were very costly to those countries, especially in Western Europe, which depend on US export markets (approximately 15 per cent of British exports go to the USA). Secondly,

Table 1.4   *Increases in real GDP per person employed 1960–1982*

	1960–68	1968–73	1973–79	1979–82
		% changes		
USA	2.6	1.3	0.2	−0.1
Japan	8.9	7.9	2.9	3.1
West Germany	4.3	4.2	3.0	0.7
France	4.9	4.8	2.9	1.2
UK	2.7	3.0	3.0	1.4

SOURCE: OECD, *Historical Statistics 1960–82*, 1984, p.47.

Table 1.5   *Index of wholesale price of oil in OECD countries 1975–1983 (1975 = 100)*

1975	1976	1977	1978	1979	1980	1981	1982	1983
100.0	102.3	104.3	99.1	116.0	149.3	163.8	157.2	146.7

SOURCE: OECD, *Economic Outlook* **34**, December 1983, p.143.

and even more significantly, it is thought that the recession has been prolonged more than necessary by the maintenance of comparatively high US interest rates. These have remained particularly high since 1980, under President Reagan, increasing in real terms by 45 per cent between 1980 and 1983.

High interest rates allow the USA to finance its own budget deficit, caused mainly by large increases in defence and space expenditures. For purposes of maintaining currency stability, no other country can afford to allow its real interest rates to get too out of line with those in America. If, for instance, British rates fell disproportionately to those of her competitors, there might well be an outflow of capital from Britain to a country where investors could be assured of a greater return on their capital. Whilst this poses a disincentive for countries to lower their interest rates in advance of the USA, continuing high interest rates tend to compound the recession. Companies experiencing financial problems find it more expensive to borrow money to see them through a difficult period, and are thus more likely to make lay-offs and closures, or to collapse, with obvious consequences for employment levels. In their defence, the Americans point out that the federal deficit has assisted economic growth, and that this in turn has produced a large trade deficit, which has helped Western Europe by sucking in exports. It can also be argued that the so-called 'huge deficit' is not so huge after all – at only 6 per cent of US GNP, and on some calculations below that figure.

Another international development has been the change in the international terms of trade brought about by the increased production in Third World and Pacific countries. This has had two important distinct but related effects; first, traditional export markets for western manufactured products in Third World countries have been taken over by either home or Third World producers. In some cases these markets were closed to western exports for reasons of demand deflation within Third World countries, as their own export earnings have fallen with the international recession and as they have struggled with continuing debt burdens. Secondly, the increased economies of scale which have developed as a result of the first effect, and the competitive labour costs, have combined to make increasingly sophisticated products, especially from South Korea, Taiwan, Singapore and Hong Kong highly competitive in western markets. It is therefore reasonable to suggest that fairly fundamental *structural* changes in the world economy are taking place with the continued success of newly industrialised countries (NICs). In this sense, all the western industrialised nations are going through an extremely painful process of readjustment, as their 'smokestack' industries disappear or undergo drastic reduction, as their service sectors continue to grow and as they develop new technologies. It is not surprising that the combination of these massive shifts in production patterns and the oil crisis have produced unpleasant side-effects. The UK record in the 'motor vehicle and spares' sector illustrates this point. In 1971, there were over 500,000 employees in this industry; by January 1984 this had dwindled to just under 300,000. Similarly, the 'metal manufacturing, ore and other mineral extraction' industries reduced the number of employees from 822,000 in 1971 to 456,000 in January 1984 (Department of Employment, 1984 May: S8, S9). More specifically, the British Steel Corporation employed some 228,000 people in April 1975, whereas it currently employs under 75,000.

A further problem for both the USA and Western Europe has been that the trend of penetration of western markets by Japanese goods begun in the 1960s has continued, and in some areas escalated over the last decade. This is due to combinations of low labour-costs, absence of industrial disputes, high levels of investment in new manufacturing processes, an under-valuation of the yen, and effective marketing strategies – as well as more than a hint of outright protectionism by the Japanese.

In summary then, there are several international pressures which have been instrumental in bringing about recession and increased unemployment in all advanced western economies. Turning then to the UK, let us consider some of the factors that have compounded these international effects.

1.2 Unemployment and government economic policies

Unemployment in the UK during the 1950s and 1960s remained at what were considered 'acceptable' levels, rarely exceeding 3 per cent of the total workforce. The proportion of these who remained unemployed for over one year rarely exceeded 15 per cent of the total unemployed. It was commonly believed by most politicians and economists of the time that this was achieved by the adoption of Keynesian techniques of fine tuning the economy. Quite simply, if a government considered that unemployment was rising towards a level which would be popularly deemed unacceptable, it would reflate the economy to increase demand. This was achieved by reducing taxes and interest rates, and by raising public expenditure levels. The additional purchasing power which was subsequently released into the economy seemed to lead to the desired reduction of unemployment levels. However, after a short period, the reflation would get out of hand, and the government would then face the task of exerting a brake on the economy in order to correct balance of payments deficits and to protect the international value of sterling. The cyclical process of reflation followed by deflation became known as the 'stop-go' cycle. Whether this happy ability of governments to control unemployment levels, apparently at will, was solely due to the responsiveness of the economy to the pulling of budgetary levers is less certain in retrospect. Keynesian techniques seemed to work because of the coincidence of a number of other critical factors: especially, lower real oil-prices, stable Commonwealth markets for British exports and comparatively low US interest rates.

The criticisms which the Conservative opposition under Edward Heath made of the Wilson Government's economic policies in the sixties did not really include any analysis of the economics of unemployment. As mass unemployment had been avoided between 1964 and 1970, the issue was not yet on the political agenda (see Chapter 2.2), although considerable restructuring had taken place (e.g. in coal-mining, in which the numbers employed fell from 602,100 in 1960 to 287,200 in 1970–1). As the first surge towards 'unacceptable' levels of unemployment occurred during 1971–2, it was the Heath Government's misfortune to have to develop, whilst in power, an economic policy in response to the problem.

The Conservatives had been elected to office promising to reduce government intervention in the economy, to reduce public expenditure, and thereby to permit reductions in taxation. It was thought that this would provide a moderate reflationary stimulus and a shot in the arm to British industry. It was assumed that any short-term rises in unemployment caused would be swiftly mopped up by a regeneration of British industry unshackled from government intervention and trade union power (to be facilitated by the reform of industrial relations).

This scenario did not follow in the first year. No upsurge in industrial activity took place; rather, business profits and industrial investment declined (much potential industrial investment was channelled into property). Thus Anthony Barber, then Chancellor of the Exchequer, attempted, in his April 1971 budget, to further reflate the economy by reducing income tax, corporation tax and selective employment tax deductions, and by increasing child allowances and other welfare benefits. These measures appeared to be ineffective. Coupled with this absence of recovery had been a steady rise in unemployment, which by January 1972 was approaching the then symbolic one million mark. This, it was considered, would spell electoral danger and the government abandoned its initial intentions and introduced a much more determined reflationary budget in April 1972, aiming at a 5 per cent growth rate. This was to be achieved by reductions in taxation, further increases in welfare payments, and the reintroduction of industrial investment incentives. Although there was a short-term reduction in unemployment levels, these measures did nothing to arrest inflation which had been rising simultaneously with unemployment, and thus undermining the accepted wisdom that inflation and unemployment were inversely related.

The irresistible rise in levels of inflation appeared to be due to a combination of the long-term effects of the 1967 devaluation, bringing about higher import prices, the deficit financing of US involvement in Vietnam (having the effect of inflating money supply of many US trading partners), and comparatively-high average wage settlements (in money rather than real terms). Although the real value increases in wages were negligible, the effect of the appearance of more pay, plus relaxed HP restrictions was to increase demand. Rather than fuel a national recovery, this rapid rise in demand led to a common British phenomenon – imports: British producers were unable to exploit this rise in domestic demand. Here we see perhaps the most central and difficult problem facing the UK – its international competitiveness – or lack of it (see Tables 1.3 and 1.4). Hence we have witnessed UK industries lose traditional markets overseas at the same time as seeing high penetration of home markets by foreign imports. Table 1.6 indicates the increasing penetration of the UK market of motor vehicles, traditionally thought to be one of the country's industrial strengths. In a period of six years the market share of imports rose from 23 per cent to 39 per cent. Whilst this is something of a special case, it is symptomatic of an overall trend. In 1975 there was 22.2 per cent import penetration of the total UK market in manufactured goods. This had risen to 30.8 per cent by September 1983 (CSO, various).

In order to combat continuing high levels of unemployment, the

Table 1.6   Import penetration of UK vehicle market 1974–1980

Imports as a percentage of home market

1974	1975	1976	1977	1978	1979	1980
23	26	29	34	36	41	39

SOURCE: Central Statistical Office, *Digest of Statistics,* December 1981, p.138.

government introduced a three-stage counter-inflation policy, with statutory limits on wage increases. (The policy did incorporate a threshold system which provided for additional wage increases if inflation exceeded specified levels, and also provided additional incentives for productivity achievements.) Whilst the scheme had advantages as a short-term counter-inflationary measure, it was unable to provide a means for certain groups of employees to solve problems of wage relativities. Thus, the National Union of Mineworkers (NUM) first went on an overtime ban from November 1973 and then threatened an all-out strike in February 1974, although this was suspended when Prime Minister Heath called the February 1974 General Election.

Because of the country's decreasing dependence on coal, the effects on the economy (and indeed upon the political system) of this dispute might have been less serious had it not coincided with the shock which reverberated throughout the industrialised world: the impact of the Arab–Israeli war of October 1973. This first precipitated reductions in oil supplies from Arab to western countries, of about 15 per cent, and then, drastic price increases. These combined had the effect of quadrupling the price of oil in Britain. The oil-price increase caused steep rises in the costs of production and severely depressed demand in all but the oil-rich Arab countries.

The conjunction of the international oil crisis with the NUM's industrial action (exacerbated by overtime bans by ASLEF and the electricity power workers) made for special problems for the British economy. The short-term impact on unemployment levels was minimal, but the longer-term effects were more serious. Due to the acute shortage of energy over the winter of 1973–4, the government not only had to curb domestic use of electricity, but also to introduce a three-day working week in industry. This resulted in reduced output (see Table 1.7), loss of regular overseas orders for British manufacturers (due mainly to fears of further industrial disruption), import penetration by their overseas competitors, and a disastrous balance of payments deficit by early 1974.

By the end of the Heath administration the rises in unemployment which occurred over 1972–3 had been reversed if not erased. However, seeds had also been sown which would raise future problems in restraining increasing unemployment. Britain, like her competitors, suffered the depressive effects of the embargoes and price increases on oil. These were compounded by the industrial conflict between government and key

Table 1.7   Index of GDP at constant market prices 1970–79 (1975=100)

1970	1971	1972	1973	1974	1975	1976	1977	1978	1979
91.3	93.0	96.1	103.0	101.0	100.0	102.6	105.1	109.1	111.2

SOURCE: CSO, *National Income and Expenditure*, 1982, p.14.

workers, leading to loss of markets and the balance of payments deficit.

The government resorted to heavy borrowing from overseas. The repayment of these loans was to prove a major additional burden on the country over the following five years. Finally, the inflation problem persisted – also largely due to increases in oil prices – despite the three-stage anti-inflationary strategy. Thus the immediate economic concerns of whichever government was elected in February 1974 would be tackling the balance of payments and inflation problems.

The Labour Party took office again in February 1974, but, with the two major parties doing equally badly, this was mainly due to the refusal of the Liberal Party to maintain Edward Heath in office. Having no working majority in Parliament was clearly a major difficulty for the new government, and it was clear that another General Election would soon be in the offing. However, the Chancellor of the Exchequer, Denis Healey, wasted no time in bringing in his first budget, which simultaneously attempted to reduce inflation and to improve the balance of payments situation by proposing a £1,500 million reduction in the public sector borrowing requirement of 1973–4 and by making large direct and indirect tax increases, which fed directly into the Retail Price Index. Harold Wilson reports that by the time the bill received its Royal Assent in July 1974

...the Chancellor was forced to advise the Cabinet that further measures were needed. The oil-generated inflation, the turn-down in investment and industrial activity which had begun even before the action of the oil producers, a world-wide loss of confidence; all these were combining to threaten employment. Men were being laid off. (Wilson, 1979: 27–8)

Whilst Healey's first budget had attempted to deflate the economy, it was soon apparent that this could have the effect of precipitating a further recession. Thus, the second budget was an attempt at a mild reflation of the economy, by reducing VAT from 10 per cent to 8 per cent, by increasing the domestic rate relief allowances, by increasing the Regional Employment Premium and by increasing subsidies on household flour. These measures, of course, cancelled out the efforts to reduce public expenditure.

Joel Barnett, Chief Secretary of the Treasury 1974–9, commented that February to October 1974 was

a period when public expenditure was allowed to increase at a pace we could not afford, leading inexorably to the enormous political and practical problems of having to make large cuts later, particularly difficult for a Labour Government. (Barnett, 1982: 33)

Rises in unemployment levels were temporarily restrained in the second quarter of 1974, but despite the attempts to stimulate demand in the second budget, and the other attempts made to help industry by planning agreements, investments, regional aid and *ad hoc* interventions, unemployment levels soon started increasing again, rising from 2.3 per cent in June, to 2.8 per cent in November, and to 3.3 per cent in January 1975.

In addition to budgetary measures, the Labour Government also maintained that it was fighting unemployment by means of the Social Contract, although this was mainly an instrument to control wage rises. In the belief that excessive wage demands by some groups of workers caused others to lose their jobs, the government attempted to achieve a *voluntary* prices and incomes policy. Harold Wilson recalled negotiations with trade union leaders where the Cabinet members tried to impress upon their audiences that economic realities were changing:

In all these meetings, whether annual trade union delegate conferences, or ad hoc meetings, my colleagues and I stressed at first the fact that existing living standards would be impossible to maintain, and, as time went on, what had become the inevitable truth, that they must fall. The only offset we could hold out was the marked improvement in the provision of the social service 'family bonus'. Above all we emphasised *that every single point in the inflation index would inexorably mean a worsening in unemployment.* (Our emphasis.) (Wilson, 1979: 111)

In short, this Social Contract consisted of trade unions agreeing to seek annual wage increases which should only compensate for price increases over the previous year. In return, the government would do its utmost to restrict price increases, by operating a price code and providing subsidies, and to maintain employment. This objective was quickly undermined by successive unofficial strikes in the motorcar industry, and strikes among railway drivers and hospital workers.

The year 1975 saw unemployment rise by another 335,000, average wage rises of 30 per cent – almost twice the OECD average (OECD, 1983:90) – a further balance of payments deficit (£1,513 million), and a widening Public Sector Borrowing Requirement (PSBR). (The actual outturn of public expenditure in 1974 – 5 had been £5 billion more than was planned, in real terms.) Hence, another stringent budget was introduced in April 1975, and though a brake was exerted on rising unemployment, jobs could hardly be described as Healey's immediate priority. In order to reduce the country's debt he made further tax increases (both on income tax and by selective VAT increases) and further public expenditure cuts (notably defence spending and subsidies on nationalised industry prices, housing and food). Though some special measures were introduced for retraining workers and subsidising the employment of those threatened with redundancies (see Chapter 3), these did not compensate for the deflationary effects of the overall package. The other main tool in the fight against inflation was Stage II of the Social Contract, which entailed a more stringent price code with penalties, and provided for a maximum wage rise of £6 per week for those earning up to £8,500 a year. Despite these policies, not only were there further rises in unemployment, but also, in

1976, there emerged another pressing factor in the government's macro-economic equation: the fast-falling value of sterling. Despite the recent 'turning on' of the North Sea oil pipe-line, international confidence in the British economy was waning.

This was a frightening performance. It could not simply be blamed (or explained) either on Britain's balance of payments deficit or on the high internal rate of inflation. The real explanation lay in a fear of the future course of the economy – and in particular of the Government's apparent inability to contain the Public Sector Borrowing Requirement . . . (Sked and Cook, 1979:343)

The pound, when still worth more than $2, was recognised by many to be undermining British competitiveness, and 'a prevailing view in the Treasury favoured progressive depreciation in order to offset the escalation of our domestic industrial costs' (Pliatzky, 1982:148). What was clearly unexpected, however, was the chaotic slide in the value of the pound. Thus, in order to secure a credit agreement with the IMF, a package was put together by Healey, coming into effect in July 1976, to cut public expenditure. This consisted mainly of overall reductions in the Regional Employment Premium, cutbacks in capital expenditure of nationalised industries and an increase in the employer's National Insurance contributions. It was complemented by an increase in interest rates, making capital available to the government and discouraging consumer spending. But even these measures did not stop the slide in the value of the pound.

Finally, in September, Healey, on his way – ironically – to an IMF conference, turned round at Heathrow airport to make speedy plans to halt the pound from sliding below $1.64. The government was obliged to seek assistance from the IMF in the form of a $3,900 million loan (see Keegan and Pennant-Rea, 1979). However, the IMF would only agree to give this loan if further cuts were made in public expenditure and taxation increased, to reduce the Public Sector Borrowing Requirement (PSBR). The cuts of about £3,000 million were planned to take effect during 1977 and 1978, and threatened further job losses. There was some opposition within the Cabinet to the package, specifically on the unemployment issue (rather than on spending cuts *per se*), notably from Tony Benn and Peter Shore. The latter commented that 'There is no will in this Cabinet to tell the IMF to take a running jump, even if unemployment rose to 2 million' (Barnett, 1982:109). However, ultimately the impact of these measures upon employment was subordinate to the objective of stabilising Britain's currency, which required reducing her international debts, and in turn reducing what Barnett referred to as these 'four damned letters': PSBR. The government's final package to secure the loan was considerably less severe than first expected, and consisted primarily of selling £500,000 of BP shares, making cuts in defence expenditure and overseas aid, abolishing food subsidies and the Regional Employment Premium (except in

Northern Ireland), and making cuts in certain capital expenditure programmes. Pliatzky quoted the comment of the Expenditure Committee on this.

The Government is thus acting like those industrialists it criticises for failing to invest. Indeed, even worse, it appears to be cutting capital expenditure and selling off productive capital assets (e.g. BP shares) in order to sustain current expenditure, the classic action of an ailing industrial company. (Pliatzky, 1982:157)

It simply proved politically easier to cut capital expenditure than current expenditure.

Considering the traumas of 1976, the effects of measures taken were less dramatic over the subsequent years of Labour rule than had been expected. This was largely due to the benefits of North Sea oil which enabled many of the cuts made to be restored. One senior Whitehall official is reported as saying that, 'Not only did the IMF not get the cuts they wanted, but subsequently most of them were quietly restored, with no ill effects on the Pound' (Keegan and Pennant-Rea, 1979:169). Further, the effects of North Sea oil were to provide small balance of trade surpluses in 1978 which had the effect of strengthening the pound, and some reduction in interest rates. It should be pointed out, however, that this state of relative health was also somewhat due to the unpredicted shortfall in overall public expenditure (using the cash limits system) during 1977 – 8 of the order of twice the size of the planned public expenditure cuts of 1976!

During 1978, it must have appeared to the Cabinet that the pressure was off: inflation had been brought down to single figures (though the rate of decrease in inflation was slower than in most other economies) and the incomes policy remained intact; the dramatic rise in unemployment levels had been arrested (if not reversed); and a small balance of payments surplus was recorded. With North Sea oil flowing in larger quantities, this might have appeared to be a recipe for growth and a downturn in unemployment. Indeed, the April 1978 budget saw small reductions in personal taxation levels and suggested that a policy of controlled expansion would follow.

One element in this policy would be to continue with the incomes policy which had appeared effective in bringing down the level of UK wage increases (although unit labour costs still increased at a faster rate than in other OECD countries). The level of increase which was announced for Stage IV of the Social Contract was 5 per cent, which could perhaps have been a bargaining offer for a 7 or 8 per cent settlement with the unions. It has been suggested that Healey and Callaghan went for 5 per cent in order to match the West German achievement of keeping wages and price inflation to 5 per cent (Pliatzky, 1982:172). However, in what became known as the 'winter of discontent', the pay policy was broken by several groups of workers, but most notably by the road haulage workers, who conducted extensive secondary picketing at the country's ports. Not only did this contribute to signs of rising inflation in early 1979, it provided the launch pad for Mrs Thatcher's election victory in 1979 (see Chapter 2). Ironically, whilst the Conservatives had argued against a government wages policy, it was Labour's failure to achieve this in 1978–9 which provoked fears of hyper-inflation, singled out by Mrs Thatcher as the greatest evil facing the country.

If the Labour Government had at least made some rhetorical reference to unemployment as the country's major problem, the incoming Conservative Government of 1979 spelt out rather different priorities. The first of these was to bring down inflation by reducing the public sector borrowing requirement and restricting the money supply. Secondly, the new government pledged itself to restore incentives, notably by reducing taxation. Thirdly, it was promised that public expenditure would be compatible with these borrowing and taxation targets. Leo Pliatzky pointed out when discussing the new government's White Paper *The Government's Expenditure Plans 1980–81* (Cmnd 7746) that:

Not only was there no mention of full employment as an objective; the word 'employment' did not appear at all in the short White Paper except in the section heading 'Industry, energy, trade and employment', and in one of the paragraphs in that section which stated that 'No provision is made for the extension of the Small Firms Employment Subsidy'. (Pliatzky, 1982:177)

In short, the Conservatives believed that whilst governments are able to create a healthy economic climate, the actual achievement of economic growth and subsequent high levels of employment is the responsibility of all those in industry.

As has often proved to be the case for incoming governments espousing simple and radical solutions to the various problems facing them, the Thatcher administration's real macroeconomic strategy has not been able to follow this vision. As will be related below, the Conservative Government initially was unable to achieve its objectives due to a combination of international economic factors, domestic economic factors, and domestic political constraints, which, acting upon the government have obliged it to compromise its vision. This has been particularly evident in the case of public expenditure, which the Conservatives have failed to reduce significantly, and consequently taxation has risen in respect of VAT, direct personal taxation and national insurance payments. Even more recently as the international recession has eased, it has had policy successes only on some fronts, e.g. inflation and money supply.

However, as suggested earlier, initially the Conservative economic policies appeared consistent with doctrines unfolded during the opposition years, e.g. in *The Right Approach* (Conservative Central Office, 1976). Thus:

Whereas under Mr Healey monetary policy had been juggled alongside incomes policy and measures to hold down unemployment in an uncertain mix, the early Conservative approach was more straightforward. There was a vision of how the economy did (or should) work, and it was applied. (Riddell, 1983:60)

Sir Geoffrey Howe's first budget was announced on 12 June 1979, and presented as a complete change in attitude towards the way in which the economy worked. Income tax was reduced by £3.5 billion (£2.5 billion of which was compensated for by increases in indirect taxes). Cuts in public spending were announced, representing reductions in the PSBR from 5 per cent to 4 per cent of gross domestic product. This was to be achieved by cuts in increased expenditure planned by Labour and totalling £1,618 million, further squeezes on cash limits for planned programmes to save £1,000 million, and estimated receipts of £1,000 million from the disposal of assets (Treasury, June 1979). The main burden of these economies fell in the fields of energy, housing, training and employment and regional development grants.

At the same time, other measures were introduced which were intended to increase incentives for economic recovery. These consisted of reductions in taxation on capital, the ending of controls on pay, prices and dividends, and the first stage of the abolition of exchange controls (completed later in 1979). As it was believed that the single most important factor in causing inflation was the money supply, the Minimum Lending Rate was raised from 12 per cent to 14 per cent. It was intended that this should enable the 1979–80 rise of the money supply measure, M3, (i.e all cash and bank accounts) to be kept to the 7 per cent to 11 per cent range.

It was not long before it was clear that implementing the new economic strategy would prove far more difficult than composing it. Even though the government had anticipated a small initial rise in inflation prior to its predicted fall, it had not anticipated the developments of the ensuing months. In retrospect, it does seem extraordinary that, for instance, the inflationary effects of the increase in VAT (adding 4.5 per cent to the Retail Price Index) were not recognised. The inflation rate exceeded 20 per cent during 1980, and was still running at 12 per cent at the end of 1981. Another international oil crisis had followed swiftly in the wake of the Iranian revolution, causing an inflationary pressure on prices as well as a brake upon economic growth. In addition, considerable inflationary pressures were already in the pipeline arising from awards made by the Clegg Commission on Pay Comparability set up by the Labour Government in order to resolve its political difficulties. Various budgetary measures introduced by Howe served only to compound these inflationary effects, notably the impact of VAT increases and the increase in nationalised industry prices (particularly electricity and gas), resulting from cuts in their budgets to reduce the PSBR. In fact, rather than decrease the money supply, the 1979 budget had the effect of increasing it. The raising of the Minimum Lending Rate (MLR) to 17 per cent (an all time record high) only compounded rather than solved the problem.

Although MLR was suspended in 1981, officially – as a demonstration of the government's confidence in market forces – interest rates remained high. This was partly explained by high US interest rates, but it was also a result of the government's belief in restricting the money supply to combat inflation. The effects of this policy have been significant in employment terms, both directly and as a result of the appreciation of sterling, leading to increased industrial costs. Also, rather than reduce inflation, high interest rates have been thought to have increased prices, as people did not adjust their expenditure patterns.

How did the Conservative Government respond to the early experience of failure to control money supply and inflation and to the simultaneous deepening economic recession? In some areas, policy changes and even policy reversals have been made, whereas in others the government has stuck doggedly to its principles. Despite consistent pleas from industry, the government made no effort to reduce artificially the international value of sterling, which was particularly high during the first few years of Conservative office, mainly because of Britain's oil reserves. This made the task of British exporters more difficult, and gave comparative price advantage to importers. Whilst the value of the pound against the American dollar has come down (largely due to the comparative oil glut), the damage to British order books sustained between 1979 and 1981 as a result of the overvalued currency is thought to be significant. On this measure, competitiveness is now back to its 1979 level, but still worse than in the mid-1970s. Until 1985 exporters argued that sterling was over-valued against other currencies. The abolition of exchange controls provoked a considerable outflow of investment. Although some outflow was expected in the form of portfolio investments, it was not expected that direct investment overseas would so easily outstrip inward direct investment. In 1980 an outflow of about $100 million was recorded, compared to an average net inflow of $4½ billion over the three years up to 1979 (OECD, 1981:24). Whilst there are some commercial benefits of such overseas investment for British companies, and the British economy, the decline in inward direct investment poses a threat to Britain's industrial infrastructure and employment levels.

Despite the rhetorical claims by the Prime Minister that 'this lady at least is not for turning' and 'there is no alternative', the government has made significant changes in its economic strategy. Indeed, after the December 1981 budget measures, the Thatcher Government was described by *The Economist* as being 'as rigid as an eel' (5.12.81).

Following initial reductions in taxation made in Howe's first budget, the overall burden of taxation has steadily risen from 39.6 per cent of GDP in 1979 to 45.7 per cent in 1982 (Treasury, October 1983). For all groups (single and married) earning between 75 per cent and 200 per cent of the national average earnings the combination of income tax and National Insurance contributions has increased between 1978 – 9 and 1983 – 4, and the lower income groups have suffered disproportionately. Only those earning well over twice the national average income have enjoyed reductions in taxation (Riddell, 1983:71 – 2). Table 1.8 indicates that tax levels have increased in the UK at a considerably faster rate than the OECD average. The reasons for this overall increase in taxation are twofold: the high levels of inflation referred to were, according to monetarist mores, due to an excessive supply of money; income tax increases were designed to reduce the spending power of consumers and reduce the PSBR.

More importantly however, increases in taxation arose because public expenditure continued to exceed government targets, and in some cases rose in real terms. The policy alternative of increased borrowing to finance this expenditure was rejected. Although the Conservatives have not achieved their initial objectives in this field, they have adhered comparatively closely to their policy principle that the PSBR should be reduced. Table 1.9 illustrates the relative magnitude of recent public expenditure increases.

What factors accounted for this irony, that whilst political debate raged over the government's *planned* public expenditure reductions, *actual*

Table 1.8 UK and OECD average increases in levels of tax and N.I. as a share of GDP 1978 – 1982

	UK	OECD average
1978	33.9	34.4
1979	34.7	34.9
1980	36.2	35.8
1981	38.2	36.8
1982	39.1	36.7

SOURCE: OECD, *Economic Outlook* **34**, December 1983, p.36 and *Economic Survey 1983 – 84 UK*, January 1984, p.17.

Table 1.9 Total government expenditure on goods and services at 1983 prices (£million)

1975	1976	1977	1978	1979	1980	1981	1982	1983
14,745	17,550	19,131	21,390	24,879	31,661	35,535	39,125	43,429

SOURCE: CSO, *National Income and Expenditure*, 1984, p.67.

levels of government spending exceeded these plans? (For a full discussion see J. J. Richardson, 1982.) First, the Conservatives had agreed during the 1979 General Election campaign to honour pay agreements made by the Clegg Commission and were obliged to accept findings of the Civil Service comparability machinery, before abolishing both of these systems of assessing wage demands. More recently however, pay comparability has become fashionable again. Thus, public sector pay (which amounts to about 30 per cent of total government expenditure) rose initially in excess of private sector pay and of the current inflation rates. Although since then the government has had greater success in establishing public sector 'pay norms' which are more akin to expected inflation levels, some higher settlements have had to be tolerated. For example, in 1981–2, whereas the public sector pay target was 4 per cent, there were significant 'special cases': local authority workers received a 7 per cent wage increase, the police 13 per cent, firemen 10 per cent, water workers 9 per cent, and miners just over 9 per cent.

Whilst the government did resist demands and strike action for higher pay for the extremely low paid National Health Service workers, this should not disguise the difficulties it has had in achieving public sector pay settlements which correspond to public expenditure targets. In 1984 the government had found itself having to assent to wage increases well above the 3–3½ per cent 'preferred range', to nurses, railwaymen and teachers, and indeed, in May, real earnings had risen by 7¾ per cent over the previous year – nearly 3 per cent higher than the then rate of inflation.

A second major problem area has been in reducing expenditure on nationalised industries. Although the government has been criticised for not doing enough in some such sectors, it has been forced by the recession to fund expenditure way above initial targets. For instance, expenditure on assistance to the coal industry more than doubled, from £232 million in 1980 to £495 million in 1981 (CSO, *National Income and Expenditure,* 1983:45).

The sale of some public corporations funds the PSBR in the short-term (but does not of course really reduce it), although clearly this policy must be limited to those very public sector organisations which are capable of paying their own way! The threat of privatisation has certainly had some beneficial effects, e.g. in improving the trading performance of British Airways, but the government is left with responsibility for the major loss-making industries and services, and has – hitherto at least – overridden public expenditure targets to sustain them.

The third factor which has undermined the government's plans for public expenditure, and which is of particular relevance in the present study, is the financial demands made upon the public purse by increased unemployment. As early as November 1980, the Chancellor of the

Exchequer had estimated that over £1 billion had then been added to the PSBR as a result of recession being deeper than had been expected. The first element of this additional expenditure is in the sheer costs of social security benefits and lost tax revenues. Even though the government abolished the earnings-related unemployment benefit in order to reduce public expenditure, the costs of mass unemployment remain a considerable burden. Estimates as to the precise additional costs of unemployment do of course vary according to which factors are taken into account. In 1982, the Manpower Services Commission suggested that 'each additional 100,000 unemployed is estimated to cost well over £400m, (current prices), in benefit payments and the revenues foregone' (MSC, 1982a:4). It has also been roughly calculated that, on the basis of indicators of social security payments and lost tax revenues, the annual cost to the country of three million unemployed would be about £15,000m, (at 1982 prices): one-and-a-half times the annual public sector borrowing target for 1981 − 2 (Institute of Fiscal Studies, 1982).

The government has shown considerable political courage in resisting the rather simple-minded view, often expressed by the Labour opposition, that it would be cheaper to keep people in their existing jobs by subsidising them. This argument misses the point that the UK has to increase its competitiveness and has to go through restructuring, and that often markets do not exist for non-competitive British goods, e.g. Bathgate. Also, the government has decided that these costs are worth bearing in order to achieve what they see as much-needed changes in working attitudes. Further unexpected costs have been incurred as a result of mass unemployment: the costs of the various job-protection and job-creation schemes (see Chapter 3 for full details). These were initially contracted after Geoffrey Howe's first budget in 1979, but with rapid increases in unemployment levels the government soon resorted to following the pattern of its predecessor in trying to use such schemes to ameliorate this trend. In particular, with the onset of the politically sensitive issue of mass youth unemployment, James Prior, then Secretary of State for Employment, and, also one of the Cabinet's leading moderates, succeeded in securing increased expenditure on the Youth Opportunities Programme. There was an increase in the number of entrants to this scheme, from 210,000 to 360,000 − 100,000 more than the original target. Similarly, whilst the numbers projected for the job-creation scheme Short Term Employment Programme in 1980 − 1 were 12,000 to 14,000, the actual number entering the scheme was in excess of £18,000. Even under the more hard-line Secretary of State for Employment, Norman Tebbit, expenditure on these sorts of schemes continued to rise: £1,000 million was initially committed to the first year of the Youth Training Scheme (though this may not in fact all be spent). Overall, the expenditure of the MSC (including that on behalf of the Department of Employment) rose from

£727.1 million in 1979–80, to an estimated £1343.2 million (MSC, 1983:34). At constant prices, this represents a rise of around 20 per cent. It now looks as though the government is prepared for further increases in expenditure in this field. The estimated expenditure increase of the MSC between 1982–3 and 1986–7 (at 1982–3 cash limit prices) is around 65 per cent (MSC, 1983a:36).

It is clear that any single characterisation of the politics of either the Labour or the Conservative Governments since, say, 1970 is very difficult. When in office, Labour was actually committed to what are now called Thatcherite policies. Following the rapid expansion of the money supply which contributed to further inflation between 1973 and 1975, Denis Healey's policy was officially described as follows:

...the focus of monetary policy is now specifically the control of the money supply for which a formal target – in the form of a preferred range for annual growth – was announced in 1976. Control of the money supply, in helping to rebuild a climate of confidence and stability in financial markets and to reduce expectations of future increases in prices, is now seen as one of the two main strands of counter inflation policy, the other being policy in pay and prices. (Treasury, July 1978:4)

This statement, with the exception of the reference to pay and prices, could equally have been issued by Mrs Thatcher's Government, some three years later.

In practice, Mrs Thatcher has had to be less Thatcherite than her public image suggests. Her government has been a fascinating mixture of contradictions, and it is thus important to ask what have been the achievements of the Conservative Government since 1979. It was endemic to the 'Thatcher approach' that there should be some short-run costs to be paid, in order to put the British economy back on a stable and competitive footing. However, the employment costs have certainly been greater and longer-lasting than expected. The official figures, which constitute the most conservative estimates, indicate that unemployment is currently in the region of three million, of whom over one million have been without work for over a year. Although the levels will probably not rise a great deal above this level within the forseeable future, equally there is little sign of any major reduction in these figures. Moreover, the gross domestic product declined in real terms below pre-1979 levels: in 1980, GDP fell by 3 per cent on the previous year, and the 1981 figure was a further 2 per cent lower than 1980. Whilst, prior to 1979, the figures for UK industrial production increases were about the same as the OECD average, during the early 1980s, when the UK GDP was in decline, the average OECD figure for 1980 and 1981 was a 1.4 per cent increase.

Most significantly perhaps, whereas output from North Sea oil and gas rose by 72 per cent between 1979–83, manufacturing production fell by 15.75 per cent over the same period. The period has also been characterised by record levels of company closures. In the first nine months of 1981 alone, 6,223 British companies went bankrupt, and company liquidations during 1983 in just England and Wales totalled 12,466 – 51 per cent higher than the equivalent figures for 1981.

One of the main aims of the Conservative Government was to increase productivity in industry, and this is one thing which could be achieved with a significant drop in employment. Between 1980 and mid-1982, productivity increased in the manufacturing sector at an annual rate of 7.5 per cent. Of course, productivity improvements are most significant when contrasted with achievements of trading competitors. The OECD reported that, during 1983 Britain had fallen from thirteenth to fourteenth in the ladder of international industrial competitiveness among OECD countries. International competitiveness does not just take into account comparative industrial productivity levels, but also the trade-weighting of currencies. While the relative value of sterling has recently declined against the dollar, the damage was done to Britain's international trading position between 1979 and 1982, when the government tolerated a pound artificially inflated by the existence of North Sea oil. It was argued in some quarters that the pound's value against other European currencies and the yen continued to undermine the country's competitiveness.

In the realms of taxation and public expenditure, (though not the public sector borrowing requirement), it has been demonstrated that the Conservative Government has failed to meet its objectives. After initial failures, more recently the rate of monetary growth has been reduced from about a 20 per cent rate in 1979 to about a 10 per cent rate in 1983. The one clear policy success that the government can claim in the economic field is that of bringing down inflation to single figures in the spring of 1982, and as low as 3.7 per cent in the spring of 1983. By the end of 1983, the underlying rate of inflation was around 5 per cent. Thus, although inflation initially continued to grow under the Conservatives, it has now been reduced well below the level of May 1979.

It remains to be seen whether the government is correct in its original prognosis that, once inflation was brought under control, the economy would stabilise, attract greater investment and achieve sustained economic growth, thereby diminishing present unemployment levels. Certainly, consumer demand has increased and a recovery has begun. However, whilst the OECD predicts better prospects for the world economy during 1985, it expects the British economic recovery to continue, but at a slower than average pace.

Perhaps the most disturbing prospect pertaining to unemployment is the apparent decoupling of the traditional link between economic growth and employment. A survey by the CBI Special Programmes Unit in 1981 suggested that a high percentage of employers could increase output significantly *without* increasing their labour forces (Richardson, 1983:29).

It is particularly pessimistic that, in early 1984, firms such as Ferranti which were supposed to be operating on a sound footing, should still be making redundancies. The OECD also confirms this pessimism as to the likely levels of economic growth making any significant inroads into unemployment levels. Indeed, it has suggested that as the output of the manufacturing sector has been so limited since 1980, the increase in demand is more likely to lead to further import penetration than to the creation of new jobs in the UK. It is as yet too soon to assess the impact of recent exchange rate shifts upon UK employment levels.

The government's 1984 budget, described by Chancellor Nigel Lawson as a 'budget for jobs', sought to make some impact on unemployment by means of reducing the cost of labour. The CBI finally had its plea met for the abolition of the National Insurance Surcharge (this 'tax on jobs' was originally introduced by Labour and initially increased by the Conservative Government), along with a reduction in corporation tax. These measures might be expected to give employers some incentive to take on new staff. However, employment in the building industry, already suffering after cutbacks in grants towards housing renovations, is likely to be further hit by the imposition of VAT on building alterations in the 1984 budget. Indeed, when pressurised in the House of Commons, Norman Tebbit admitted that he could not give an assurance that the budget would lead to a fall in unemployment.

In summary, the Conservatives were initially failing in almost all their economic goals, but more recently they have had more success in reducing inflation, the PSBR and monetary growth. There have been productivity improvements, though to some extent these were inevitable after a period of high unemployment and recession. The likelihood of these achievements leading to a downturn in unemployment in the short term remains in doubt.

1.3 The distribution and impact of unemployment

It is well known that in the post-World War II period, until about ten years ago, Britain, like most other advanced Western industrial countries, succeeded in restricting unemployment to what were considered to be acceptable levels. Although successive governments claimed this to be a major policy success, more favourable terms of trade and relatively low oil prices also contributed to this happy situation.

Table 1.10 illustrates that since 1970, this state of relative employment equilibrium has been savagely disrupted. The first such disruption occurred in 1971 – 2. The unemployment figures were approaching the one million mark in the early months of 1972, and the seriousness and novelty of this state of affairs swiftly provoked a determined reflationary budget in March of that year. Whilst this was accompanied by costs in

Table 1.10 *UK unemployment 1970–1984: average numbers and percentages of total workforce*

	1970	1971	1972	1973	1974
Numbers (000's)	603.4	755.4	844.1	597.9	599.7
Percentage	2.6	3.4	3.8	2.6	2.6
	1975	1976	1977	1978	1979
Numbers (000's)	935.6	1,304.6	1,422.7	1,409.7	1,325.5
Percentage	4.1	5.6	6.0	6.0	5.6
	1980	1981	1982	1983[1]	1984
Numbers (000's)	1,794.7	2,733.8	2,916.9	3,104.7	3,159.8
Percentage	7.4	11.3	12.2	12.9	13.1

SOURCE: Department of Employment Gazettes

[1] From 1983 figures reflect changes made in the system of counting in 1983 budget, and are thus about 400,000 lower than they would have been.

terms of inflation and an adverse balance of payments, the figures for unemployment had dropped to an average of 2.6 per cent over 1974: around 600,000 people. However, since then there has been a steady increase in the numbers and the proportion of the workforce without work. For both these indicators, the figures doubled between 1974 and 1976, and have doubled again between 1979 and 1981. In January 1982, the number of people out of work in the country exceeded 3 million for the first time, and this had risen to over 3.3 million by January 1985. Estimations of future trends vary, usually according to political persuasion. There is agreement, however, that the present levels of unemployment are likely to continue, if not increase. The incidence of long-term unemployment (i.e. of over twelve months) is thought likely to increase.

Besides giving a brief précis of the overall national problem of unemployment, it is also necessary to outline certain special characteristics of contemporary British unemployment. This is not simply for their intrinsic interest, but because certain features of the problem may be particularly pertinent to the nature of the political debate and to the specific measures introduced by government.

The first such feature of importance is the extent of regional disparity in the unemployment levels. Table 1.11 indicates that unemployment in the West Midlands, the North, Wales, Scotland and Northern Ireland regions of the United Kingdom is at least 4.4 points higher on the national scale than in the South East or East Anglia. Indeed, in real terms the proportion of the workforce unemployed in Northern Ireland is more than twice that in the South East. Further, certain inner-city areas are characterised by markedly higher levels of unemployment than the surrounding areas. Relatively low levels of unemployment in the latter may mask disproportionately high levels of unemployment in the former. For example, the Chatham office in the South East region recorded a rate

Table 1.11   *Regional unemployment levels, 1983*

	Rate of unemployment %
South East England (including Greater London)	9.5
East Anglia	10.6
South West England	11.3
West Midlands	15.7
East Midlands	11.7
Yorkshire and Humberside	14.1
North West England	15.7
North England	17.3
Wales	16.1
Scotland	15.0
Northern Ireland	21.0

SOURCE: *Department of Employment Gazette*, April 1984:S26-S29.

of 16.7 per cent unemployment in March 1984: 75 per cent higher than the average for that region (*Department of Employment Gazette*, April 1984:S30).

Although until recent years it was thought that a high number of the unemployed had not had work experience prior to registering as unemployed (see W. W. Daniel, 1981), more up-to-date evidence suggests that now 71 per cent had been in full-time and 6 per cent in part-time employment (Economist Intelligence Unit, 1982:39). At the same time, people are now more likely to remain unemployed longer than was previously the case. Whilst in April 1980, 38 per cent of the unemployed left the register within three months of joining it, this had fallen to 27 per cent by April 1982 (MSC, 1982c:11). By January 1985, 38.2 per cent of the total unemployed had been so for over a year (*Department of Employment Gazette*, February 1985:S33).

One of the most significant structural features of contemporary unemployment is the high proportion of young people without work. Maurice Peston has estimated that whilst in 1966 about a quarter of people unemployed fell into the under-25 age group, by the end of 1980 almost half of the unemployed were within this age group (Peston, 1981:29). By October 1982 the proportion of the unemployed who were under 25 had fallen to just over one-third (1.3 million out of 3.3 million), mainly because this age group has been the major beneficiary of government 'mopping up' schemes. Over half a million school-leavers entered Youth Opportunity Programmes during 1981–2 (MSC, 1982a:14). Despite the increase in numbers on YOPs and the advent of YTS, by October 1983 the proportion of the total unemployed taken up by this group had risen again to 40 per cent, though the absolute numbers remained just under 1.3 million.

The seriousness of youth unemployment is brought home when one considers that the 16 to 25 years age group only constitutes about a fifth of the working population. In September 1973, only 14,000 school-leavers still had no job; in September 1981, 280,000 school-leavers were still unemployed, despite the increase in entrance to further and higher education. It should be added that the pressure on youth unemployment might slightly ease during the 1980s due to declining birth rates in the late sixties and early seventies, although this does also depend on them improving their performance in the job market. The length of time spent unemployed by members of the 16 to 25-years age group is increasing rapidly. In October 1982, 30.1 per cent of those unemployed for six months or over were in this age group. A year later this had increased to 38 per cent.

A further important characteristic of contemporary unemployment is the proportion of racial minorities without work. This feature often overlaps with the themes of inner-city and youth unemployment. It has been estimated that the rate of unemployment among black and Asian workers is almost twice that for all workers. (Sinfield and Showler, 1980:16). A survey by the Commission for Racial Equality found that six out of ten black and four out of ten Asian teenagers were unemployed: a finding which the Commission blamed mainly on discrimination rather than educational disparities. Perhaps even more significantly, over 80 per cent of those interviewed, including some white youths, believed that some employers discriminated against ethnic minorities (Commission for Racial Equality, 1982).

The 1982 Annual Report of the Commission for Racial Equality backed up these findings. A further survey found that 50 per cent of employers still discriminate against black applicants for jobs, contributing to a situation which the report described as 'potentially explosive' (Commission for Racial Equality, 1983). Further, a survey of Bradford Asians who had left school over a year earlier indicated that only 28 per cent were in real, paid employment. The rest were either unemployed (41 per cent) or were taking part on YOP schemes (31 per cent). In short, 'Asian school-leavers were more than twice as likely to be unemployed or on YOP as school-leavers in general' (Campbell and Jones, 1982:4).

This outline of the extent and distribution of contemporary UK unemployment does not of itself demonstrate why it is a problem. Indeed, there exists a belief (usually unspoken) that it is not of itself a problem; the argument being that, in the short term, mass unemployment will reduce relative labour costs, so providing increased employment in the long term in commercially viable enterprises, and providing the lubricant to gain much-needed improvements in productivity. This point aside, what are the social consequences of high levels of unemployment?

First, despite those who argue that the Protestant work ethic has been undermined, it does appear that the unemployed still wish to work. (Economist Intelligence Unit, 1982:39). This finding was most poignantly illustrated recently when about 400 men and women besieged a Midlands Jobcentre in snow and rain, after it was rumoured that the Austin Rover plant at Longbridge was looking for more workers. Sadly, most of these hopefuls will have been disappointed as the 800 vacancies which did exist were mainly filled by those who had worked previously in the firm, and who had been contacted privately (*Guardian*, 4.1.84).

This inability of citizens to fulfil their modest ambitions of finding work poses a potential problem for society, but also reflects difficulties which the unemployed and their families may encounter. First, although it is true that *some* jobs are not much more remunerative than unemployment or social security benefits, one of the main problems faced by the unemployed (particularly the long-term unemployed) is their low standard of living. The MSC have calculated that, on average, social security benefits provide unemployed people with about 65 per cent of their former net weekly income. A recent government report indicated that the gap between the average income of a household whose head is out of work is about £50 per week lower than the average household whose head is in work (Central Statistical Office, 1983).

Such is the potential political sensitivity of the lot of the long-term unemployed that it is suggested that an MSC report on the subject was censored in order to give prominence to government responses, rather than to the material difficulties faced by this group. Illustrative of the material cut from the draft is the following: 'The relative poverty of the long-term unemployed is emphasised when their benefit is expressed as a proportion of income of all male workers. Single person only 32 per cent, married 57.3 per cent of male net income' (de la Cour, 1983). A recent United Nations study found that the benefits for the unemployed in Britain are a lower proportion of national average earnings than in any other major western country. In 1982 the unemployment benefit as a percentage of earnings for a worker with three children was 47 per cent. Although comparisons are difficult, due to different systems of payment, in France and West Germany the comparable figures would be more in the region of 65 per cent.

It has also been argued in some quarters that prolonged unemployment has an adverse effect on health. A recent report indicated that death rates among unemployed men were considerably higher than among comparable groups of employed men. Although unemployment may not be a prime causal factor in all cases, it was thought likely to be in the case of accidents and violent deaths (including suicide), which occur twice as frequently among unemployed as employed men (Office of Population, Censuses and Surveys, 1983). Preliminary research on the relationship between parasuicide (non-fatal deliberate self-harm) suggests that the unemployed in general were almost twelve times as likely to commit parasuicide as the employed. This likelihood rose to nineteen times in the case of those unemployed for over a year (Platt, 1983).

A report commissioned by the Department of Health and Social Security concluded that the children of the jobless suffer from stunted growth. The director of the research reported that, having accounted for relevant biological factors, the social factors potentially contributing to lack of growth were 'dominated by the effect of unemployment and its associated factors' (*The Times*, 30.12.83).

Such personal costs may also rebound upon society with respect to diminishing work skills and capacity to work, and in terms of cynicism towards the system, which has been linked with increase in crime, racialism and civil unrest. The riots of the summer of 1981 were linked in the minds of many with unemployment. Certainly the government assumed a connection, and dispatched the Minister for the Environment, Michael Heseltine, to Liverpool with a brief to open up job opportunities. One of the findings of a recent research investigation among unemployed youths in the West Midlands was that there was a propensity for some white youths to be attracted by fascist organisations because of the sense of alienation (Taylor, 1983). It should be noted that in all of these instances it is difficult to establish conclusive causal relationships. Nevertheless, the correspondence of unemployment with crime (especially among the young) and other instances of unrest cannot be ignored.

Unemployment is also an economic problem in terms of its impact upon demand, its impact upon the national purse, and in terms of the various remedies postulated. Unemployment presents an economic burden to the state. (The impact of mass unemployment upon public expenditure patterns was discussed in the previous section.) In addition, high unemployment means lower absolute levels of production. The MSC has estimated that 'each 100,000 increase in registered unemployment is associated with about £590 million of output foregone. Unemployment of 2.5 million would represent foregone national output of about £10.7 billion' (MSC, 1981a:7).

The lower living standards endured by the unemployed must also have a significant (if unquantifiable) feedback effect on demand for home produced goods and services. For example, in a recent review of the food and drinks manufacturing industry, it was reported that

there is agreement that the decline in the value and volume of food and drink consumption is directly related to the erosion of net disposable incomes, in particular, the impact on lower income groups most affected by unemployment . . . Consumption of beer and whisky slumped over the past two years and areas of higher unemployment have been especially hard hit. These are generally areas of heavy industry where per capita consumption among those doing strenuous manual work has traditionally been high. The continuing decline of jobs in these areas is likely to reduce consumption further. (Food and Drink Manufacturing EDC, 1983:2, 3)

1.4 Summary

We have sought to portray the problem of unemployment in three broad contexts: first, as a function of international economic factors; secondly, as one of the several factors in the equation of national economic policy-making facing successive governments; and thirdly, as an issue contributing to further social and societal problems. The unemployment issue seems to be a feature of what we call a 'cycle of deprivation'. The British economy has tolerated inefficiencies for many years, cushioned by little international competition and cheap energy costs. However, these inefficiencies have been exposed as the world economy went into recession and as other countries' competitiveness improved. The rise in unemployment has coincided with this 'exposure', and so it has been harder for British governments to provide relatively generous benefit levels (compared to France and West Germany). Recognition of this problem does not easily lead to a solution. As we have indicated, a 'jobs at any cost' policy may actually hasten the decline in the country's wealth, accelerating the cycle of deprivation. Increases in taxation to pay for higher benefit levels are usually thought to be politically unpopular, and may stunt further investment by business. In addition, there has been some attempt by the Conservative Government to increase the attractiveness of work, not by increasing wages (given its other objectives) but by lowering the real value of benefits. If spending on social security had continued at the same real rates as in 1979, government expenditure would be £6.5 billion higher than it was in 1984: the equivalent of more than 2p on income tax.

In what ways has the unemployment issue impacted upon the political debate, and how have politicians sought to present the issue to the country are questions that are taken up, as the main focus of this book, in the following chapters.

2 The Politics of Unemployment

2.1 Party perspectives on unemployment

Anyone living in Britain today can be in no doubt that the political parties pay special attention to the unemployment issue, an issue that has caused conflict not only between the major parties but also within them. It is important to draw a distinction between the rhetoric of party debate and the actual behaviour of parties in government. It is also important, however, to be aware of the nature and content of party debate. In this section we provide brief summaries – snapshots – of the party political perspectives on the unemployment issue, putting some of the pet theories and slogans into context. We do not propose to provide concerted critical accounts of these perspectives, but rather, a broad overview of the debate and issues of controversy. The political impact, or salience of unemployment, will be considered later in the chapter.

The Conservative Party

As was indicated earlier, the Thatcher leadership of the Conservative Party has been characterised by a radical rhetoric, especially in the fields of economic and industrial policy. A major element in this rhetoric has been an adherence to the tenets of monetarism, which, put most simply, blames inflation upon excessive increases in the money supply, and unemployment upon government mismanagement of factors which should best be left to the direction of market forces. In some ways it is ironic that the Conservative Party should have become so closely associated with this new creed, as in practice the 1974 – 9 Labour Government was already giving greater attention to restricting money supply in its fight against inflation. In 1976, James Callaghan had told the Labour Party

We used to think you could just spend your way out of recession and increase employment by cutting taxes and boosting government spending. I tell you, in all candour, that the option no longer exists, and that insofar as it ever did exist, it only worked by injecting bigger doses of inflation into the economy followed by higher levels of unemployment as the next step. That is the history of the past twenty years. (Labour Party, Annual Conference, 1976)

Further, the close, philosophical adherence to monetarist principles by the Tory Party is very much associated with its present leader Margaret Thatcher, and her elevation of Sir Keith Joseph within the Party. It is interesting to note that Thatcher herself was elected in somewhat freak circumstances, after Edward Heath resigned rather than face a second ballot, and William Whitelaw declined to fight against his old leader.

Once she was elected to the leadership of the Party, economic liberalism became its ascendant philosophy. Thus the views of Milton Friedman came to dominate the debate within the Conservative Party.

What are his views on the question of unemployment? For Friedman, each country has a 'natural rate' of employment which is dependent upon such factors as 'the effectiveness of the labour market, the extent of competition and monopoly, the barriers or encouragements to working in various occupations and so on' (Friedman, 1977:15). He continues to illustrate this point with reference to the USA, where he points to the entry of new groups (e.g. women, teenagers, and part-time workers) into the labour force, and the generous levels of assistance to unemployed workers, as determinant factors of the US natural rate of unemployment. Friedman goes on to argue that although high inflation does not necessarily imply either high or low unemployment.

the institutional and political arrangements that accompany it, either as relics of earlier history or as products of the inflation itself, are likely to prove antithetical to the most productive use of employed resources – a special case of the distinction between the state of employment and productivity of an economy. (Friedman, 1977:23)

The danger to society of high inflation for Friedman lies in the reaction of the public to the uncertainties produced by price instability. Thus spending, rather than saving, becomes rational which, he argues, leads to a polarisation of society. Equally, it may contribute, in two different ways, to a higher natural rate of unemployment. First, the necessity to introduce price-indexing on contracts introduces rigidities and reduces the effectiveness of markets; secondly, it renders market prices a less efficient system of co-ordinating economic activity, undermining the use of the system of absolute prices as a method of exchange.

Having briefly summarised the views of Friedman on the unemployment question, we should add that we see no necessary *direct* link between his theories and what the Conservative Government has done. It is unlikely that many Conservative MPs will have even read any of his work. However, the views of Friedman, and other 'new right' economists have contributed to the ideas of opinion-formers within the Conservative Party, and thus to an overall change in the climate and language of opinion.

A further example is the work of Friedrich Hayek and the Austrian school, who have also contributed to the new Conservative sphere of ideas. Their proposed remedy to the problems of unemployment and recession is an all-out attack on inflation *at all costs,* by means of strictly limiting the money supply, thus creating higher levels of unemployment in the short-term than have ever been experienced in the UK. Equally influential in the realm of ideas have been what can be called 'supply side' economists, who are critical of the more abstract work of Friedman and

Hayek and argue that higher taxation increases the cost of work and reduces the price of leisure to the individual, resulting in higher unemployment and reduced production.

This range of new-right economic ideas made its impact upon several important economic journalists, including Samuel Brittan and Peter Jay, but most significantly, in the case of the Conservative Party, upon Sir Keith Joseph. In his now legendary Preston speech, in September 1974, he argued that by printing money, government had caused inflation, which whilst in the short term arrested increases in unemployment, in fact created even higher rates of unemployment in the long term. After, by a quirk of fate, Mrs Thatcher had been elected leader, in choosing to elevate Joseph within the Party she achieved a mixture of new-right economic theory and her own brand of 'traditional values', such as hard work, thrift, and individual responsibility and reward.

The application of this mix of views was most clearly directed specifically to the issue of unemployment in a paper written by Keith Joseph (1978). He argued that governments could only create the right conditions for high employment by encouraging competitiveness, entrepreneurialism and profits. In contrast, Socialist governments, in attempting to use the state to maintain jobs in unproductive sectors, had undermined these very pillars of a healthy economy, as essential to the workers as to the employers. This was due, he argued, to a misunderstanding of the nature of work.

Once the concept of a job is divorced from its social function of creating value by satisfying wants, a job is transformed from a factor of production into an article of consumption – something to be given for the recipient's benefit – and at the expense of others. In consequence, the whole economic nexus on which full employment and rising living standards depends is distorted and disrupted. (Joseph, 1978:15)

He argued that

We must, therefore, encourage enterprise and adaptability if we are to approach full employment. Alas, we are far from doing so. Inflation, high government spending and borrowing; high personal taxation on income and capital; price, pay, dividend, rent controls; untaxed benefits; non-productive jobs with attractive perks; over-regulation; Luddism; all cumulatively suppress enterprise and adaptability.

Council housing policy and government destruction of private rented housing discourage mobility. Effective minimum wage norms under the Equal Opportunities and Employment Protection Acts price some least-skilled and least-qualified workers – the very workers meant to benefit – out of work. Price controls squeeze out jobs and add a further hazard to investment and expansion. Regulations and their bureaucracies constantly harass and divert management. (Joseph, 1978:9 – 10)

This catalogue of complaints against factors which Joseph saw as raising unemployment above its natural rate has been reproduced in various forms by the Prime Minister and other Cabinet spokesmen to explain their policy of attempting to reduce the role for government and to fight inflation as a means to the end of reducing unemployment.

Debate continues within the mainstream of the Conservative Party on the question of unemployment. In the foreword to a 1981 Conservative Research Department paper on unemployment, Norman Tebbit, then Secretary of State for Employment, gave emphasis to the need for competitiveness and profitability: 'The priority of today must be to restore profitability to British industry. Without it, there will be little new investment, little job security and few new jobs' (Rouse and Hobson, 1981:354). In the paper that followed, the authors blamed unemployment on poor productivity and competitiveness, which are in turn functions of managerial ineffectiveness, over-concentration on large plants (exacerbating strikes and management problems), overmanning and restrictive practices, poor industrial relations and a failure to adapt to changing consumer requirements. Special attention was given to the effect upon the problem of increased trade union powers. Since 1967 trade unions had won 'excessive' pay awards, it was argued, pricing some employees out of work, and contributing to losses in competitiveness and profitability. The paper concluded that, although government can create conditions for fuller employment by reducing its own spending and borrowing, cutting taxes and encouraging enterprise, and reducing the burden of the public sector, changes were still needed in industry to achieve increases in employment.

Another source of ideas on the unemployment question within the Conservative Party is Patrick Minford, Professor of Economics at Liverpool and an economic adviser to the government, who is quickly becoming one of the chief British economic theoreticians of the right. In his recent book, *Unemployment: Cause and Cure,* he acknowledges that UK unemployment is partly a function of the world recession and of the Conservative Government's attempts to reduce inflation. However, he argues that it is not these cyclical factors, but the underlying factors which explain the very high levels of unemployment. Minford first singles out excessively high wage costs, whether as a result of high real wages, or low productivity. But, the book gives greater attention to 'two major distortions in the UK labour market which prevent real wages and productivity from adjusting naturally to shifts in technology, demand and industrial structure, and relocating those freed from one sector into other sectors' (Minford, 1983:2). These, according to Minford, are, firstly, the benefit system, due to the relatively high level and indefinite nature of which, he argues, insufficient incentive is provided to enter employment. Thus, although shift in economic conditions may warrant a reduction of real wage costs, because unemployment benefit levels act as a 'floor' to the whole wage structure, such a shift may actually result in higher unemployment. There is thus insufficient wage flexibility in the UK economic system. Minford's second major factor in explaining high levels of UK unemployment is

the power of unions to raise wages relative to non-union wages. Given the way the benefit rate sets a floor below the non-union wage, as unions raise wages for their members, the workers who then lose their jobs cannot all find alternative work in the non-union sector because wages there do not fall sufficiently; the overall effect is increased unemployment. (Minford, 1983:3)

On the basis of his analysis, Minford proposes policy changes in four areas. First, he suggests that rather than using the flat-rate benefit system, a ratio system is used, such that maximum levels of benefit would be calculated as a percentage (70 per cent was suggested) of net income in work. Secondly, it is suggested that after a certain period the unemployed should be obliged to do community work, or risk losing their benefit. Thirdly, and to complement the first proposal, Minford advocates raising tax thresholds and child benefits for those in low-paid occupations, to provide a greater incentive to work. Finally, he proposes that the means-tested benefits in kind be abolished and replaced with a more generous Family Income Supplement, which as well as being administratively simpler and cheaper, would undermine the 'poverty trap'.

In addition to these proposals, Minford also suggests a weakening of trade union power, such that unions would be subject to common law, that no contracts should be contingent on the union status of employees, and that a Labour Monopolies Commission be formed to investigate and remedy breaches of public interest in labour market competition. To complement these policy proposals, Minford advocates (i) the abolition of Wage Councils in order to prevent wage rises which might lead to unemployment, (ii) the raising to economic levels of council house rents, and the de-control of the rentals in the private sector, to improve labour mobility, and (iii) the introduction of a regional employment subsidy based on regional unemployment rates in order to reduce such disparities, using EEC regional fund finance.

We have suggested that there is no necessary direct causal link between this range of ideas of economic liberalism (which are at times contradictory – see Ashford, 1984) and the policies of the Thatcher Government. Indeed, it is as likely that the economic theory and practice 'feed' off each other. More importantly, in this context, the Thatcher Government is subject to other pressures, both in the realm of ideas and in that of practical politics. As a result, few of the strategies outlined above have been consistently and thoroughly pursued. Overall, income tax had risen until the last year, and even then the lower paid did not gain disproportionate benefit. Although earnings-related unemployment benefit has been cut back and there have been reductions in the real levels of benefit, there has been no attempt to introduce the more sophisticated strategy suggested by Minford. Similarly, changes in trade union law have not gone as far as Minford advocated. The government was initially unable to control growth in the money supply, despite successive re-definitions of the concept, as it has had to meet other political pressures. It has had more success in recent years. The total weight of regulation has probably not changed very much under Mrs Thatcher. Ironically, in the fields that have been privatised and liberalised, it has probably increased.

The ideas of neo-liberalism certainly had some significance in the formation of government policy towards unemployment, notably in encouraging it to tolerate high levels of unemployment without making a rush for growth as Heath and Barber did in 1972. Also, considerable lip service is still paid to its tenets. In an interview with Julian Haviland, Margaret Thatcher said:

I cannot accept responsibility for those who strike themselves out of jobs, who insist on having over-manning or restrictive practices, who refuse to accept new technology, or who have not good management, or who don't design products which other people want to have. What I do accept responsibility for is creating the right financial framework and the right legal framework. I believe we've done that. (*The Times*, 5.5.83)

In her speech to the new Parliament in 1983, she said that the government will pursue its strategy for recovery and jobs with a five point strategy: (i) helping business to cut costs (ii) encouraging small business (iii) support for new technology (iv) increasing training and (v) increased trade union reform.

It would, however, be foolish to overstate the influence of theories – ministers are usually under too much pressure to have time to conjecture on the ideas of theoreticians. In any case, the demands of the ministers, respective civil servants and policy communities (see Chapter 4) provide more immediate sources of perspectives on the problem. Thus neo-liberal doctrine has had a significant impact on the Conservative approach to un-employment, but not a comprehensive one. It is also, of course, as mis-leading to suggest a cohesion of views of Conservative MPs and ministers as it is to assert a unity of neo-liberal economic theories regarding unem-ployment. In fact, a great array of opinions prevails, although it would be fair to say that these now coalesce more around the views of Friedman than Keynes. We will now proceed to examine more briefly the dissident views on unemployment of a small, but senior number of Conservative politicians.

The Conservative Party dissidents

In terms of parliamentary and governmental policy outcomes, the Conservative Party has had views broadly synonymous with those of the Conservative Government. However, this should not disguise the fact that opinion persists within the Party which is critical of the approach the leadership has taken towards the issue of unemployment in particular and the economy in general. This group has become known as the 'wet' wing of the Party. Such labels are always misleading in that they hide policy differences within the group; however, the term is generally applied to those towards the left of the Party on economic and social matters.

From the time that he was sacked from his position as Foreign Secretary and member of the government after the 1983 general election, Francis Pym has joined the group of other former Conservative Cabinet ministers in questioning the government's strategy. In an article in *The Times* summarising a speech he made in Oxford in November 1983, Pym argued that greater compassion was needed from the government. He suggested that, because of the potential of social divisiveness resulting from unemployment, a more humane social policy should be introduced: thus, the Government's economic strategy need not be abandoned, but tempered (Pym, 1983).

A more thoroughgoing critique has been made in the speeches and articles of Sir Ian Gilmour. In another *Times* article summarising a speech he made to the Tory Reform Group during the 1983 Conservative Party Conference, Gilmour's theme was that the pursuit of monetarism was an impediment to reducing unemployment. He argued for a reflation consisting of a reduction of various costs to industry, greater capital investment within public expenditure, and easier industrial borrowing. The reflation would be tempered by an effective incomes policy to prevent excessive price inflation (Gilmour, 1983a). In his recent book, *Britain Can Work*, Gilmour complains of the way monetarism has taken over the Conservative Party, and argues that putting people back to work is the best way of ensuring political stability for the country (Gilmour, 1983b).

In an interview with James Prior, then Secretary of State for Northern Ireland, in which he was asked about the government's policy on unemployment, he maintained that he was not disloyal to Mrs Thatcher on this issue, but expressed concern for those

vast numbers of people in Britain who are intensely patriotic and proud of what they are doing but don't actually aspire to greatness in society; they just want to go about their ordinary task and live with their families in reasonable conditions ... Sometimes I think we tend, for reasons of economics or because of our backgrounds, to think that everyone has got to be tremendously efficient and tremendously able and enterprising and so on. That isn't what society is made up of. I can play a part in putting forward our policies in a sensible, reasonable, understanding way. Sometimes we don't always do so. (*The Times*, 12.10.83)

Similarly, Peter Walker, Secretary of State for Energy, warned that the Conservatives would not be elected for a third term if high levels of unemployment persisted. He said that the government had done a great deal to help the young unemployed, but warned that for many the training schemes will be coming to an end and they (young people) will become exceedingly frustrated if there is no active opportunity for them. If we continue with sustained unemployment of the young the repercussions will be profound on society and the economy. (*Financial Times*, 16.11.83)

Indeed, Walker has been something of a persistent thorn in the side of the government on this issue. This was illustrated by a speech to the Tory Reform Group during the 1982 Conservative Party Conference in which he argued for economic growth and government investment to create jobs.

It is difficult to identify any particular impact of these Tory critics upon policy outcomes. Their role with Cabinet appears muted, and it is certainly the case that the overwhelming majority of Conservative MPs – especially the new cohort – display strong allegiance to the Party leadership. They have shown little inclination to polarise around the critics who are, after all, closely associated with the policies of former Prime Minister Edward Heath. What the critics have achieved is to keep the issue of an *alternative* Conservative strategy on the agendas of the Conservative Party and the right-wing press.

The Labour Party

If the Conservative victory in the 1983 General Election posed something of a point of interest for students of politics, given the high levels of unemployment, it was a cause of considerable depression within the ranks of the Labour Party (see Foot, 1984). Not only was the Thatcher Government re-elected, but in terms of 'the average share of the constituency vote going to Labour candidates, this was Labour's poorest showing since the party was founded in 1900' (Crewe, 1983).

In the aftermath of this disaster, blame was variously attributed to the leadership, the Party's right wing (notably Callaghan, Healey and Hattersley who publicly criticised the Party's manifesto), the media, and the SDP – Liberal Alliance. Although these all had significant impact, they cannot hide the fact that Labour did so badly despite such high unemployment and the issue's prominent standing in the minds of the electorate. One possible inference is that without mass unemployment the Party might have fared even worse. Apart from the factors that worked in the Conservative Party's favour, which have already been discussed, what, we might ask, were the particular factors within the Labour Party approach to the unemployment issue that contributed to this state of affairs?

Clearly they are very complex, but collectively they ensured that Labour have not presented a credible alternative on the unemployment issue. In the first place, disregarding questions of presentation, Michael Foot's criticism of unemployment having doubled under the Thatcher Government almost invariably invited the retort that it had also doubled under Labour when Foot himself was Secretary of State for Employment.

Thus, to simply criticise the Government for high unemployment was never going to be enough to increase electoral support. What was needed was the presentation of a perspective and a programme on the issue which could be understood and believed. This, however, the Party appeared to fail to provide.

To explain this gap, we should first look briefly at the development of broader economic outlooks within the Party. What is quite clear is the absence of any consensus within the Party on the solution to the problem. Now, of course, all political parties of whatever hue are always characterised by 'factions' and 'tendencies' (see Rose, 1964), and as was noted earlier the Conservative Party currently has a small but distinct group of dissidents. However, for whatever reasons – possibly the strong Tory bias within the press, the more open nature of debate within the Labour Party or the relative lack of deference to the leadership – the divisions within Labour appear more serious.

Among the many different perspectives within the Party, the most important cleavage lies between those advocating broadly traditional Keynesian responses to the problem, modified by adherence to competition goals, and those on the left of the Party – notably Tony Benn and the adherents to the Cambridge School of Economists – who have argued for a more thoroughgoing revision of Keynesianism, involving greater state activity in the control of the movement of finance, regulation of trade, and an extension of state ownership. (This takes no account of such factions as the Militant Tendency. For a Marxist critique of the Labour Party's approach to unemployment, see Jordan, 1982.) Thus internal division became a major obstacle to Labour's exploitation of the issue. During the run-up to the election campaign, these factors were compounded by what one senior party official privately described as 'over promising', whereas in fact the electorate's faith in the national governments' ability to solve major economic problems was in decline (see opinion poll data in 2.3 and 2.4).

A further problem which the Party – and especially its right wing – has faced has been adjusting to the shift of the 'battle ground' of economic debate. As has been illustrated by Callaghan's 1976 speech and the economic policy pursued by Healey, the practice of classical Keynesianism had been eschewed by the last Labour Government. Yet the Party's main solution to the current crisis, which it is argued is primarily caused by the pursuit of monetarism, is economic expansion. Indeed, the current Party leader, Neil Kinnock, seems to have recognised this problem, and that of over promising. In a television interview in January 1984, he abandoned the Party's previous commitment to bring unemployment down to one million in the lifetime of one Parliament, and said that it might be a mistake to set a target figure. He suggested that even if four million jobs were created, there might still be two million unemployed.

He further indicated his belief that during the 1983 election Labour had problems in securing an 'accurate perception' of its approach to such policy problems (*Financial Times*, 23.1.84).

The solution to the unemployment problem advocated by Labour is most clearly summarised in a 1982 edition of its *Economic Review*:

> ... there is an urgent need to stimulate the economy by raising demand in particular through increases in public spending, cuts in taxation, lower interest rates and a lower pound. The initial boost to demand will have a 'multiplier effect' on the economy as higher spending feeds through to higher incomes and then to further spending. This process of 'reflation' will entail a temporary increase in public borrowing, which will then fall as the economy responds, as tax revenues rise and spending on benefits falls. There is no reason why an increase in demand should produce higher prices since there is plenty of spare capacity in industry. Reflation, therefore, will produce more jobs, and higher output. Provided we take further measures to deal with imports, capital movements, training and industrial investment; and provided the expansion is carefully planned; there is no reason why the initial expansion should not lead on to sustained growth. (Labour Party, 1982a:15)

In the 1983 statement by the Shadow Chancellor and Labour's Treasury team, the right to work was described as a 'fundamental principle of democratic socialism', which would be achieved by 'securing a realistic wage rate' to improve competitiveness, by strengthening the public sector, especially in the construction and capital goods sectors, and by setting up new structures for 'democratic planning' to decide upon how the economy should be directed (Labour Party, 1982b). In another document published earlier in the same year, emphasis was given to the waste of unemployment, in terms of the people and skills which were not being utilised (Labour Party, 1982c). In the subsequent discussion, emphasis was given to the nature and distribution of the problem itself. Conservative economic policy was criticised, with the suggestion that its real intention was to use unemployment as a means of reducing trade union power, and to provide the rich with profits at the expense of the poor.

Finally, the paper presented the 'socialist alternative' to the Conservative policy, whose corner-stone was economic expansion. This would be achieved by increasing spending power (public and private) to enable goods to be bought, and production and demand for labour to increase. The goal of reducing unemployment would be complemented by greater economic and industrial planning, common ownership, more training schemes, and industrial democracy. In order to distinguish the Labour programme from those of other reflationary proposals, the document concluded that

It is not going to be easy to climb out of the economic morass we have been dragged into by the Tories. We certainly will not get far with the kind of half-baked ideas and half-hearted tinkering favoured by the SDP, Liberals and Tory 'wets'. Their proposals for 'modest expansion' will be barely sufficient to stop unemployment rising and even their limited measures will run into difficulties if they are not prepared to deal directly with rising imports and prices, and to plan industry. (Labour Party, 1982c:19)

This however does not enable the Party leadership to escape from the problem of wishing to distinguish itself from other reflationists, without at the same time alienating its own potential electoral supporters.

Illustrative of this aspect of the Labour Party's position was a recent speech by Roy Hattersley, deputy leader of the Party, who maintained that it was unconvincing for Labour to argue for a massive increase in demand as an automatic remedy for unemployment: a party which provided an inadequate or unconvincing response to the unemployment crisis, he said, would not win. He asserted that the public doubted Labour's ability to restrain inflation, and was suspicious of the view that unemployment could be easily solved. Indicative of the impact of the neo-liberal language on the political battleground, Hattersley placed emphasis on the need for a 'vigorous competition policy' within the framework of indicative planning and public spending on infrastructure (*The Times*, 16.5.84). So far, however, there has been little apparent move by the Labour leadership – unlike the Austrian and Swedish Social Democratic Parties – towards an agreement with trade unions over an incomes policy as part of a policy package to fight unemployment (see Webber, 1984).

The Liberal/SDP Alliance

As in many aspects of its economic and industrial policy, the Alliance has advocated something of a middle way in its policy proposals to meet the problem of unemployment. For example, a press release commented on the one hand that:

Mrs Thatcher and her Government have set their faces against any real help for the jobless. With unemployment showing no sign of falling, Ministers have even started making a virtue of the hardships for which they are overwhelmingly responsible.

On the other hand, the Alliance's own programme to get unemployment down was described as

a carefully costed realistic programme of special measures designed to reduce the number of jobless by one million within 2–3 years. Its effect on public borrowing would be an increase of only £3–4 billion, and it would not, like Labour's programme, lead to a wild increase in spending, a collapse of the exchange rate or an acceleration in inflation. (Liberal/SDP Alliance, 1983)

The interim report of the Alliance's Commission on Employment and Industrial Recovery published in 1982 also illustrated this attempt to win the theoretical middle ground. It stated that 'The main task of an Alliance

Government would be to restore the competitiveness of British industry'. This language echoes a major theme of Margaret Thatcher, yet competitiveness was to be achieved by 'a controlled reduction in the exchange rate, linked to moderate wage growth and improved productivity'. Aware of the dangers of runaway inflation for the economy, the document stated that their aim would best be achieved by means of a prices and incomes policy – something which the Conservative Government has attempted to achieve without actually admitting as much. Reminiscent of the Labour programme, the Commission advocated substantial capital investment in the public sector, but, it was added, this was not to be an end in itself, but to act as a stimulant to the private sector. In addition to expanding the Community Programme (see Chapter 3), other job-creation proposals were made: an Environment Improvement Programme and a Low Cost Jobs Creation Programme. Finally, an increase in training opportunities, and wider eligibility for the Job Release Scheme were advocated (Liberal/SDP Alliance, 1982:44 – 6).

One interesting proposal that has been adopted by the Alliance is the Counter-Inflation Tax proposed originally by the Liberal Party, and resurrected by an LSE Economics Professor and SDP Economic Policy Committee member, Richard Layard (1982). He presented the problem faced by West European governments, that they fear responding to unemployment in the traditional Keynesian manner because of its inflationary consequences, and suggested that the problem was not so much one of reducing inflation levels, but more one of restraining them once reduced. The tax is thus proposed as an alternative to the means of controlling inflation which Layard ascribed to the Conservative Party (that of mass unemployment) and the Labour Party (some form of centralised incomes policy). To summarise, a tax would be levied on firms making wage increases of over a nationally agreed norm, unless they could prove productivity increases. However, free collective bargaining would persist at local and national levels, and mass unemployment would not be needed to contain inflationary pressures. In addition, as the tax would increase the elasticity of demand for labour, union monopoly power would be less likely to act as a hindrance to new employment. Shirley Williams has argued that such a tax should be adopted in concert with improvements in consultation processes in industry and rewarding restraint by profit sharing (*Financial Times*, 20.10.83).

Having discussed the nature of the problem of unemployment, its place in British politics, and varying political perspectives on the issue, our study will now continue by identifying the main policy responses to the problem.

2.2 Unemployment and British electoral politics

The intrinsic importance of particular issues is not necessarily matched by their political salience (Moon, 1983). The *apparent* importance of issues is often a reflection of the attention devoted to them by politicians and the media: political issues are, after all, their stock-in-trade. However, in democratic systems the high salience of issues can provide a cue for governmental action. Sir Edward Boyle once commented that:

The Cabinet increasingly, as the years go on, tends to be most concerned with the agenda that the press and media are setting out as crucial issues before the nation at any one time. (Kogan, 1971:109)

Jose Harris has demonstrated that, around the turn of the twentieth century, the issue of unemployment was subject to significant shifts of salience, the objective nature of the problem aside (Harris, 1972). She demonstrated that despite high levels of unemployment in Britain during the nineteenth century, unemployment was not treated as a serious economic or political matter until the very end of the nineteenth and the beginning of the twentieth century. With the increasing enfranchisement and organisation of the working classes, the issue rapidly became a central one in the political arena, and appeared as such in the 1906 Liberal Party manifesto. The explanation which Harris offered for the adoption of the issue by the Liberal Party was that the Party feared the consequences of being politically outmanoeuvred by either the Conservative or Labour Party. In other words, it was perceived as important to be seen to be doing something about unemployment in order to avert the threat of a loss of political support to a competitor for government.

After the Second World War it became established political wisdom that mass unemployment would spell electoral disaster for a British government. Precisely why this shibboleth developed is less certain. The post-war generation had been haunted by the spectre of mass unemployment during the 1920s and 1930s and, perhaps most significantly, by the accompanying levels of deprivation and despair, most forcefully brought home by the Jarrow marchers. Although Keynes' *General Theory of Employment, Interest and Money* was first published in 1936, the view that governments could increase demand in an economy by lowering interest rates and create jobs by investing in public works did not acquire widespread legitimacy until towards the end of the war. This new feeling was summed up in an article in *The Times* during 1943: 'Next to war, unemployment has been the most widespread, the most insidious and most corroding malady of our generation. It is the specific social disease of western civilisation in our time' (quoted in Allen *et al.*, 1981:49). Such a view was further legitimised in the coalition government's 1944 White Paper, *Employment Policy,* which opened thus: 'The Government accept as one of their primary aims and responsibilities the maintenance of a high and stable level of employment after the war'. This White Paper, accepted by all of the political parties, proved to be a major policy commitment of governments until the present unemployment crisis. Indeed, over-adherence to this principle has been seen by some as a damaging constraint upon British economic policy, as it has obstructed flexibility in the labour market.

The success of the Labour Party in the 1945 General Election has been put down to several factors. One important factor was, surely, that large sections of the electorate were fed up with the old ways which had, among other things, been characterised by the toleration of high levels of unemployment by pre-war governments. Apart from the relatively higher levels of unemployment in the snow-bound winter of 1946 – 7, the experience of the immediate post-war years was in accord with public expectations about employment. Indeed, as Alan Deacon points out, the Attlee Labour Government was faced with acute labour shortages, such that the Cabinet even considered banning football pools in order to divert women employed therein into more useful employment (1981:63). The comparatively happy employment circumstances of post-war Britain (in contrast to the high levels of unemployment in the years following the end of World War I) together with the economic strategy pursued by the first post-war Tory Chancellor, Rab Butler, served to cement the view that governments were able to control levels of unemployment, and that they would continue to do so for reasons of electoral expediency.

It should be pointed out that despite *beliefs* as to the relationship between government performance (e.g., with respect to unemployment, inflation and consumption levels) and its popularity among the electorate, research suggests in fact the situation is far more complex. Goodhart and Bhansali concluded that 'the apparent sensitivity of political popularity to economic conditions, as shown by the equations, seems almost too much to credit' (1970:86). However, it has been pointed out by Frey and Garbers that the correlation of two such variables does not imply causation: government popularity might cause unemployment, and unpopularity might oblige a government to reduce unemployment. They further suggest that each month's findings for government popularity may be a function of the previous month's popularity modified by some random shock (Frey and Garbers, 1971). Further analysis led Miller and Mackie to conclude that:

The evidence is against a simple view of politics in which the electorate choose between competing teams of economic managers, base their choice on only two economic variables, and take no account of the politician's verbal interpretations of these economic statistics. (Miller and Mackie, 1973:279)

Miller and Mackie also suggested that the use of government economic statistics in model building was probably misleading anyway. The media's and politicians' presentations of the economic condition of the country were far more likely to be the potent cue for the electorate's perceptions of economic reality. Although recent, more advanced research has continued to suggest that relationships between economic performance and voting intentions remain significant (see Frey and Schneider, 1978), Pissarides concluded that:

> Governments may be able to learn something about the influence of their policies on voting by studying the way the Gallup poll responded to policy in the past, but too much concern with it (perhaps elevating it to an 'objective' of short-run economic policy) does not appear justified ... (Pissarides, 1980:579)

We will continue our analysis by looking more closely at the status and the impact of the unemployment issue in British politics, focusing on two periods, 1970–9 and 1979–84.

2.3 Politics and unemployment 1970 – 1979

Unemployment had started to rise during the mid-sixties, but the issue did not achieve significant political salience due to the Labour leadership's success in presenting this as a function of the process of industrial change which the country was experiencing, and the concentration of media and public attention upon the simultaneous problem of Britain's growing balance of payments deficits (see Deacon, 1981:71).

Reference to Table 1.10 illustrates that during 1970 the level of unemployment (seasonally adjusted) was 2.6 per cent. Whilst this represented one of the highest levels of unemployment in post-war Britain, it did not constitute a sharp increase on the figures for the previous three years. An average of more than 500,000 people were unemployed during the year, but this was not deemed worthy of debate in the House of Commons (see Table 2.1). Prior to the election campaign of 1970, only 5 per cent of the electorate saw unemployment as 'the single most important problem facing Great Britain today'. This contrasted with 27 per cent and 16 per cent for problems of the cost of living and strikes/industrial relations respectively (National Opinion Poll, May 1970).

The low figure matched the low level of salience attached to unemployment by the Labour Party in its campaigning: only 12 per cent of the Labour candidates mentioned the question in their election addresses (the 26th most frequently mentioned issue). The speeches of the Labour leader, Harold Wilson, totally ignored this matter (Robertson, 1971). The only context in which employment was raised in the Labour Manifesto was in connection with training and manpower planning for the needs of modern industry (Labour Party, 1970). The Conservative Party, however, attributed greater importance to the question.

Of all the Conservative candidates, 76 per cent mentioned the problem (second only to inflation – 92 per cent) in their election addresses, though their leader, Edward Heath, only devoted about two per cent of the total content of his speeches to Labour's record on unemployment (Robertson,

Table 2.1   Annual proportions of House of Commons business taken up
with question of unemployment 1970–1979[1]

	Columns occupied by unemployment	Unemployment as a percentage of total debate
1970		
May–Dec	—	0.00
1971	561	1.59
1972	419	1.18
1973	178	0.58
1974	57	0.22
1975	230	0.64
1976	141	0.40
1977	398	1.23
1978	698	2.12
1979		
Jan–April	18	0.17

[1]Both for Hansard columns indexed by 'unemployment' or 'unemployed' for the total annual columns, the figures have been rounded up where a partial column occurred. Columns devoted to written questions have been excluded in both cases.

1971). The Conservative Manifesto did refer back to the last Conservative administration when 'unemployment was low', but this did not constitute a major policy platform (Conservative Party, 1970). On the basis of these findings it can be concluded that whatever were the motives of the Conservative candidates in giving emphasis to the issue, it was a short-lived phenomenon having no distinct impact upon popular opinion or the parliamentary agenda. The issue was not discussed at either the Conservative or the Labour Party Conference of that year, and was the subject of a relatively small number of items and special articles in *The Times* (see Table 2.2), during the second half of 1970. During the early years of the Heath administration the issues of industrial relations, Barber's economic strategy, inflation and the Common Market were the predominant issues on the domestic front.

Table 1.10 indicates that over the years 1970–2 the levels of unemployment rose dramatically from 2.6 per cent to 3.8 per cent. This was matched by a distinct rise in the salience of the issue. In Parliament, 561 and 419 columns were taken up with debate on the matter, roughly equivalent to 1.59 per cent and 1.18 per cent of the respective total annual debate (Table 2.1).

The question became a major item of debate at the conferences of the Labour Party during these years, with several motions being discussed and voted upon. The 1971 Conference passed a resolution stating that the return to full employment should be the first priority for a next Labour Government (Labour Party, 1971:383). The Scottish Labour Party

*Table 2.2   Survey of news items and articles devoted to unemployment by
The Times*[1] *1970–1979*

	Total news items[2]	Index of news items	Special articles
1970 July – December	27	100	7
1971 January – June	102	377	18
July – December	123	455	17
1972 January – June	94	348	17
July – December	56	207	5
1973 January – June	33	122	6
July – December	20	74	4
1974 January – June	57	211	2
July – December	65	241	9
1975 January – June	68	251	9
July – December	138	511	28
1976 January – June	72	266	5
July – December	148	548	12
1977 January – June	196	725	12
July – December	177	655	18
1978 January – June	239	884	13
July – December	176	651	10
1979 January – June[3]	91	337	6

SOURCE: Times Index 1970–1979

[1] After 31 December 1972 figures include items in THES, TES and TLS.
[2] Includes leader articles, news items and special articles, but excludes correspondence.
[3] During suspension of publication (1.1.79–12.11.79) references in *The Times* Index were made to *The Daily Telegraph, Sunday Telegraph* and the *Telegraph Sunday Magazine,* in order to maintain a continuous newspaper index.

Conference was recalled on 16 November 1971 for a special debate on unemployment. In the following year a motion was passed at the national conference advocating that unemployment was 'the first priority on which the Labour Party should campaign nationally ...' (Labour Party, 1972:258).

The question of unemployment was also raised at the National Union of Conservative and Unionist Associations Conferences of 1971 and 1972. At these conferences, motions were put expressing 'serious concern' (Conservative Party, 1971:81) and regretting 'that despite the present intolerable level of unemployment Her Majesty's Government has still failed to evolve an effective regional policy' (Conservative Party, 1972:109), but both were easily defeated. None the less unemployment was the subject of major debate on both occasions, involving speeches by John Davies (Secretary of State for Trade and Industry). In passing, it is interesting to note that at the 1971 Conference, in his closing address,

Edward Heath blamed the rising unemployment on the old uneconomic ways of socialism. A year later John Davies symbolically declared, 'We have reached the clear conclusion that market forces will not unaided reverse in time the deterioration of our remoter and less favoured regions' (Conservative Party, 1972:115).

Not only did the salience of the issue increase in the fora of Parliament and of the political parties, Gallup poll findings showed a distinct peak in popular estimations of the importance of the problem of unemployment corresponding with the peak in the figures for the unemployed (Table 2.3). Similarly, the coverage by *The Times* of the unemployment issue reached a peak during late 1971 (Table 2.2).

Table 2.3   *Perceptions of public regarding importance of unemployment: response to question 'What would you say is the most urgent problem facing the country at the present time? 1970–1979*

	% Respondents	Rank of issue
December 1970	3	6=
April 1971	15	3
August 1971	28	1
December 1971	43	1
April 1972	27	1
August 1972	14	3
December 1972	11	3
April 1973	5	6
August 1973	2	9=
December 1973	1	6=
April 1974	2	8
August 1974	2	5=
December 1974	1	8=
April 1975	10	5
August 1975	14	2
December 1975	2	6
April 1976	19	2
August 1976	21	2
December 1976	14	3
April 1977	13	2
August 1977	23	2
December 1977	23	2
April 1978	36	1
August 1978	33	1
December 1978	24	2
March 1979[1]	18	3

[1] Due to General Election campaign, no poll taken in April.

SOURCE: Gallup Political Index 1970–1979

The decline in the proportions of the working population who were registered as unemployed from 1972 to 1973 and 1974 was matched by a marked decline in parliamentary attention to the issue during these latter two years (Table 2.1), as well as by a decline in popular perceptions of the importance of the issue (Table 2.3) and a decrease in the items and special articles devoted to it in *The Times* (Table 2.2). The question of inflation figured more prominently than unemployment during both the February and October 1974 General Elections, though both major parties dealt rather more at length with unemployment in their second manifestos of the year (Butler and Kavanagh, 1974 and 1975). In October 1974, Labour gave emphasis to regional employment schemes, an increased role for the Manpower Services Commission and retraining of redundant workers (Labour Party, 1974). The Conservatives, blaming inflation for rising unemployment, argued in their manifesto that they would seek to reduce inflationary wage demands in order to combat unemployment (Conservative Party, 1974). In addition, special mention was made of regional policies and youth programmes. However, to reiterate, the unemployment issue did not figure significantly in the campaign, nor did it achieve a prominent rank in the public's estimation of important election issues.

From 1974 to 1977 and 1978, there was a steady increase in the proportion of the workforce unemployed with a slight reduction in 1979. Examination of Table 2.1 shows that there was yet again an overall concomitant increase in House of Commons attention to the matter. Two qualifications should, however, be made. First, despite the fact that the unemployment level in 1976 exceeded that of any previous year under analysis, there was a significant fall in House of Commons attention to the question from 1975 to 1976. Secondly, although unemployment levels in the years 1975, 1976, 1977, 1978 and 1979 exceeded those of 1971 and 1972, the degree of parliamentary attention devoted to the matter only exceeded the 1971 and 1972 levels in one year, 1978.

The issue assumed increasing importance at the conferences of the TUC and the Labour Party, with considerable criticism developing of the Labour Government's record in this field. The Conservative Party conferences during these years did not pay as much attention to it as might have been expected from an opposition party. Whilst there were instances of Tory criticism of the government's record on unemployment, this was increasingly for too much state intervention rather than too little.

Under the Labour Government, despite the fact that the levels of unemployment were considerably higher than in the 1971−2 period, the public's estimation of its importance at no point exceeded that of the last three months of 1971. Joel Barnett comments on this in his memoirs:

If anybody had told us in 1974 a Labour Government would preside over levels of unemployment of that size, we would have derided them. But not only did we do so, we did so for years and despite criticism from the trade union movement and our activists inside and outside the House of Commons, we did so with comparatively little trouble. Remarkably enough I do not recall a single letter in the whole of that time complaining specifically about this terribly high level of unemployment. I know from talking to other Ministers and back-benchers that the same quietist mood applied in their constituencies. Although the subject came up from time to time in my constituency party meetings, frequently we went many months without referring to the subject. (Barnett, 1982:50)

Several explanations for this can be offered. First, the high levels of unemployment under the Heath Government were novel in the post-war period and thus provoked a more dramatic public response. By the mid 1970s, the public had become more used to high unemployment, though this argument would have to be qualified in the light of the 1979 – 84 period. Secondly, the other prominent issues in the mid-1970s, e.g. inflation and the social contract, might have weighed more heavily in the minds of the public, thus 'pushing out' concern for unemployment. In passing, it is interesting to note the sharp decline in public perceptions of the issue's importance between autumn 1978 and early 1979, when the issues of inflation and industrial relations assumed prominence. It is, therefore, important to recognise the complexity of the political agenda at any one time. As Downs (1972) argues, issues are competing for attention; new issues drive out the old (something Mrs Thatcher discovered to her good fortune during the Falklands War). A third type of explanation could be posed along the lines that the government, by virtue of its various schemes to help the unemployed, successfully persuaded the public that it was doing all it could to meet the problems and that, beyond this, the problem was out of its control. Barnett himself mentions the relatively high level of unemployment benefits (which were then related to earnings for the first six months) which helped to cushion the blow, and reduce the militancy of the unemployed; the increase in married women on the register (which was less politically sensitive); and the increase in 'moonlighting' (Barnett, 1982:50).

All these explanations may contain an element of truth, but the role of the opposition in this matter was also crucial. Whilst it would be misleading to suggest that the Conservatives were not concerned with unemployment during the period, they did not focus the concentrated attention upon it that the Labour opposition did in 1971 – 2 or has done since 1979. Increasingly, the new Conservative leadership in opposition saw unemployment as the consequences of other evils such as high wage rates and excessive government intervention in industry, resulting in overmanning in non-competitive industries. It was these themes which were the subject of high-level Conservative attention. At the 1975 Conservative Conference, having jibed at Labour's record in the employment field, Mrs Thatcher spoke of reducing public expenditure, rebuilding profits and restoring incentives as the best hope for the unemployed. At the 1978

Conference, Sir Keith Joseph made it clear that 'the Conservatives were not in the business of using taxpayers' money to rescue companies crippled by lack of co-operation or bad management' (quoted in *The Times*, 13.10.78). He spoke of the problem of overmanning (bolstered by government intervention), which meant that new jobs were not opening up. The proper role of the government, he argued, was to create conditions of prosperity and fuller employment. In summary, a party whose attention was increasingly focused upon the market, monetarism, public spending cuts and cash limits, could not at the same time attack the government for not doing enough to alleviate unemployment by means of traditional and conventional Keynesian responses. The whole philosophy of the Conservatives was to create a new economic order, the logic of which inhibited them from fully exploiting the unemployment issue.

Unemployment was not attributed major importance by the political parties during the 1979 General Election campaign either. The Labour Party manifesto was dominated by the themes of a caring society and notions of equality and socialist ideology, whereas the Conservative manifesto devoted most attention to unions, a caring society, and the economy. Ironically perhaps, jobs, employment and unemployment were mentioned two-and-a-half times more often in the Labour than the Conservative manifesto (Pinto-Duschinsky, 1981: 314 and 321), though the Conservatives did exploit the issue with the poster of a fabricated dole queue and the caption 'Labour isn't working'.

An analysis of the Party leaders' speeches during the campaign shows that the issue of jobs, employment and unemployment ranked fifth in James Callaghan's speeches, below caring society, families, prices, and national unity; in Margaret Thatcher's speeches it ranked sixth, equal with law and order/uphold Parliament, but below freedom, unions, caring society, socialism, and British tradition/unity (Pinto-Duschinsky, 1981: 315 and 322). The Liberal manifesto and the speeches of the Party leader, David Steel, gave even less emphasis to this issue.

How did the issue impact upon the campaign itself? Given that television has increasingly assumed the function of the country's major news and information source, it is important to assess the issue's salience within that medium. An analysis of BBC and ITV early and main news bulletins shows that individual policy coverage accounted for between 53.4 per cent and 62.4 per cent of their election coverage, the remainder consisting of coverage of polls, party prospects and other features of the campaign in general (Harrison, 1982:72). Disregarding the categories of 'general praise and blame' and 'unclassified', only in one of the four broadcast categories – the ITV main news bulletin – did the employment issue achieve prominence (coming second equal with 'wages and prices') in the amount of attention it received (see Table 2.4). Even so, the most prominent issue in this category, industrial relations, received almost twice the attention of the second two. The theme of the 'winter of discontent' had the effect of distracting attention from unemployment issues. In the other three categories of broadcast, the employment issue came sixth twice and fifth equal in order of salience, and was consistently less salient than 'industrial relations', 'wages and prices', and 'other economic'; in two out of three cases it was less salient than 'taxation'.

Table 2.4   Most important policy issues in election coverage in evening TV news bulletins, 1979

| | Early bulletin | | Main bulletin | | |
	BBC % time	ITV % time	BBC % time	ITV % time	Average % time
Industrial relations	8.0	9.0	9.1	10.5	9.15
Wages and prices	10.7	6.7	7.6	5.8	7.70
Taxation	1.6	3.7	6.2	3.2	7.20
Other economic	4.2	3.3	3.5	3.4	3.60
Employment	2.9	2.9	2.7	5.8	3.58
Immigration/Southall	4.9	2.9	1.9	1.3	2.75
Law and order	3.2	0.8	1.2	3.4	2.15
EEC	0.8	2.9	2.6	2.0	2.08
Northern Ireland	1.7	1.3	2.9	1.3	1.80

(Derived from Harrison, 1982:72)

What impact did the unemployment issue have upon the behaviour of the electorate? Explaining electoral outcomes is never a simple matter, as elections turn on combinations of underlying social structural shifts, events immediately prior to elections, and popular perceptions of politicians, as well as relative assessments of issues. In attempting to explain the Conservative victory in the 1979 General Election, Ivor Crewe (1981) highlighted several factors which accounted for Labour's poor performance. First, the 'winter of discontent' undermined the credibility of Labour as the only party who could deal with unions, and provoked a drop in the popularity of James Callaghan. William Rodgers confirms this latter point in identifying the Prime Minister's visit to Guadaloupe during the ice- and strike-bound January of 1979, and his apparent insensitivity to the 'crisis' on his return, as leading to a loss of popular confidence in him (Rodgers, 1984). Crewe adds that an underlying trend against Labour was already in process, consisting primarily of working-class desertion of their traditional party. Turning to particular reasons for Conservative success, he cites the superior party organisation – especially at the local level – and the Conservative's better performance in relation to key issues in the campaign.

Unemployment was identified as the second most important issue by 27 per cent of respondents, behind prices (42 per cent of respondents). However, those selecting these issues only marginally identified Labour as the preferred party to cope with them. In contrast, the 21 per cent of respondents who selected taxes and the 11 per cent who selected law and order as the most urgent issues clearly identified the Conservatives as the preferred party to deal with these problems. Thus, whilst unemployment was identified as the second most urgent issue, its impact upon the election outcome was less significant because Labour, it seemed, was no longer the party particularly identified with full employment. This could be regarded as a very significant shift in electoral attitudes. As we shall see, even in the midst of mass unemployment the Labour Party failed to benefit during the 1983 election campaign. Crewe calculated that between the October 1974 and the May 1979 General Elections there was an 8 per cent swing from Labour to Conservative among those identifying unemployment as the most salient issue (Crewe, 1981:288). This effectively wiped out any potential advantage to Labour of the unemployment issue achieving high salience.

Having seen that both the salience and the political impact of the unemployment issue differed between the 1970–4 and 1974–9 periods, we will move on to assess the stature and political effect of the issue under Mrs Thatcher's administration. In many ways this is, politically, the most remarkable period in the history of unemployment.

2.4 The unemployment issue under Mrs Thatcher 1979 – 1984

As is now well known, the Conservative Party won the General Election of 3 May 1979 with an overall majority of 44 seats in the House of Commons, excluding the Speaker. Margaret Thatcher thus became the country's first woman Prime Minister. Since her election as leader of the Conservative Party she had acquired an image of a hardliner, (the 'iron lady', as the Russians had dubbed her), and indeed Labour Party spokesmen had warned during the campaign that unemployment would rise under her government. Callaghan himself foretold 'deserts of unemployment'. Mrs Thatcher, on taking office, was evidently trying to dispel this image when she quoted a prayer of St Francis of Assisi:

Where there is discord, may we bring harmony. Where there is error, may we bring truth. Where there is doubt may we bring faith. Where there is despair, may we bring hope.

It is hard to imagine what impact this must have had on the unemployed! In any case, at the same time as insisting that the government would be compassionate, Mrs Thatcher also emphasised that it would be single-minded in pursuit of its goal of restoring British competitiveness via its clearly stated policies of attempting a strict monetary policy and reducing

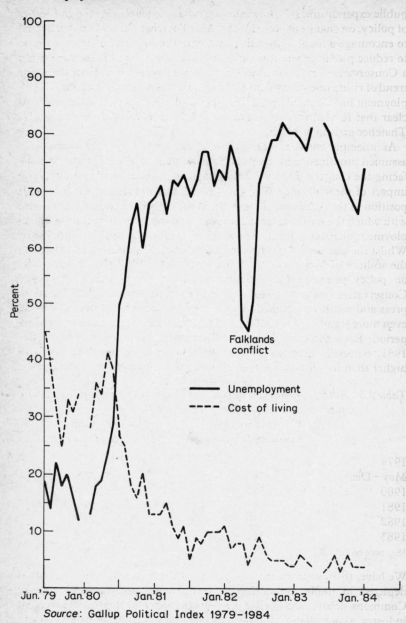

Source: Gallup Political Index 1979–1984

Figure 2.1   Public perceptions of importance of unemployment and cost of
living issues 1979–1984

public expenditure. It is, however, important to emphasise the continuity of policy, on change of government. Mrs Thatcher has done much herself to encourage a tough unbending image, but monetary policy – the desire to reduce public expenditure and cash limits in the public sector – is not a Conservative invention. Moreover, as we suggested in Chapter 1, the trend of rising unemployment had certainly started under Labour. Unemployment had doubled under the previous Labour Government, and it is clear that fundamental economic forces were at work by the time Mrs Thatcher arrived at No 10.

As unemployment increased dramatically from 1979 onwards, so it assumed prominence in the public's perception as the most urgent issue facing the country. Figure 2.1 illustrates that, since June 1980, only the impact of the Falklands War knocked the unemployment issue off pole position in the public consciousness. What is also impressive is the speed with which the public returned to its view of the importance of the unemployment question after the cessation of hostilities in the South Atlantic. Whilst the war with Argentina markedly changed popular perceptions of the abilities of Mrs Thatcher, it appeared to do nothing to change views on policy priorities (see Miller, 1984). As the period of post-1979 Conservative rule proceeded, unemployment became a central feature of press and media coverage, and as Table 2.5 illustrates, it has become an even more significant matter in parliamentary debate than in the 1970 – 9 period. Even though its proportionate status dropped somewhat after 1981, especially between 1982 and 1983, the figure for 1983 was still higher than for all but one year in the 1970 – 9 period (see Table 2.1).

Table 2.5   *Annual proportions of House of Commons business taken up with question of unemployment 1979 – 1983*[1]

	Columns occupied by unemployment	Unemployment as a percentage of total debate
1979		
May – Dec	82	0.52
1980	537	1.62
1981	552	2.36
1982	449	2.23
1983	321	1.71

[1] See note on *Table 2.1.*

We have, then, seen the further growth of the issue of unemployment as depicted in public opinion polls and content analysis of House of Commons debate, and fuelled by the emergence of the 'unemployment industry' a constellation of groups campaigning and becoming involved in delivering schemes for the unemployed (see Moon and Richardson, 1984). The question arises of how the Conservative Party in the 1983 General

Election managed to lose only 1.5 per cent of its share of the vote cast in 1979. This would have seemed remarkable ten years previously, given the long-established political wisdom that mass unemployment would spell electoral disaster for a British Government. It could be argued that this was not so remarkable, as during the 1930s when unemployment levels were high the Conservative Party (taken singly and in partnership with National Liberals) enjoyed notable electoral success in the 1931 and 1935 General Elections. Our point however is that it was *after* the War, with hindsight, that the consensus emerged, that the 1930s experience should not and *could not* be repeated.

Of course, the Conservative parliamentary majority after June 1983 was largely a function of the existence of *two* main opposition parties, but this is a separate question from the one which we are addressing. Of greater interest in the context of growing unemployment is that millions of people continued to support the Conservatives. Indeed, although some supporters were lost since 1979, these losses were largely complemented by some Labour and Liberal voters of 1979 switching to Conservative! (Miller, 1984:13). The explanation of this puzzle does not lie simply in the fact that the electorate was distracted from its view of the importance of the unemployment question during the period of the election. Clearly, other factors played a part in the campaign: public perceptions of the abilities of competing parties and their leaders, issues such as defence, inflation, nationalisation and the Common Market, and more general evaluations of the abilities of the Thatcher administration. No single factor can fully explain the electoral outcome, but none the less the question remains, how did the Conservative share of the vote more or less hold up given the electorate's dogged identification of unemployment as overwhelmingly the most important issue?

Closer examination of opinion poll data around the time of the 1983 election suggests some complexity in the electorate's perceptions of unemployment as the most important issue facing the country. Indeed, there has been a breakdown in the conventional corollary to this – that the government should get the blame for the problem – without which the Conservatives might not have fared so well at the polls.

For a number of months prior to the election there had been a decrease in the public's propensity to attribute blame for the high levels of unemployment to the Conservative Government. Indeed, during the election campaign the polls indicated that the Conservative Party drew level with the Labour Party in answer to such questions as 'Which Party do you consider to be best equipped to fight unemployment?' (Miller, 1984). Even the publication of the draft report of the House of Commons Treasury and Civil Service Committee chaired by a senior Conservative MP, Edward du Cann, which suggested that government monetary policies were partly to blame for Britain's higher than average unemployment levels, failed to undermine the government's standing.

Gallup poll findings provide interesting insights into new subtleties in the way respondents view the issue. Since the end of the Falklands conflict, over 75 per cent of respondents had identified (unprompted) unemployment as the most urgent issue facing the country (Figure 2.1). Yet, in December 1982, 43 per cent said that unemployment could sometimes be justified as necessary during a period of adjustment, and only 57 per cent thought that high unemployment could be solved if a government really tried to apply the right measures. Thirty-six per cent further believed that no government could really solve the problem (Social Surveys, December 1982). When asked how long it would be before unemployment would be drastically reduced, only 12 per cent of respondents chose any of the specified periods of three years or under; 47 per cent chose periods between three and four years; 22 per cent said 'never' and 19 per cent did not know (Social Surveys, February 1983). Further, when asked whether they thought that the level of unemployment in the country would change over the next year, on three successive occasions, over 70 per cent thought it would increase sharply or slightly (Social Surveys, January – March 1983). Thus, whilst high unemployment has consistently been seen as the most important issue facing the country, popular expectations as to its solution were low, and the government has less and less been singled out as the sole cause of the problem.

We would readily acknowledge that inept campaigning by the Labour Party, more effective and polished campaigning by the Conservatives, the role of the third party, personalities, and the interpretative role of the popular press all played a part in 'presenting' the unemployment issue to the electorate. However, the political success of the government, given such high levels of unemployment, owes much to its handling of the problem whilst in office. The introduction of special anti-unemployment measures, the playing of 'the numbers game', and of the lowering the level of demand for jobs have coincided with changing views about unemployment among the electorate.

As illustrated in the previous chapter, in 1979 the new government did not view solving the problem of unemployment as its main task. However, as unemployment continued to rise steeply, threatening to undermine its credibility, the government committed, if not a U-turn, at least a major redirection of policy. This was reflected in the development of schemes it had initially contracted, and more recently in the introduction of a new set of job-creation, training and labour-subsidy schemes (see Chapter 3). Whilst these have all had the effect of removing greater numbers from the unemployment register, they clearly are not a permanent solution to the problem, nor have they arrested the upward trend of unemployment – even using the government's own figures.

However, the revitalisation of old schemes and the introduction of new ones played a significant part in a story of successful political and social management of the unemployment issue by the government. It has been sufficiently active in providing short-term responses to unemployment to be seen to be doing something about the problem, thus deflecting potential criticism, and has at the same time been able to pursue its own broader economic objective of increasing Britain's international competitiveness.

There has been a second major area of government activity designed to deflect criticism over the unemployment issue, and thereby to enable it to pursue its other policy objectives. This could be called 'playing the numbers game', or, to put it another way, reducing the real and the apparent demand for jobs. After all, the figures published indicating the monthly levels of unemployment possess enormous symbolic significance in today's politics. The government has therefore introduced additional measures to reduce the actual supply of labour. First, it has continued with the Job Release Scheme introduced by Labour, whereby subsidies are given to women over 59 and men over 62 who retire and are replaced by workers who until then had been unemployed. Thus, one job is maintained and one person is effectively removed from the labour force for good. The Job Splitting Scheme gives subsidies to employers who split jobs, creating part-time jobs both for the original employee and for one other person who until then had been unemployed. Again, no new work is created, but another person is removed from the register and brought into gainful employment. This scheme also allows the possibility of the perfectly reasonable desire, from some sections of the workforce, for part-time employment. However, the initial response was disastrously low: in the first five months of the scheme only 251 of the 50,000 places were taken up. It is possible that employers and employees need greater incentives. The Chancellor announced, in his 1983 budget speech, that a Part-Time Job Release Scheme would be introduced, having the same effect as the Job Splitting Scheme. These schemes have the potential to provoke fairly fundamental changes in society – towards earlier full or partial retirement, part-time employment, job sharing, and 'community' projects.

The method of counting those who remain without work is also relevant here. In common with past practice, everyone participating on the various government schemes for the unemployed is excluded from the count (about 750,000 over 1983/4). The present government has made several changes to the counting method, which will have the effect of producing figures lower than would otherwise have been the case. From October 1982, the count has no longer included those *registering* for work, but only of those who *claim* unemployment benefit, supplementary benefits and national insurance credits. Although, for the first time, the severely handicapped unemployed who claim such benefits have been included in the count, the Department of Employment estimated that, had the new system been used during 1982, the figures would have been between 170,000 and 190,000 lower than was the case. In his 1983 budget speech, the Chancellor announced that those men over 60 who currently sign on to protect their pension rights when they reach 65, will no longer have to do so. Similarly, those men between 60 and 65 who are a year or less away from becoming entitled to a higher rate of supplementary benefit and are currently signing on in order to claim this, will be treated as if they had already become entitled to it. Together, it is estimated that these schemes will remove 132,000 from the register. The government has come in for considerable criticism for this 'massaging' of the figures, though we should not expect another government to 'improve' the counting system so as to increase the numbers of unemployed! In France similar controversy has surrounded the use of unemployment statistics.

These three political strategies pursued by the government have not of course eroded the problem of unemployment. In the case of the job-creation, training and labour-subsidy schemes, they have conveyed the impression that the Thatcher administration is not wholly unresponsive to the plight of the unemployed. In the case of the second two strategies, they have slowed up the increase in the official figures of unemployment which would otherwise have broken through the three-million mark earlier, and would by now have possibly reached four million. The fact that the official levels of unemployment were just under three million for quite a long time, dissipated some of the political symbolism of this figure.

Whilst we see the introduction of new schemes and the reduction of apparent demand for employment as important features of the current acceptance of unemployment, there are also other important factors. The government seems to have had considerable success in getting across its view that UK unemployment is largely the reflection of a world problem. The public continued to see unemployment as the major issue facing the country, but opinion polls also confirmed the decoupling of the link between the problem of unemployment and government responsibility for it. Although the level and rate of increase of unemployment have been worse in the UK than in most industrial countries, voters seem to have recognised that Britain's unemployment problem was by no means unique. Even in a sample of the unemployed, almost half blamed unemployment on the world economic recession (Economist Intelligence Unit, 1982:34), a point that was emphasised by the Conservatives in their campaign. Sir Geoffrey Howe said in an election broadcast that at least half of the rise in unemployment since 1979 was due to world recession, and the other half due to conditions which Britain had generated for herself. It obviously proved difficult for opposition parties to convince enough voters that UK unemployment has been Mrs Thatcher's fault, and that a different government could have done significantly better.

Another major factor in explaining the electorate's political response to unemployment is that, although between three million and four million people are currently unemployed, over 80 per cent of the workforce are in work. It is undoubtedly true that a larger number of the employed workforce will at some time have experienced unemployment, but in a climate where high levels of unemployment are becoming more commonplace and less of a novelty, those in work may be likely to consider any previous periods of unemployment (for most people, still under one year) to be less an injustice and more something that is to be expected. As the proportion of people who suffer long-term unemployment (over one year) is only just over one third of the total, and largely confined to the relatively politically inarticulate, this further detracts from the likelihood of the unemployed *themselves* raising the political cost of the issue for any government.

Further, whilst we would not wish to underestimate the seriousness of long-term unemployment for workers and their families, especially in terms of decreased living standards and loss of morale, those who suffer short-term unemployment today do not suffer financially as badly as was the case during the 1930s – the very period which served to build up postwar expectations that no government could seriously countenance high levels of unemployment. For some people – though clearly not all – another factor in their acceptance of unemployment may be that they are able to take up other interests (so long as they are not too expensive), or engage in comparatively profitable activity within the black economy.

In summary, the Conservative Government has managed to survive the potentially politically disastrous threat of mass unemployment. We have suggested that there have been important changes in public perceptions about the nature of the issue and that the government has tempered the political symbolism of the issue by virtue of its own initiatives and by artificially slowing the official rate of increase in unemployment. We would, however, acknowledge that the hypothesis that this government strategy is somehow causal in this respect is difficult to prove, and warrants further study. It is also possible that the present, relatively quiescent attitude of the population may not continue. The tolerance of government training schemes by the young may wear thin if large numbers of trainees are subsequently unable to find work. The government, having built up high expectations of the Youth Training Scheme, for example, may pay political costs if these are not matched by results. Secondly, it is possible that there might be a recoupling of the link between unemployment and government responsibility for it, if the government's overall standing declined, whether as a result of banana skins or more effective opposition politics. This possibility will be considered further in the concluding chapter.

3 Governmental Policy Responses to Unemployment

This chapter is primarily devoted to what we term direct responses to unemployment: job-creation schemes, employment-subsidy schemes, training schemes, and schemes which are designed especially for youth and draw upon the three aforementioned types. We refer to them as 'direct' because they are implicitly or explicitly aimed at preventing individuals from joining the ranks of the unemployed, or removing individuals from the employment register by providing them with work and/or training. As will be seen in the discussion that follows, other very significant policy objectives may, at particular times, be combined with that of minimising unemployment levels, e.g., providing industry with a more skilled workforce, or improving productivity by de-manning or reducing wage levels. The success or failure of these other policy objectives may, in the long run, be among the most important determinants of longer-term levels of unemployment and employment.

There are also, of course, what might loosely be described as indirect policy responses, which could have potentially far greater impact than the direct ones to which we give prime attention. Macroeconomic policies as they impact upon employment levels were discussed in Chapter 1, and regional policies are discussed later in this chapter. Similarly, governments have also committed *ad hoc* interventions, most of which could be described as rescue missions, in order to prevent large-scale redundancies. For example, Mrs Thatcher intervened to prevent an accelerated pit-closure plan in the coal industry in 1980. In contrast, she took the opposite viewpoint in 1984! By giving prime attention to the direct policies, we would not wish to underestimate the importance of regional and *ad hoc* initiatives, and budgetary policies. These however are fairly long-established features of the policy land-scape, whereas most of the types of initiatives outlined in this chapter have emerged only in the last decade. Further, many of these schemes, and their main sponsoring organisation, the MSC, have become significant features of the life-experiences of literally hundreds of thousands of our citizens. At times of course, the direct/indirect distinction becomes blurred: for instance, there are 'direct' regional policies.

The discussion of direct government policies which follows will provide a basic description of different schemes, the reasons for their introduction, and general indications of their differing implementation

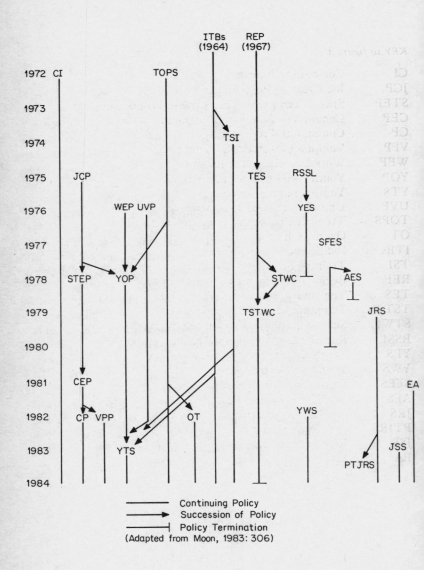

Figure 3.1   Policy change in job creation, work experience, training and employment subsidy schemes

KEY to figure 3.1

CI	Community Industry
JCP	Job Creation Programme
STEP	Special Temporary Employment Programme
CEP	Community Enterprise Programme
CP	Community Programme
VPP	Voluntary Projects Programme
WEP	Work Experience Programme
YOP	Youth Opportunities Programme
YTS	Youth Training Scheme
UVP	United Vocational Programme
TOPS	Training Opportunities Programme
OT	Open Tech
ITBs	Industrial Training Boards
TSI	Training Services to Industry
REP	Regional Employment Premium
TES	Temporary Employment Subsidy
TSTWC	Temporary Short Time Working Compensation
STWC	Short Time Working Compensation
RSSL	Recruitment Subsidy for School Leavers
YES	Youth Employment Subsidy
YWS	Young Workers Scheme
SFES	Small Firms Employment Subsidy
AES	Adult Employment Subsidy
JRS	Job Release Scheme
PTJRS	Part Time Job Release Scheme
JSS	Job Splitting Scheme
EA	Enterprise Allowance

effects. More detailed consideration will be given to the local delivery methods of the most important of these schemes in Chapter 4.

Figure 3.1 gives some indication of the number of direct government initiatives in this field, and also of the number of policy changes: normally in the form of 'policy successions' (see Moon, 1983a). The speed of these policy changes is rapid by any standards, reflecting the growth of the problem facing governments: rising levels of unemployment, and the accompanying imperative upon successive governments to be seen to be doing something in response to this key political issue.

3.1 Job creation schemes

The notion of creating temporary jobs for the unemployed at low rates of pay and usually with some community or environmental benefit in mind has been a strategy adopted by most Western governments facing mass unemployment. Indeed the MSC, which had been instructed, when first established, to prepare for a national job-creation programme, looked closely at such a Canadian scheme in drawing up the Job Creation Programme, which commenced in 1975. It was designed to

provide worthwhile work for those who would otherwise be unemployed . . . and that the local community should benefit from the work done, whether through the enhancement of the local environment or through projects tackling social or community problems. (MSC, 1976:23)

This type of response has the advantage of appealing to the common sense of the electors, who may be puzzled by the length of the dole queues on the one hand, and the shortage of people to clean streets, beaches and so on, on the other. The MSC reimbursed the project sponsors for the approved wages of the participants, the employer's national insurance contributions and up to 10 per cent of each project's running costs. The scheme was open to the unemployed in the 16 to 24 and over-50 age groups, who were felt to be suffering disproportionately from the recession.

In 1978, the Job Creation Programme (JCP) was succeeded by the Special Temporary Employment Programme (STEP) when the unemployed 16 to 18-year-old cohort was transferred to the Youth Opportunities Programme (see below). Thus STEP was an 'adults only' form of JCP, undertaking similar work, with similar sponsorship and organisational arrangements. However, indicative of the mounting pressure of unemployment upon the government machine was the fact that entrants to STEP had to have been previously unemployed for over a year, or over six months in the case of the 19 to 24-years cohort.

On assuming office in 1979, the Conservative Government made reductions in planned expenditure on STEP, and restricted its application to areas receiving regional aid. Subsequently, however, in January 1980, the government made an early U-turn and announced it was to launch a new Community Enterprise Programme (CEP) to replace STEP, coming into operation in February 1981. This was initially intended to provide 25,000 jobs of benefit to the community, sponsored by private firms and nationalised industries. However, in 1981–2 more than 34,000 such opportunities were provided, costing £89.6 million, compared with £45.7 million for STEP in the previous year. CEP differed from STEP in that sponsors were reimbursed for any training they provided for participants, and the MSC made special efforts to encourage sponsorship from private and nationalised industries.

In October 1982 yet another change took place and CEP was replaced by the similar Community Programme (CP). This was intended to provide 130,000 places in its first year of operation (almost four times as many as CEP) and over 200,000 places between April 1983 and April 1984. However, this response was more sophisticated. Due to the lower weekly allowances provided under CP, and the fact that the hourly rate for any job had to reflect local wage rates, there is an in-built pressure for sponsors to take on part-time participants. This enables the government to make a bigger impact on the unemployment figures, at a lower cost per head than was possible under CEP. Also, the training element provided in the earlier scheme was withdrawn in the CP.

Finally, at the same time as launching CP, the government announced the Voluntary Projects Programme, which provides the unemployed with constructive activity for community benefit. Most participants receive no allowance for this, but continue to draw their normal levels of benefit, although some opportunities have been created for paid supervisory work.

Table 3.1   Entrants and expenditure on job creation schemes

Financial year	Scheme type	Entrants Number	Expenditure on JCS Total £m
1975–76 [1]	JCP	14,100	30.0
1976–77	JCP	79,300	37.1
1977–78	JCP	106,100	71.7
1978–79	STEP	19,700	86.2
1979–80	STEP	22,400	55.9
1980–81	STEP	18,400	46.2
1981–82	CEP	34,300	86.7
1982–83	CEP/CP	39,572	177.0
1983–84	CP	112,886	(399.4)

[1] Six month period from Oct 1975
()Projected

Table 3.1 indicates the participation levels and costs of the job-creation schemes. The total number of participants only represents a small fraction of the unemployed in the respective age groups for each year. Assuming, however, that not many participants return for a second spell on these schemes, around half a million of the long-term unemployed will have had relief from unemployment for up to one year. As such, these schemes can best be described as holding operations, but they have enabled other policy objectives to be met, which in a period of recession may not otherwise have been achieved. Most notably these have been in the fields of environmental improvement, the provision of social amenities, and social and cultural work. Examples of work done under the Community Programme include the operation of outward bound centres for deprived children, landscaping of recreational areas, redevelopment of waste land, running educational and leisure day centres, and insulating homes of the old.

These schemes have all been subject to a certain amount of criticism, notably on the levels of allowances paid. The most recent scheme, CP, for instance, provides for only an average weekly allowance of £60 per week, which is less than many – especially those with families – could claim in welfare benefits. It is too early to say whether participants enjoy working on CP, and whether the opportunity to work part-time (albeit at low rates) is attractive. In 1983 – 4 the number of applications for CP places proved to be well in excess of the target number of places. Evidence from an independent study of the Community Enterprise Programme shows that, despite poor employment prospects, among participants it was indeed a popular scheme:

The study showed us that there was a great deal of enthusiasm for the programme. A large amount of the enthusiasm was, no doubt, due to the fact that CEP provided its entrants with what they most wanted: work. However, for some the enthusiasm was a reflection of the job satisfaction which they got from doing work which was entirely new to them, which they found challenging and interesting and from which they learned new personal or vocational skills. It is ironical that some enjoyed their jobs on CEP more than any job they had done before. (MSC, 1982d:51 – 2)

Another criticism of such programmes is that they only provide for a small percentage of those eligible, the long-term unemployed. Even the Community Programme target figure of 130,000 places in a year would only cater for about one in ten of those unemployed for over one year in 1983 – 4. Of course, temporary job-creation schemes do not significantly affect the root problem of unemployment, apart from providing relatively permanent supervisory and managerial positions for those overseeing the projects. It could be asked whether, if the tasks achieved by these programmes have been worth doing, why not employ people on a permanent basis to perform them? On the other hand, if, say, 200,000 people were thus employed, it would be more difficult to provide respite, albeit temporary, to the remaining hundreds of thousands of long-term unemployed. Thus the only real alternative to providing the present forms of relief from unemployment (other than do nothing) is a massive public works programme which would take on a wider range of tasks than are presently met by the CP. The Thatcher Government would object to this because it would have the effect of increasing public sector employment. If wages on such a programme were made comparable to other public sector wage levels, this would greatly increase public expenditure and would presumably undermine the government's objective of bringing down British wage levels in the interests of international competitiveness.

3.2 Employment subsidy schemes

Various different types of employment subsidy schemes have been introduced by Conservative and Labour Governments, although the varying terms of some of the individual policies do betray the differing policy objectives of successive administrations. We can at the outset distinguish two broadly different types of employment subsidy: those designed to defer redundancies and those designed to create jobs.

In considering the first group, policies designed to defer redundancies, it should be noted that although the most important of these schemes were introduced from the mid-1970s onwards, a form of employment subsidy had operated under the Regional Employment Premium since 1967. This, however, was in the form of a tax rebate rather than a direct payment and applied only in assisted areas (see 3.5 below). The first form of direct subsidy was the Temporary Employment Subsidy (TES) introduced in 1975, and this too was initially to apply only in assisted areas. With unemployment levels rising fast however, it was extended after only two months to have a national application. TES provided employers with a subsidy per worker if it could be proved that without that subsidy a specified number of employees would be made redundant. It was introduced initially to last for one year, but was extended until 1979. At the same time the qualifications for receiving the subsidy were gradually eased while the levels and duration of the subsidy increased (see Moon 1983a for full details). Over the three-and-a-half years of its operation, TES subsidised just over 540,000 jobs (see Department of Employment, November 1979:1122–3). In retrospect it is felt by Department of Employment officials that this scheme, although a valid 'fire fighting' measure, was too undiscriminating and was open to the criticism that non-viable jobs were being maintained. Indeed, it is generally felt that the scheme had limited long-term value in preserving jobs. Further, the scheme came in for criticism from the EEC Commission for undermining the Community's laws on competition. Thus it was superseded, initially in 1978, by the Short Time Working Compensation Scheme. This was restricted to the textile and footwear industries, and provided 75 per cent wage reimbursement for employees put on short-time working.

The more important successor scheme was the Temporary Short Time Working Compensation (TSTWC) scheme introduced in April 1979. This was designed to preserve jobs which were threatened in the short term, but had long-term viability. TSTWC provided a reimbursement of a percentage of wages of employees who had been put on short-time working, as long as they were given one full day's work after a maximum of seven consecutive days without work. The level of the subsidy and its duration have varied, as the Department of Employment has had to respond to Treasury cutbacks (see Moon 1983a for full details). These have had a marked effect on the number of jobs supported: whereas in the first two years of operation, almost 720,000 jobs were supported, only 175,000 were supported in 1981–2 (Department of Employment, November 1982:471). Applications for TSTWC were closed in March 1984, and last payments made in the autumn of 1984. On this occasion the government has stood by its word and will presumably be reluctant to introduce a successor scheme, unlike other schemes which have been extended beyond initial targets or succeeded by similar programmes.

Employment subsidies to avert redundancies have several advantages. First, they have an obvious impact on the aggregate potential level of unemployment and maintain a continuity of employment for the individual. Also, by sustaining even minimum levels of output, such schemes may assist the country's balance of payments. The maintenance of equipment and of working skills would of course be advantageous if an upturn in Britain's economy did occur. The net expenditure on private-sector employment subsidy is of course low, as the country might otherwise be paying full social security and unemployment benefit payments to the workers made redundant. It might, however, be the case that the government is paying for workers who might still be employed had the scheme not existed, and thus substituting public funds for private. Analysis of the Temporary Employment Scheme suggested that such a displacement effect 'represented only a small part of the output supported' (Deakin and Prattern, 1982:149).

A more substantial problem, and one which it is difficult to quantify, is that employment subsidy schemes impair the adaptability of British industry to turn to new products, plant and skills. This view is a reflection of a belief that Britain is passing through a much needed restructuring of its employment patterns. Any public policy designed to slow this down could be considered to be harmful to long-term prospects for the economy as a whole. However, an evaluation of the TSTWC concluded that 'the majority of redundancies were at best delayed rather than averted' (House of Commons, 1983:15). This would seem to raise doubts as to the long-term value of the £800m spent on the scheme over five years, though there were obvious political benefits in its cushioning effect within declining industries.

Turning to employment subsidies designed to create rather than simply maintain jobs, we will see that there has been considerable variety in the schemes introduced. From July 1977 the innovatory Small Firms Employment Subsidy provided wage subsidies to small manufacturing firms in assisted areas who took on additional full- or part-time workers. This was expanded in January 1979 to apply nationally to small manufacturing firms, and in assisted areas to small non-manufacturing firms. However, as a result of Treasury cutbacks in July 1979, it reverted more or less to its original parameters. During the scheme's first and most effective year 1978–9, just over 82,000 jobs were supported (Department of Employment, November 1979:1124). The short-lived Adult Employment Subsidy was designed to subsidise the recruitment of adults who had been unemployed for at least a year in the Merseyside, Tyneside and Leeds areas. The take-up was so low (1,460 in all) that the scheme was brought to an end in June 1979, after just one year of operation. It appeared that employers did not find the subsidy sufficient to warrant taking on unemployed members of the workforce.

Less conventional types of subsidies for the creation of employment have also been introduced. The Job Release Scheme (JRS), introduced in 1977, was designed to encourage older workers to retire *if* they could be replaced by unemployed workers, by providing weekly allowances to the retirees. Like other Department of Employment schemes, this was initially only applicable in assisted areas, but within sixteen months it had become national. From October 1983, a supplementary scheme, the Part-Time Job Release Scheme, has been in operation working within the same broad parameters as the JRS. It allows the older workers to switch to part-time work, and also provides unemployed workers with part-time work. Presumably, this will only be attractive to the latter if they are able to earn more than they would have received in the way of unemployment benefits. By February 1984, the number of unemployed helped by the JRS had reached 250,000 (*Employment News*, 117, March 1984), but after three months of operation, the PTJRS had only 37 participants.

This is similar to another scheme running on an experimental basis since early 1983, the Job Splitting Scheme, which provides block grants (currently £750 paid in four instalments) to employers who split a full-time job into two part-time jobs, one of which should go to a person who had previously been unemployed. Despite an expensive and high-profile advertising campaign, the initial take-up for the scheme has been disappointing: whilst provision was made to finance the splitting of 50,000 jobs, after four months only about 500 new part-time jobs had been created. In view of the low response, the government announced in July 1983 that greater flexibility would be provided, particularly in giving employers time to find suitable recruits from the pool of unemployed (Department of Employment, August 1983:365). By March 1984, the total of part-time jobs created had risen to 1,672, at an advertising cost alone of £423,208.

Finally, the Enterprise Allowance, which operated on a pilot basis from 1981, was expanded and became nationally available in 1983. This scheme reflects the frequently proclaimed faith of the Conservative Government (in common with all of the Western democracies) in small businesses, by providing an allowance of £40 per week for a year to those unemployed for at least thirteen weeks who want to start up their own business. Like the Job Splitting Scheme, it was initially under-subscribed, so the rules were amended, notably the requirements of £1,000 capital for the business has been relaxed to permit a £1,000 bank loan as a suitable qualification. It was intended that about 25,000 unemployed people could be helped by this scheme. The initial response to the scheme was beyond all expectations, with queues up to six months long of those wishing to take advantage. So great was the response that the Treasury agreed to provide additional finance to expand the scheme.

In this field of employment subsidy to create jobs, there has been a development from the rather crude forms of subsidy introduced in the late seventies, to more sophisticated subsidies, building upon the experience of the Job Release Scheme introduced at the same time as the Small Firms Employment Subsidy. In this sense, we are, as a society, on an upward learning curve in terms of direct responses – hence the common phenomenon of 'policy succession' as improvements are built into the redesigned policy. For example, the Small Firms Employment Subsidy was found to have a marked 'dead weight' effect, that is, it was found that only about two out of every five subsidised jobs were created as a result of the subsidy, the inference being that three out of every five jobs would have been created anyway without the help of the subsidy (Department of Employment, May 1978:551). In contrast, the JRS is thought to be 80 per cent effective (House of Commons, 1983:ix).

In contrast to the JRS, the Enterprise Allowance is designed to have a multiplier effect. It is hoped that for the cost of creating one job for the small businessman (which is no more, and often less, than benefits which would otherwise be paid should the individual have remained unemployed), other jobs might in turn be created in the successful firms. There is of course a potential dead weight effect here too, in that those benefiting from the scheme might have gone into business anyway, though this is likely to be minimal given the obstacles to starting a business for most of the unemployed.

The Job Release Scheme, its part-time variant and the Job Splitting Scheme represent attempts to reduce unemployment by the comparatively sophisticated means of trying to meet changing societal values –

namely, demands for more leisure time and early retirement – with schemes which could simultaneously reduce the numbers out of work. Of course no *new* work is created. The possibilities for dead weight still exist even in these schemes, and it was reported recently that this together with replacement by someone who did have work probably accounted for about 20 per cent of the JRS expenditure, though efforts have since been made to tighten up the rules (House of Commons, 1983:18). As was indicated earlier, the response to the JSS was initially disappointing.

Thus it may well be that greater efforts will have to be made in the way of incentives for employers and employees to opt for these schemes. There is certainly plenty of scope for a *transfer* of work both in the realm of reduced working hours and in that of early retirement. A recent report indicated, firstly, that the average number of hours worked by the British is considerably higher than in other West European countries, and secondly that a significantly greater percentage of British men aged 60 to 64 were still in the workforce, in comparison with other West European countries (*Financial Times*, 24.1.83). However, if hours of work are to be reduced – an attractive proposition in terms of the demands for and job creation effects of increased leisure – then this will need to be matched by reduced wages and/or increased productivity, if Britain's competitive position is not to deteriorate as a result. Similarly, if our retirement habits are to be brought in line with the rest of Western Europe, then this may have an adverse effect on public expenditure on pensions. One of the main policy problems facing most of the western world is that relatively smaller workforces will be expected to support relatively larger retired proportions of their populations.

3.3 Training policies

Although, when first introduced, government training policies bore little direct relation to those designed to combat unemployment, one of the most interesting developments accompanying the succession of policies in response to mass unemployment has been the merging of these two policy areas. Training policies have not simply been used as a means of preparing members of the workforce for new jobs, but also as a means of removing large numbers of people from the unemployment register. This merger has been most obvious in the case of schemes for youth, and as such these will be dealt with in the next section. However, there have also been important training initiatives affecting adults.

Although government had been operating its own training centres since 1919, it was not until 1964 that it made its first concerted effort to influence the volume, distribution and nature of industrial training, with the introduction of the Industry Act. This created a number of statutory Industrial Training Boards (ITBs) consisting of employer, trade union and educational interests. These were responsible for ensuring the adequate provision of training in a specified industrial field, by making levies upon constituent firms and providing grants to those employers offering recognised training. The costs of these grants were met by raising a levy from all firms in that industry. During the last few years the number of ITBs has been reduced due to a combination of some employer dissatisfaction and changing government priorities.

The most significant development in the merging of the unemployment and the training policy areas, however, was in the creation of the Manpower Services Commission in 1974, under the 1973 Employment and Training Act. The MSC was not only given responsibility for operating the employment placement service, the Job Centres, and for introducing the pioneering Job Creation Scheme, but also took over responsibility for the co-ordination of the Industrial Training Boards and for the newly created Training Opportunities Scheme (TOPS).

TOPS had been introduced in 1972 to enable individuals to acquire additional skills which would better equip them in the increasingly competitive job market. Grants were paid to participants who attended courses at Further Education Colleges, MSC Skillcentres, employers' establishments and residential centres. Whilst the scheme was not formally directed at the unemployed, as time went on TOPS places were increasingly taken up by those who had been on the unemployment register. During the mid-1970s, the TOPS programme was considerably expanded (Table 3.2).

Table 3.2 Completion of TOPS courses 1973 – 1984

1973 – 4	39,930
1974 – 5	45,416
1975 – 6	60,724
1976 – 7	89,651
1977 – 8	98,964
1978 – 9	70,187 [1]
1979 – 80	74,489
1980 – 1	66,418
1981 – 2	61,400
1982 – 3	59,300
1983 – 4	66,200

[1] Young people taken out, and put into YOPs.

SOURCE: MSC Annual Reports

A range of craft, clerical, commercial, secretarial, management, catering and trading skills were taught at government centres in addition to those taught in employers' establishments and residential colleges for the disabled. The numbers fell in 1978 – 9 because young people were no longer eligible due to the commencement of the Youth Opportunities

Programme (see section 3.4). Even so, adult figures from this point on did not match those targeted several years earlier (MSC, 1977:23).

On achieving office in 1979, the Conservative Government immediately made cuts of £22.3 million in the planned expenditure on TOPS, especially affecting the commercial and clerical subjects. A reduction of almost 18 per cent in those completing TOPS courses took place between 1979 and 1980. Whilst this has obviously had a detrimental impact upon the overall levels of unemployment, the government has however introduced another adult training scheme, the Open Tech. This differs from TOPS in that no grants are paid to participants. The emphasis within Open Tech, on training in technical skills, reflects a trend that was already in progress within TOPS. Open Tech operates an 'open learning' system, whereby participants have considerable choice in what they study and where they study it. Approved schemes are intended to provide open and distance learning systems, closely relating course content to specific industrial and occupational skill needs.

At the time of writing however, the question of adult training is in a state of flux, with the MSC currently considering a successor to TOPS. A discussion document on this gave emphasis to more closely matching the skill needs of industry and retraining those in employment (MSC, 1983). If this policy were to be pursued, given the steady reduction in TOPS places, the link between the training policy area and simple responses to adult unemployment might be weakening. This theme has been confirmed in the recent government White Paper on the subject, which suggests a redirection of skill training away from the unemployed, and expanding the work of Open Tech among those in employment, e.g. at the technician and supervisory levels. However, the proposals have not proceeded very far as yet.

The MSC is currently attempting to expand its activities in the field of training not only among the unemployed and the employed, but also among schoolchildren and students at colleges of further education. In the case of the former, it launched fourteen pilot projects of the Technical and Vocational Education Initiative (TVEI) in the autumn of 1983. This foray of the MSC into the administrative territory of the DES was devised by the government to try to improve the preparedness of schoolchildren for work in industry. The TVEI, which has already expanded to operate in another 46 local authorities, is designed to teach a series of modular courses of special relevance to the working world, *within* the school curriculum, and to give schoolchildren regular experience of working on the premises of a local employer. It caters for only a small proportion of schoolchildren even within the pilot areas. Thus, at the moment it can only be considered to be a catalyst project for long-term change within the secondary education system (see Moon and Richardson, 1984 for a discussion of the emergence of the TVEI).

3.4 Youth schemes

It should first be pointed out that the term 'youth' does not officially refer to a specific age group. Generally the term youth denotes sixteen and seventeen year olds, although occasionally reference will be made to schemes catering for those several years older.

The problem of youth unemployment first appeared in Britain during the mid-1970s. Whereas the overall unemployment rate in October 1983 was 13.0 per cent, for 20 to 24-year olds it was 19.8 per cent, and for under 20-year olds, 26.9 per cent (Department of Employment, March 1984:S39). This takes no account of those participating in job creation, work experience and training schemes, some indication of which is provided in Table 3.1. Further, these tables disguise the fact that there are concentrated areas of youth unemployment even higher than the national average. For example, in the Strathclyde region of Scotland, about 60 per cent (30,330) of sixteen and seventeen year olds have no permanent job, and in some areas within this region the figure has reached almost 80 per cent.

What then has central government attempted to do in response to escalating levels of youth unemployment? In the following analysis we shall distinguish work experience and training programmes from youth employment subsidies. The first direct response to the problem of youth unemployment – Community Industry – was in fact the brainchild of the National Association of Youth Clubs, which continues to administer the scheme, though it is funded by the Manpower Services Commission. CI was set up in 1972 during the first significant wave of increased unemployment in post-war years. The scheme was very small at the outset (see Table 3.3) and, although it has grown since then, it continues to offer a relatively small number of places. CI was devised not only as a part solution to unemployment, but also as a contribution towards solving the problems of disadvantaged young people by offering them opportunities to do work for community benefit. Initially CI was only available in eight specified areas, but since 1980 it has operated in 56 areas.

With the more serious advent of mass youth unemployment in the mid-seventies, the Labour Government responded with a range of policies. First, it introduced a labour creation subsidy for youth, the Recruitment Subsidy for School Leavers, which is considered later, and then the Job Creation Programme (JCP). As was outlined in section 3.1, the JCP, whilst giving precedence to those over 50 years old, in effect did the same for 16 to 24-year olds. Not only did JCP remove almost 200,000 people from the unemployment register during the 30 months of its operation, but surveys indicated that about two-thirds of ex-JCP employees obtained jobs within six months of leaving (MSC, 1977: 30).

As the levels of youth unemployment continued to rise, the government introduced the Youth Opportunities Programme (YOP), which removed

Table 3.3 Participation rates on youth job creation and work experience
schemes 1972–1984

Financial year	Community industry	Job Creation Programme (youth element)	Work Experience Programme	Youth Opportunities Programme	Youth Training Scheme
1972–3	800				
1973–4	1,700				
1974–5	2,000				
1975–6	3,500	7,200			
1976–7	4,500	22,254			
1977–8	5,500		59,725		
1978–9	7,000			162,000	
1979–80	6,000			216,000	
1980–1	7,000			360,000	
1981–2	7,000			553,000	
1982–3	7,000			543,000	
1983–4	7,000				354,000[1]

[1] Includes those transferred to YTS in September 1983 (estimated).

SOURCE: MSC Annual Reports

16 to 18-year olds from JCP and TOPS schemes in an attempt to provide
both work experience and training. YOP also drew upon the small Work
Experience Programme (WEP) which had been introduced in 1976 in
order to offer young people a positive alternative to unemployment:
'opportunities to learn about different types of work and, on a modest
level, scope for "learning by doing" under supervision' (MSC, 1978:30).
Employers were invited to offer work-experience facilities, and participants were paid a flat rate maintenance allowance and National Insurance
by the MSC.

YOP, however, was designed as a much larger and more comprehensive
scheme. Its intention was that no July school-leaver should be still unemployed at the following Easter, without having been offered a place on
YOP. The first component of YOP, reflected the aims of WEP: work
experience on employers' premises. The second component was training,
and this drew upon the Training Opportunities Programme. In 1977–8,
about 20,300 (i.e. just over one-fifth) TOPS places were specifically
designed for young people. These went under three headings, (i) short
industrial courses, (ii) occupational selection courses and (iii) wider opportunities courses. The all-round objective of the scheme was to improve the
employability of unemployed 16 to 18-year-olds by means of work
experience and work preparation.

As the problem of youth unemployment got worse during the early

1980s, the effectiveness of YOPs was looking increasingly shaky. First, despite early success in placing trainees in employment, the rate dropped from 70 per cent in 1980 to 41 per cent in 1983. At the same time, there was an increase in job substitution within the Work Experience on Employers Premises element of the course, such that, by 1983, there was a risk, in about 30 per cent of places involved, that existing employees might lose their jobs. Survey evidence confirmed this to be so in 5 per cent of the cases. Finally, such training which had been permitted in the original YOPs design was evidently not being provided in practice.

Without doubt, the most ambitious policy initiative by the MSC to date has been the launching of the Youth Training Scheme. This policy constituted a consolidation of several previous schemes, notably YOP and WEP, but differed in certain significant respects. First, the scheme was heralded as a permanent feature of the training/work preparation land-scape for school leavers: the previous initiatives had all been explicitly introduced as temporary measures. Secondly, YTS was designed to provide places for all sixteen-year-old school leavers and unemployed seventeen-year-olds: previous schemes had never been able to match places available with the number of eligible young people. Thirdly, YTS was designed not only for those without work, but also for all sixteen-year-old school leavers with jobs, and a financial incentive was provided for employers to place two of their youngest permanent recruits for every three one-year trainees on to the scheme. This was because YTS was presented as more of a training scheme than a reservoir for unemployed youngsters, and the YTS design at least reflected this. Each scheme must include a minimum of thirteen weeks off-the-job training, either at a college or in an employer's own training department. This is intended to provide certain basic social skills and to back up some of the job-related skills. The on-the-job component of YTS should consist of both work experience and training.

Two different models of YTS have been proposed by the MSC: Mode A and Mode B. Mode A was planned to cater for the majority of the trainees: 300,000 out of the initial target of 460,000. Under this Mode individual employers (public or private) provide the places, either as sponsors acting directly with the MSC or via Managing Agents who organise the delivery of a group of schemes among different employers. Under Mode B1 the MSC has greater responsibility for organising the delivery of schemes on community projects, training workshops or colleges. Under Mode B2 these 'providers' act more independently on the behalf of the MSC. Each of these alternatives entails a different system and different levels of funding provision. The main difference between Modes A and B is that the former is more specifically oriented towards the needs of employers, and the latter towards the needs of those least likely to succeed in the job market. This point should be qualified however, as the likelihood of those who attend Mode B courses at Information Technology Centres entering employment is considerably higher than most. All of the different schemes are expected to include particular core elements, including basic numeracy, communication, problem solving and planning, manual dexterity and an introduction to computers. In addition each scheme must provide an induction period, guidance and counselling, an assessment of the trainees, and a certificate for them on leaving the scheme.

Clearly, at this stage, it is too soon to make a conclusive assessment of the impact of the scheme, but some early indications of the way it is working in practice are discussed in Chapter 4.

Turning to youth employment subsidies, three main schemes have been introduced: the Recruitment Subsidy for School Leavers and the Youth Employment Subsidy, both introduced by a Labour Government, and the Young Workers Scheme introduced by the Conservatives.

The Recruitment Subsidy for School Leavers (RSSL) provided a subsidy for employers taking on school-leavers with no full-time work experience. The weekly subsidy was paid for six months. A survey of employers taking part in the scheme indicated that 76 per cent of them would have taken on the school-leavers had the subsidy *not* been in operation. This high 'deadweight' effect was not, however, matched by a high 'displacement' effect: only 14 per cent of the firms indicated that the RSSL had provoked the reduction of recruitment of other groups of workers. Despite the deadweight effect, if was felt that

Since unemployment amongst young people in general continues to be a problem it can be maintained that special help should be concentrated on the least advantaged amongst this age group. (Department of Employment, 1977:696)

Thus, the Youth Employment Subsidy (YES) was introduced to replace the RSSL in October 1976, giving an increased weekly subsidy for six months to employers recruiting young people under twenty years old who had been unemployed for at least six months. The scheme was originally designed to last for six months, but was subsequently extended twice, and was finally wound up at the end of March 1978. A survey of the scheme indicated that about three-quarters of the subsidised young people would have entered the jobs anyway. Among the remaining quarter for whom there was no deadweight effect, half of these took jobs which would not have gone to another person. Thus, in the case of one-eighth of the recruits there was no deadweight or displacement effect (Department of Employment, 1978, 425). There was no immediate youth employment successor to YES; instead, another remedy was introduced in the form of the Youth Opportunities Programme discussed earlier.

The Young Workers' Scheme (YWS), introduced in 1982, was designed to provide some advantage to young people in the job market. Under

YWS, employers are paid with subsidies for employing those under eighteen years of age for the first year of their employment. However, consistent with the Conservative Government's view that problems of British industry stem largely from her uncompetitive wage levels, the YWS also encourages lower weekly wages. Thus, the current subsidies provide employers with £15 for each employee they take on whose gross average earnings are less than £42 per week, and £7.50 for each employee whose gross earnings are between £42 and £47 per week.

It is doubtful that such a scheme could have any significant impact on national wage levels (see Makeham, 1980), but even if this were the case the scheme may not have a significant effect on gross employment levels. In a recent report by the Comptroller and Auditor General, it was estimated that there was a 77 per cent 'deadweight' effect, though it was thought by Department of Employment officials that this might decrease as the scheme became established (House of Commons, 1983:20). There have also been some instances of flagrant abuse of the scheme by employers who pay young workers much less than the *national minimum wage* (which the Department of Employment is responsible for enforcing), yet still receive the full government subsidies under YWS for doing so!

We have seen how there has been considerable policy development in the field of policy responses to youth unemployment, indicative of some capacity to learn and adjust to the changing magnitude and nature of the problem. The early attempts at youth employment subsidies (RSSL and YES) were discarded at the same time as YOP was set up to provide a work experience and training scheme. The shortcomings of YOP first became apparent during the early 1980s, and YTS was designed to counter its problems of inadequate training, suspicions of job substitution, and general declining confidence in the scheme amongst the young unemployed. The YWS was introduced not only to improve the chances of employment for young people, but also to have a wider impact on wage levels. Ironically, in the first year of operation, one of the reasons for the shortfall in recruitment was put down to the preference of young people to take up positions under YWS, so in 1984–5 the latter will no longer be available for sixteen-year-old school leavers.

Schemes in response to youth unemployment, as in most western countries, appear to have been given disproportionate importance by successive governments. For instance, about half of the £2 billion to be spent on all special employment measures will be taken up by the YTS alone. Further, adverse employment implications of youth schemes for the adult labour market – notably in terms of labour substitution in YOP and YWS, and depressing wage levels in YWS – have been tolerated. So too have inefficiencies in the implementation of YOP and YWS, notably concerning the lack of any extensive training in the former, and the deadweight effect in the latter. The reasons for this policy emphasis are clear:

he high-proportionate level of unemployment among these groups has
ed to real fears about a 'lost generation'. The concern is that large sections
•f the current 16 to 18-years cohort will never have jobs, which apart from
ts intrinsic seriousness, may impair normal socialisation processes and
eed wider future societal problems.

The main qualitative change in the government response to youth un-
:mployment has been to concentrate greater attention on improving the
:mployability of school-leavers. Thus, not only have we witnessed the
:mphasis of vocational training within YTS, but also the TVEI which
ittempts to provide this before the children even leave school. TVEI is
>nly an acorn at the moment, but the government has invested great hope
n its becoming an oak tree in the drive towards increasing employment
:hances of school-leavers.

3.5 Regional policies

A further important type of policy response which has long been used to
·educe instances of peak levels of unemployment, even when national
.evels of unemployment are low, is that of regional policy. Regional
policies have been designed to create conditions in which employment
night increase in depressed areas, by means of favourable rates, grants
and tax allowances, rather than directly to create jobs. The first form of
·egional incentive scheme was introduced during the 1930s and, although
:he definition of designated areas benefiting has been subject to change,
some form of area development policy has persisted since then. This has
consisted mainly of grants towards investment in the specified depressed
areas, in the hope of stimulating growth and employment. At times these
have been criticised for giving 'concentration on areas of need rather than
areas of potential' (Yuill, 1980:188).

For the early post-war period, regional policy went through what Yuill
described as a 'dormant' period (1980:187). Part of the government
reaction to higher levels of unemployment in the late 1950s and early
1960s was to designate new categories of development areas matching
instances of what was then high unemployment – 4.5 per cent! This
system was further built upon by the Labour Government. These developments included the first direct employment subsidy, the Regional
Employment Premium (REP), which was introduced in 1967. REP
provided a rebate on the Selective Employment Tax to employers taking
on workers in the manufacturing sector within designated areas. The
growth of regional policies after 1966 incurred considerable criticism
from the Conservatives, who, when returned to office in 1970, proposed
that the system be significantly pared down and the definition of specified
areas amended. It was announced that REP would be phased out over four
years (though it had only been introduced as a temporary measure).
Further, regional investment grants on plant and machinery were replaced

by differential tax allowances on machinery installed within the specified areas. However, it was the spectre of rising unemployment in 1971–2 which provoked re-appraisal of policies in both this and other policy areas. In March 1972, the tax allowances mentioned earlier were extended to apply nationally and the regional development grants on plant and machinery abolished eighteen months earlier were re-introduced, in addition to further discretionary assistance.

With unemployment steadily increasing in the mid-to-late 1970s, one might have expected the Labour Government to strengthen the apparently well established UK regional policy. This indeed was probably its intention. However, the economies required under the terms of taking the IMF loan in late 1976 signalled the abolition of the REP. What the Conservative Government under Heath had not had the political nerve to do, Callaghan's Labour Government was forced to do by economic circumstances. In the same year, certain exclusions were also made in regional development grant assistance. On the other hand, due to rises in unemployment, the Welsh, Scottish and Northern Ireland Development Agencies were all created in this period, and charged with the task of investing in new and expanding enterprise in these regions. In the Welsh case this task was described as follows:

... by developing industrial estates and sites, building factories, investing in new and expanding enterprises in Wales, providing business advisory services and promoting Wales as a location for industrial development ... (Welsh Development Agency, 1981)

Perhaps the most celebrated case of development agency activity was that of the Northern Ireland Development Agency's investment in De Lorean Motor Cars Limited. All three agencies, however, have made loans or bought shares in a wide range of private companies in their respective provinces, attempting to attract industrial investment and job opportunities.

After its victory in the May 1979 General Election, the new Conservative Government reduced the actual coverage of the assisted areas. Amongst other changes, reductions were made in the level of regional development grants. Further, overall finance for the designated areas was reduced, most particularly by reducing the percentage of total investment costs for which grants were available. Moreover, grants would now only be made available if the project would *necessarily* fail without them. But although overall expenditure has been reduced for such schemes, they persist. Indeed, original expenditure plans have been overridden in pursuance of some regional policies. For instance, in the face of mass unemployment resulting from closures in the Welsh steel industry, the government felt obliged to inject £48 million for remedial measures in affected areas, most of which are administered by the Welsh Development

Agency (Department of Employment, February 1980, p.107). More recently, the government announced a £15-million urban programme in Wales, for areas outside those affected by steel closures: a 45 per cent increase on the amount spent in the previous year.

Similar schemes have been introduced in Scotland. The Scottish Development Agency (SDA) has provided £200 million (£100 million coming from regional and local councils) for economic revival in the West of Scotland. Indeed, between 1980 and 1981 the numbers employed under SDA schemes increased by 20 per cent, the amount invested by 14 per cent, and the number of companies benefiting from investments by 30 per cent. There was a 25 per cent drop in the total amount of loans made, though by 1980 this was already a small figure compared with the figure for investments: £1.75 million and £23.7 million respectively (SDA, 1980 and 1981). The Agency acknowledged, in 1980, that there had been changes of emphasis along lines sought by the new Secretary of State, but added that '. . . there was continuity also, as the Agency's work continued to grow and strengthen on lines already established or foreshadowed' (SDA, 1980:4). A recent study of government intervention in the Scottish economy concluded that a paradox existed. Whereas the Conservative Government has adopted a rhetoric which has emphasised a rolling back of the state, various bodies such as the SDA and the Scottish Office have actually increased their intervention in depressed areas of the Scottish economy (Booth and Pitt, 1983).

Northern Ireland has continued to enjoy additional incentives to investment, with higher grants on approved capital expenditure and higher levels of grant and loan schemes. Even between 1979 and 1980 the NIDA's capital investment allowance was increased from £50 to £85 million (NIDA, 1980:5). In 1982, the Secretary of State announced a £90-million boost to the Northern Ireland economy, which represented a 3 per cent increase on planned expenditure for 1982–3.

The government has also aided a range of other development organisations, including the Highland and Islands Development Board and various English promotional bodies (e.g. North of England Development Council). It has been estimated that in 1980–1 the government spent a total of £725 million on 'regional preferential expenditure' (excluding Northern Ireland), which was in addition to the special MSC schemes in Wales and Scotland (*Sunday Times* 'Business News', 21.2.82). As in many policy areas, the tough image of the Thatcher Government (often encouraged by its own spokespersons) did not match its pragmatic activities.

In addition to these broader forms of regional aid, the government created a number of Enterprise Zones, designed to stimulate investment and create jobs in designated areas particularly hit by the slump. Industrial and commercial investments are intended to be attracted to the Zones, mainly through exemptions from the payment of rates, but complemented by a package of other exemptions grants and business services. Initially, eleven such Enterprise Zones were created, in 1981, and a further fourteen areas have subsequently been formed. A recent report has indicated that whilst jobs have been created in the first set of Enterprise Zones – 8,065 between May 1981 and May 1983 – this has been at a considerable cost, of approximately £132.9m (Roger Tym and Partners, 1984).

The report also concluded that most companies who were attracted to the Zones were from within the locality and were already in existence. Thus, the Enterprise Zones seemed most effective not in stimulating and encouraging new enterprise, but in giving existing firms several financial advantages – notably rates relief – so enabling them to expand and take on some new labour. Despite rhetoric to the contrary when the first Zones were created, they have not become a focus for private investment and initiative but have developed along conventional regional policy lines, with a heavy dependence on state subsidies. The operation of the Zones has been dubbed 'ideologically acceptable job creation' (Jordan, 1984).

However, even with such favourable conditions for industrial and regional development, disparities persist. Is this because the schemes in operation are insufficient or irrelevant? A further problem of operating a generous and flexible regional policy on British lines is that broader sectoral goals may be undermined by appeasing regional demand for investment to create new or save existing establishments. Another uncertainty exists as to whether such schemes are creating additional jobs, or are simply, by means of unfair competition, attracting investment from areas which would otherwise prove capable of supporting industry and commerce. It has been suggested that

regional policy has been effective in redirecting jobs towards the assisted areas. However, the scale of this influence appears to be very small when compared with the underlying trends in employment growth and decline at the regional level. (Keogh and Elias, 1980:174)

Recent evidence suggests that there is a real decline in the amount spent on regional aid, but an increase in urban aid. Urban aid is not specifically employment-oriented, but is aimed at improving the broader quality of life in urban areas. Further reduction on the former is likely, due to the disproportionate support given to capital-intensive industries, which have little impact upon employment patterns.

3.6 Ad hoc government interventions

In addition to using the instruments of budgetary and regional policies, successive governments have also made *ad hoc* interventions to prevent the collapse of a major employer and so avert mass redundancies. The Labour Governments of 1964–70 injected vast amounts of capital into various projects to sustain them over a difficult period, and in so doing prevented a major round of redundancies (of course, a variety of other economic and political motives also usually applied). One of the most celebrated of such schemes was the £20-million aid given between 1967 and 1970 to the five firms constituting the Upper Clyde Shipbuilders (UCS).

This trend of increasing government participation and investment, in cases where large-scale unemployment was threatened, was seen by the Conservatives in the late 1960s as laying the foundation of future economic ruin. As a major plank in its economic policy, Edward Heath's 1970 Conservative Government made it clear that it would not intervene in industry so readily as its predecessor. Such sentiments were most famously summed up by John Davies (Secretary of State for Trade and Industry), who argued that the country

needed to gear its policies to the great majority of people, who are not lame ducks, who do not need a hand, who are quite capable of looking after their own interests and only demand to be allowed to do so . . . [the majority] lives and thrives in a bracing climate, and not in a soft sodden morass of subsidised incompetence. (Hansard, Vol. 805, Col. 1211)

Clearly, if followed through consistently, such a policy would have at least the short-term consequence of redundancies and rising unemployment. Even if the policy was sound, the efficacy of such an approach would to a certain extent depend on the speed with which the changing economic climate could provide other jobs for the jobless to move to, as well as on the government's confidence in such a scenario. Would they have the nerve to take the political risk of rising unemployment in pursuance of broader objectives?

In short, the answer was no. Although not central to the policy changes which the Heath administration performed within two years of taking office, the rescue operations in the cases of the UCS and Rolls-Royce illustrated how changing economic circumstances (most notably rising unemployment) provoked important policy reversals. This was described as a result of

. . . the dawning recognition by the Government that in a modern economy capital and labour are not, as classical theory predicates, homogeneous and infinitely divisible factors of production which, if released from one employment, will flow effortlessly into another. (Stewart, 1977:137)

The 1972 Industry Act (described by Tony Benn as Mr Heath's spade-work for Socialism) was probably the most central indicator of the changing role of government in industry, giving the Secretary of State for Industry considerable powers to intervene and to provide financial assistance where he thought this would be beneficial.

Rescue missions were also conducted under the 1974–9 Labour Governments in order to maintain large-scale employers. The injection of public cash into, and the government's assumption of joint responsibility for, the British subsidiary of Chrysler, were largely due to a fear of huge redundancies and their political consequences. The activities of the National Enterprise Board (NEB) can also be seen as responses to uncertainties in the private sector, and thus state intervention would, no doubt, have been made with the possible employment consequences of non-intervention uppermost in mind (e.g. NEB holdings in British Leyland).

On winning office in 1979, the Thatcher Government made it clear that, in contrast to the Heath administration, it would keep its political nerve under difficult political circumstances. In other words, in the interests of improving Britain's international competitiveness, it would not rush in to save firms in difficulties. For the most part, it has lived up to this promise, allowing record levels of company closures with consequent large-scale redundancies. There have, however, been exceptions, when it has followed its predecessors' example, though in such cases, much stricter conditions (in terms of financial and manpower implications) have been laid down.

The government has continued to pour money into British Leyland. In 1981, the Edwardes investment plan requiring £1.4 billion over four years was approved, largely in fear of the knock-on effects of closure upon employment in the Midlands. Indeed, the recent decision of Leyland Trucks to pull out of Bathgate appeared to be more a management decision, made for commercial reasons, than the result of government intervention. A £500-million government investment in the British Steel Corporation was approved with similar fears of unemployment in mind.

The decision made by the government to purchase the British Marconi Space and Defence Systems torpedo for the Royal Navy was also with employment considerations uppermost. Rather than buy the cheaper £100 million American alternative, the Defence and Overseas Policy Committee of the Cabinet, chaired by Mrs Thatcher, chose to buy British. Marconi had said that the contract would be worth 5,000 jobs, but failure to secure it would mean the loss of 2,000 jobs. It has also been reported that, although the government favours buying American Trident nuclear missiles, it has been trying to negotiate a scheme whereby British firms could manufacture some of the parts as a condition of purchase.

3.7 The changing policy mix

The foregoing has provided a broad summary of the major policy responses to the unemployment problem and their general effects upon it. Before we can generalise about trends in this field, however, it should be stressed that there has not been a great deal of *overall* planning and co-ordination under either Labour or Conservative Governments in their responses to unemployment, although small measures have been taken, e.g. the changing of the YWS rubric because of its impact upon YTS.

There are various *political* explanations for this. First, despite the increasing inter-departmentalism within the world of unemployment, individual departments retain areas of responsibility accorded to them and imprint their own working style upon policies in these areas. Thus, whilst it has been overall government policy and the aim of branches within the Treasury and Department of Trade and Industry to achieve some restructuring within British industry, the Department of Employment's TSTWC, which was devised to preserve jobs in what were declining industries, persisted for five years of Conservative rule. Secondly, whilst there have been some attempts to reduce the amount of regional aid available, it has simply continued to *increase* under new guises, e.g. Enterprise Zones. The *ad hoc* activities of government, by their very nature, also disrupt any notion of a plan for unemployment. Thirdly, the tendency for policy development to follow a style of 'succession' from previous programmes impedes attempts to 'plan' rationally a comprehensive policy response to the problem.

Another important source of dislocation of would-be co-ordinated policy responses are other government objectives which may cut across the achievement of policy objectives in the unemployment field. Most obviously, the goals of reducing inflation and public expenditure which have preoccupied governments over the last decade (with varying degrees of success) have undermined the possibility of a concerted, national effort to reduce unemployment in the long term. Conversely, if governments do believe that improving Britain's competitiveness will provide the best chance of improvements in employment prospects for the long term, then the net additional public expenditure commitments involved in the special employment measures actually undermine the likelihood of achieving this goal. Thus, the lack of a co-ordinated national response to unemployment reflects not only departmentalism and an incremental policy style, but also the fact that governments, especially in a democracy, are not able to pursue a single policy goal at the expense of all others for fear of the political and electoral consequences. The special measures then constitute a form of political insurance on the part of successive governments.

The macroeconomic implications of the special measures are rather difficult to assess with any precision. In addition to the public expenditure implications of their running and administrative costs, there are other factors that should properly be taken into account. For one thing, it is impossible to quantify the economic and employment impact of spending the money on other government policies, or of reducing taxes. It is also difficult to assess the contribution which the various special measures make towards the total national output of goods and services. Some, such as CP and YTS, clearly account for some small addition in output, but others like JRS and JSS probably have little or no impact. Whilst it is intended that the training schemes will make some long-term contribution to the country's performance, this is not easily quantified. Given the level of expenditure on special measures, the Comptroller and Auditor General concluded that their net effect was to reduce national output, at least in the short term (House of Commons, 1983:14).

The public expenditure on these responses to unemployment not only undermines government policy to reduce PSBR; it may also detract from the efforts of the present administration to reduce labour costs in industry, by increasing pressure within the labour market and so artificially restricting the fall in wages usually associated with a rise in unemployment. If this relationship were to hold, then these unemployment policy responses might also impede a fall in inflation. However, these remain theoretical relationships which have not been empirically validated.

At first sight, the net effect of schemes upon the register seems fairly easy to calculate. Counting the number of participants on each scheme, however, does not indicate the operations of dead weight; substitution, whereby participants take the place of ineligible employees; displacement, where the subsidised output competes with output from firms who do not have the benefit of special employment measures, thus reducing their demand for labour; non-registration, affecting participants who would not otherwise have been registered as unemployed; and, in the case of the JRS and PTJRS, non-replacement, in which the retiree is not replaced by someone from the unemployment register. In his 1983 memorandum on the special measures, the Comptroller and Auditor General drew attention to the likelihood of these factors being present, to varying degrees, within the schemes, and reported that, in 1981, an evaluation working party had been set up to investigate. The precision with which the factors were calculated varied considerably from scheme to scheme, but the findings were 'generally more pessimistic than those used in the monthly Press Notice on S[pecial] E[mployment] M[easures]' (House of Commons, 1983:12). Thus, evaluating the real impact of various combinations of special measures is a difficult if not impossible task, which is further complicated by the effects of a range of unemployment-related policies like regional aid.

Even so, there have been some discernible shifts in the policy mix over about the last ten years. The increased emphasis on training within youth schemes has already been touched upon, and this looks like being a major component of change in adult schemes, although the government has yet to get its policy proposals in this field accepted by the policy network. It is not simply that *more* training is envisaged, but that skills to be taught should be more relevant to industry's needs than was the case when TOPS began. In addition, the Open Tech and the new proposals both provide opportunities for the retraining of those already in work, to enable them to adapt to technological change, rather than face redundancy.

There has also been the development of what we call 'more sophisticated' schemes, which try to reduce unemployment and at the same time meet other aspirations of the workforce, such as early retirement and job sharing. More attention, however, will need to be paid to improving the terms of the Job Splitting Scheme. The Community Programme betrays a simple attempt to get as many people off the unemployment register at the lowest acceptable cost to the public.

Similarly, there have been changes in the type of employment subsidy measures, after the abandonment of this strategy in 1980. The YWS is not justified solely on the grounds that it provides jobs for youth, but also because it attempts to create a seed change which the government believes will have longer-term employment benefits, i.e. lower wages for the young. The Enterprise Allowance, subsidising those setting up their own businesses, is fully compatible with the Conservative viewpoint that entrepreneurial flair should be encouraged. In a sense, this scheme de-centralises the unemployment problem by removing some responsibility from the government to those in receipt of the subsidies. This decentralisation theme has also been evident in the field of regional aids, notably with the creation of development agencies and enterprise zones. All in all, the precise role of government is clearly undergoing some change in responses to unemployment. Perhaps this is a reflection of the growing disillusion with the traditional role of the public sector (see Heald, 1983), and especially its centralised functions. This theme is further developed in the analysis of the wider responses to unemployment in Chapter 5.

4   The Making and Implementation of Unemployment Policy

4.1 Introduction

Two particular features of policy-making in Western democracies are usually emphasised by political scientists. Both are relevant to our consideration of the making and implementing of unemployment policy in Britain. The first is that policy-making has become highly sectorised in that the 'business of government' is subdivided into relatively autonomous compartments or sectors. Each sector seems to develop a life of its own, with its associated set of pressure groups. In Britain, a classic illustration of the sectorisation phenomenon was provided by the late Lord Boyle in his reflections on being a Minister of Education. He came to realise that education policy was made almost exclusively in the 'education world', with relatively little outside influence (Kogan, 1971:45). Most parents will readily recognise his analysis, notwithstanding recent and current attempts to increase parental power. The health sector is very similar, with the organisation of the health service (including the allocation of resources) in the hands of 'professionals'. Patients tend to be uninfluential consumers of whatever service is provided. Ministers (and governments) come and go, but the running of the health service – for instance, the balance in the use of resources between, say, heart surgery and long-stay care – seems relatively impervious to party-political or public influence. The concept of 'policy community' is important here, that is, an informal grouping or network of insiders and 'recognised' outside groups who regularly 'process' issues and problems in a given policy area.

The sectorisation of policy-making in this way is a strong force against policy co-ordination. Structures which are supposed to achieve co-ordination are usually rather ineffective. For example, the Cabinet turns out in practice to be little more than an agency where the representatives of each sector fight their respective corners, to use Churchill's expression, and where bargains are struck between the competing sectors. Each Minister is briefed by his civil servants in order to defend his departmental interests. This fragmented system can produce a set of policies full of conflicts and contradictions. Thus, for example, the objectives of the Department of Trade and Industry (DTI) in trying to encourage a viable truck industry in the UK may be in conflict with the desire of the

Secretary of State for Scotland to prevent a further erosion of manufacturing employment in Scotland.

The proposed closure of the Leyland lorry plant in Bathgate, near Edinburgh, announced in May 1984, is a brutal illustration of conflicting objectives. Those in favour of the closure saw it as a necessary step in the painful process of restructuring British industry. Those opposed to it saw it as yet another example of the de-industrialisation of Scotland and as further worsening the unemployment problem in Scotland. This 'restructuring' or 'de-industrialisation' had produced a reduction of approximately 25 per cent in manufacturing jobs in Scotland over a period of five years. Similarly, proposed changes in the regional support policy (announced in Mr Lawson's budget of April 1984) were seen in Scotland as a potentially serious threat to increased investment and employment in Scotland. Policies which may be perfectly rational in one sector, can thus have very damaging results in another.

The second important feature of the policy-making process (or policy 'style', as we would call it) is that governments usually make very great efforts to 'incorporate' outside pressure groups and to reach a consensus on what policies should be introduced. This negotiated policy style (Jordan and Richardson, 1982) is usually carried through into the *implementation* of public policies – that is, pressure groups are not only incorporated into the formulation of public policy but are heavily involved in its practical implementation. As S. E. Finer suggested over a quarter of a century ago, the whole system of public administration in Britain is founded upon the assumption that groups will actively co-operate in the administration of policy once it has been decided by Parliament (Finer 1956). In Britain, Hayward has argued that the test of a good policy is that there is broad agreement that it should be introduced, rather than that the policy should meet some objectively defined criteria (Hayward, 1974:405–7). Other writers have seen this consensual style – the 'beatification of compromise', as Lord Rothschild put it (Rothschild 1976) – as preventing any radical change at all. For example, Brown argued that it was remarkably hard to find a satisfactory example of radical innovation in the breadth of British policy-making (Brown, 1974:39).

So, how do we relate unemployment policy to these two features of our policy process: sectorisation and the search for consensus? To what extent does unemployment policy 'fit' the traditional British policy style? Is the unemployment issue special in some way, because of its high and continuing political salience and because it has been caught up in the adversarial party-political battle? In practice, policy-making and implementing in this field do appear to have some features which 'fit' the traditional style perfectly, such as the 'tripartism' of the MSC (described in the following section) and the high degree of involvement of pressure groups in such schemes as YTS.

This search for consensus and integration, centred upon the MSC, also illustrates a common view that pressure groups can sometimes exercise a veto on certain policy options. For example, the TUC and the CBI successfully resisted the proposal that participation on the YTS be compulsory for sixteen-year-old school-leavers. The emergence of new initiatives, often based upon previous policies and therefore representing policy succession rather than radical policy change (see Chapter 3 and Moon, 1983), looks very similar to the 'education world' which Lord Boyle described. That is to say, these policies are generated within the unemployment 'policy community', rather than being imported from outside. Members of the unemployment policy community seem to recognise each other's perspectives, recognise the need for compromise and consensus, and recognise that there is a collective interest in 'managing' the policy area in such a way that external policies are not imposed upon them. One particularly obvious feature of the making of unemployment policy is the virtual absence of participation by the unemployed themselves, simply because they are, as yet, unorganised.

In a much broader perspective, however, the unemployment policy sector appears to exhibit characteristics quite different to the normal British policy style. This is especially true for the period under Mrs Thatcher as Prime Minister, since 1979. As we suggested in Chapter 1, Mrs Thatcher may have broken with the post-1944 consensus, as expressed in the famous 1944 White Paper on Employment Policy, by 'allowing' unemployment to reach such high levels. Indeed, it would be ridiculous to suggest that the unemployment issue illustrates the traditional British consensual style, when there is such bitter disagreement over its causes and over possible remedies. Thus the TUC is strongly opposed to the Conservative Government's economic strategy, and has consistently argued for a more openly Keynesian reflationary policy. Even the CBI has, for several years now, been pressing government to introduce a public investment policy in such sectors as construction and motorway maintenance.

The government has been unusually steady of nerve in risking the *political* consequences of mass (and continually rising) unemployment. Its refusal to introduce a general reflationary package is certainly a radical policy, in the context of modern British economic history. The government has been pursuing overriding policy goals, such as the reduction of inflation, increasing the competitiveness of British industry and the restructuring of the economy, which have had severe cross-sectoral implications. These policies have considerably reduced the autonomy of the unemployment/employment sector, in the sense of precluding certain policy options which might have reduced unemployment, if only in the short term. It is, therefore, difficult to make a simple characterisation of the unemployment policy process. In practice, the process is a mixture of non-negotiable policies (unusual in British politics) and a very close involvement of pressure groups such as the CBI and TUC (common in British politics). This close involvement or incorporation of groups is nowhere more evident than in the work of the Manpower Services Commission (MSC).

4.2 The MSC: formation, structure and responsibilities

In this chapter, we are primarily concerned with the policy processes in which the MSC is involved, as it is these which constitute the major force of direct government responses to unemployment. First, what sort of organisation is the MSC? Its creation was announced by the late Maurice Macmillan, who was Secretary of State for Employment, under the provisions of the 1973 Employment and Training Act. It was to be a new kind of governmental organisation:

> the government attach great importance to what has become known as the tri-partite approach ... as is shown by the proposed membership ... I am not suggesting that they (board members) are mandated or delegates who must refer back on every major point, but they must carry the confidence of the organisations which helped them to be appointed in carrying out their daily functions. (*Hansard*, Vol. 852, Col. 1144)

The MSC came into operation in 1974, and was made responsible to the Secretary of State for Employment who, with help from his junior ministers, was to answer parliamentary questions on all MSC matters. Its annual budget is within the total Department of Employment 'vote' (the term used for individual departments' allocations). However, by virtue of its non-departmental status, and because of the high political salience of unemployment, the Commission is better able than the DE to make special claims to the Treasury on financial matters concerning more public political questions, (e.g., the recent appeal, in March 1984, for an extra £1 million for the Enterprise Allowance). The decision to set up the agency was partly a function of a trend of the period to create specialist MSC ('hiving off') with clearer and narrower responsibilities than those of the respective 'parent' departments, e.g., Health and Safety Commission, Advisory Conciliation and Arbitration Service (ACAS), Commission for Racial Equality (CRE). It was thus hoped that specific policy objectives would more easily be achieved in these new, more goal-oriented organisations than in the Whitehall departments which are preoccupied with a range of other policy responsibilities and day-to-day concerns.

It was the government's initial intention to 'hive off' the MSC from central government so that its staff would lose their civil service status. However, this change was strongly opposed by the relevant staff associations, and soon reversed by the government. This was also a period in which the principle of tripartism was venerated, and, in the particular context of employment and training, there was considerable interest in the comparatively successful Swedish labour market, in which employers and trade unions played a major part (Howells, 1980:306). Of course, in the field of UK industrial training, the principle of tripartism was already firmly established in the membership of the Industrial Training Boards. Thus, the Commission has consisted of ten government appointed members: a chairman, three members appointed after consultation with the TUC, three after consultation with the CBI, two after consultation with local authority associations, and one with professional education interests. The members of the Commission are formally held responsible for policy-making and oversight of all MSC activities.

A further factor to take into account in explaining the creation of the MSC was the need for the Heath Government not only to *do* something about the rising unemployment, but also to be *seen* to be doing something different. The creation of a brand new organisation, and its work (begun by the Department of Employment) in trying to upgrade the image of job seeking by creating well-furnished high street Job Centres in place of the dingy Employment Exchanges had at least some short-term advantages in this context.

Whilst the members of the Commission are responsible for the *formal* policy-making functions, it is of course the bureaucracy of the MSC which is responsible for early identification of problems and for drawing up the more detailed policy options, implementing the policies and evaluating their impact. Although there has been some recruitment from other sources, initially most of the MSC staff were simply transferred from the Department of Employment. At its inception, the MSC had a small secretariat of forty staff, and about 19,000 field staff operating in over a thousand separate establishments (MSC, 1975:i). The most recent figures indicate that, in 1982, there were just over 24,000 staff, although the highest staffing level was achieved in 1979, with just over 26,000 (MSC, 1983c:37). The bulk of this reduction from the peak was achieved as part of an overall cutback in the size of the Civil Service within the first year of the first Thatcher Government, which the then Chairman of the MSC, Sir Richard O'Brien, described as 'a difficult year for the Commission' (MSC, 1980:ii).

Initially, the work of the Commission was divided into two spheres each with its own organisational structure: the Employment Service Agency (ESA) and the Training Service Agency (TSA). The role of the ESA was to maintain and develop the work of filling employers' job vacancies and finding employment for those registered as unemployed, a task which had previously been conducted by a division of the Department of Employment. The ESA's first new strategy was entitled 'Meeting labour market needs', which consisted of widening the range of services to the job seeker (a self-service system for current job vacancies, employment advice, and specialist services, e.g., for the handicapped and the young), the physical renewal and relocation of the service, an upgrading of the service (by, for instance, more training for ESA personnel), and improved information systems about job vacancies.

The TSA's initial objectives were to co-ordinate its activities with the Industrial Training Boards (ITBs), including overseeing some aspects of ITBs' work, and to promote training in areas not covered by ITBs. In addition, it was instructed to develop TOPS rapidly, and increase the efficiency and effectiveness of government Skillcentres. As Howells (1980:309) has pointed out, the TSA had a much smaller staff than the ESA, and was a less coherent and more decentralised organisation.

During 1975 the overall role of the MSC was considerably enhanced. The MSC had earlier argued that:

> there needed to be a central authority responsible for both managing and co-ordinating the executive instruments of manpower policy and for influencing through comment and advice the manpower aspects of other policies – economic, fiscal, industrial – to ensure that they were satisfactorily related to the manpower system. (MSC, 1976:29)

The Secretary of State for Employment responded to these proposals and

> accepted that the Commission should be the main executive body operating in the labour market, develop into an authoritative centre for information and intelligence on employment matters, promote an overall manpower strategy and be an important point of influence on policies directly concerned with the working of the labour market. (MSC, 1976:29)

This development led to the appointment of a range of new staff within the Office of the MSC, and most notably, that of a Director to co-ordinate the activities of the Office, to give advice to the Commission and to maintain contacts with other relevant bodies, such as the CBI, TUC and local authorities. A further innovation was the creation of the Chairman's Management Committee, providing a nexus for senior MSC officials under the Chairman. This gave the Chairman more involvement in the day-to-day running of the MSC than other members of the Commission. Also, a Manpower Intelligence and Planning Division was created, along with a small Job Creation Unit to oversee the Job Creation Programme. Finally, in order to achieve maximum responsiveness and flexibility to the needs of employers and individuals at the local level, a network of 125 District Manpower Committees was established, to provide advisory services to the regional and local management units of the ESA and TSA. Each Committee was chaired by a Commission appointee and consisted of equal numbers of trade union and employer members, as well as representatives of educational interests and local authorities.

Further organisational changes were made in the following year, to provide opportunity for greater initiative at the regional level. First, the responsibilities for the Commission's activities in Scotland and Wales were transferred to the respective Secretaries of State for Scotland and Wales, and Commissions for these countries were established whose membership mirrored the original Commission. In 1978, a system of regional directors (Scotland, Wales and the English regions) was established, with special responsibilities for the Special Programmes and for Regional Manpower Intelligence Units.

Also, in 1978, the autonomy of both the Employment Services Agency and the Training Services Agency was weakened to enable the MSC to operate in a more co-ordinated fashion, though the main structures of ESA and TSA were retained to provide the basis for the new Employment Service Division and the Training Service Division. The Manpower Intelligence and Planning Division was retained, and the Job Creation Unit transformed into the new Special Programmes Division, which was responsible for the new schemes: Youth Opportunities Programme and Special Temporary Employment Programme. What had been the Office of the MSC became the Corporate Services Division. Each of these five national divisions had its own Director or Chief Executive, in addition to the overall Director of the MSC.

The most significant recent organisational change, completed in September 1982, has been the merger of the old Training Services and Special Programmes Divisions to form a new Training Division. This change was a reflection of the increasing emphasis, that special measures for the young should give greater attention to training and work preparation, and anticipated the Youth Training Scheme. The new division is served, at the field level, by a new structure of 55 Area Offices, complemented by a new network of Area Manpower Boards to replace the previous Special Programmes Area Boards and District Manpower Committees. Like their predecessors, the new boards operate in an advisory capacity, and consist of representatives of business, unions, local government, education, and sometimes also of the voluntary sector. The field offices of the Employment Division were also changed more or less in line with those of its training counterpart.

Figure 4.1 provides an indication of the 1983 organisational structure of the MSC, indicating different types of relationship between sections of the organisation, and distinguishing between advisory and operational bodies. As can be seen, formally constituted advisory bodies operate throughout the organisation at national and area levels, thus providing access points throughout the system for representatives of non-governmental organisations. The Training Division is responsible not only for conventional MSC training schemes, but also for the Youth Training Scheme, which is a permanent programme for work experience and training. This programme is of such significance that it has its own national advisory board, the Youth Training Board, and three sub-branches. The Training Division continues to be responsible for adult

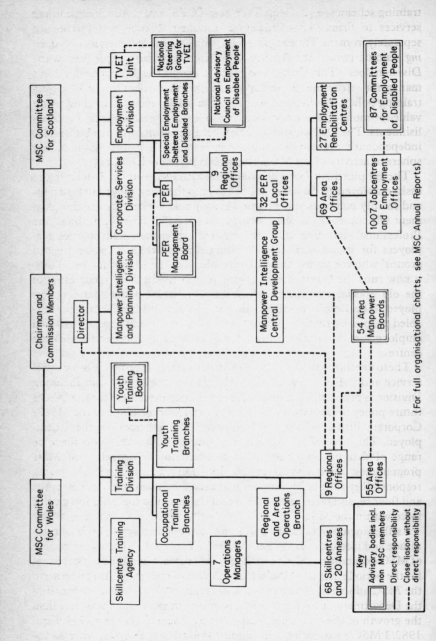

Figure 4.1   Organisational structure of the MSC

training schemes, e.g., Open Tech and TOPS, and some direct training services to firms. The Skillcentre Training Agency was established separately from the Training Division to distinguish the exercise of *delivering* training (which the Agency does) from *commissioning* it (which the Division does). This change was made to enable the Agency to develop a managerial structure most capable of being responsive to changing training policy requirements (e.g., within YTS), and of providing better value-for-money training services for industry within its training establishments. The Technical and Vocational Education Initiative Unit is also independently constituted, since it is responsible for yet another new sphere of activity of the MSC: the training of schoolchildren.

The Employment Division continues with its central task of trying to assist employers to fill vacancies and to help the unemployed to find jobs, and mainly conducts this function through its Jobcentres and Employment Offices. In addition, it provides a specialist function through the Professional and Executive Recruitment service, which charges employers for its services. The Division also provides help for 'special groups' who are having particular problems in the labour market. Thus, it now runs the Community Programme (formerly the responsibility of the old Special Programmes Division) for the adult long-term unemployed. The Employment Division is also responsible for helping disabled people, by finding them suitable work in conventional or sheltered employment, in training, employment consultancy and in rehabilitation centres.

These executive arms of the MSC are complemented by more central service and policy divisions. The Manpower Intelligence and Planning Division is primarily responsible for developing draft ideas for the MSC's future policy initiatives, and as such is a major contributor to the MSC's Corporate Plans, Reviews of Manpower and Services for the Unemployed. This necessarily involves the Division in the collection of a wide range of data on both the labour market and the operation of MSC programmes. The Corporate Services Division, as well as having responsibility for overall internal management issues, such as personnel and finance, and many external relations, also acts as the main integrative force within the MSC.

As the unemployment problem has continued to grow, both in magnitude and intensity, so too has the MSC. Table 4.1 indicates the growth of MSC expenditure relative to the overall increase in public expenditure, for the period since the MSC's first full year of operation. As can be seen, the MSC's increase in expenditure (including that incurred on behalf of the Department of Employment) has increased at a much faster rate than the growth of the total public expenditure. Indeed, between 1974/5 and 1982/3 MSC's expenditure has almost trebled in real terms, whereas the increase in total public expenditure has been relatively very modest.

Table 4.1   Total MSC expenditure compared with total public expenditure

Financial year	MSC expenditure[1]		MSC expenditure incl. that on behalf of Dept. of Employment[1]		Index of public expenditure at constant prices[2]
	£m	Index at constant prices	£m	Index at constant prices	
1974−5	125.4	63.9	125.4	63.9	95.4
1975−6	249.3	100.0	249.3	100.0	100.0
1976−7	371.4	130.5	430.4	151.3	100.9
1977−8	432.5	135.4	543.5	170.2	95.3
1978−9	507.4	142.3	641.3	180.1	94.5
1979−80	610.7	151.3	727.1	180.1	96.1
1980−1	747.8	156.4	869.3	180.2	100.8
1981−2	947.0	178.9	1117.4	211.1	99.5
1982−3	—	—	1343.2	236.8	101.6

[1] Source: Annual Reports of the MSC.
[2] Calculated from Summary Account of General Government Expenditure, National Income and Expenditure, 1983, CSO, 59.
[3] No distinction is made for MSC expenditure *excluding* that on behalf of Department of Employment.

The MSC has also increased the scope of its activities. Having initially been created largely to deliver existing Department of Employment functions, it now occupies a pivotal position in the policy making and policy delivery of schemes of very high public profile. This has been most notably achieved in the field of training. As the number of industrial apprenticeships has declined − due to a combination of reluctance of some employers to continue with apprenticeships during recession, the weakening of ITB's grants and levy powers since 1974, and the recent abolition of many ITBs − so the MSC has increased its own (different) brand of industrial and vocational training. Indeed, it has become a key factor in the direction of policy change affecting industrial training, e.g., its role as 'judge and jury' in the review of the matter in the mid-seventies (see Richardson and Stringer 1981). It has developed a wide range of schemes in the training sector, including WEEP, YTS, ITECs, as well as the range of simple job-creation schemes.

Most recently, it has further extended its administrative boundaries with the launching of the Technical and Vocational Education Initiative, which is a scheme for children still studying at school − normally the preserve of the Department of Education and Science (see Moon and Richardson, 1984a).

The MSC's almost phenomenal growth, particularly in terms of the expansion of its 'territory', has not been without criticism. But, there is no doubt that it has identified and exploited opportunities with great skill and that, as a result, it is now the repository of a growing expertise in the unemployment and training fields. As such, it is undoubtedly a powerful organisation and in its own right, raising difficult questions of accountability and control.

4.3 The Department of Employment

Having illustrated the growth of the MSC in the field of policy responses to unemployment, we should not totally lose sight of its 'parent department' the Department of Employment (DE). Whilst the MSC has undoubtedly become the main vehicle for government policy in the field of unemployment, and to a considerable degree has seized the initiative in the formulation of policy ideas, the DE, of course, retains important powers and responsibilities. First, it remains the department from which MSC expenditure is formally allocated, although, as indicated above, the MSC also enjoys independent access to the Treasury. The DE has the key role of 'fighting the corner' in the interests of employment/unemployment, in the Whitehall machine and in Cabinet, for instance, in securing resources for its unemployment schemes. Secondly, the DE is required to give approval of such policy documents as the MSC Corporate Plan, and is one of a number of departments which has a negotiated input into MSC policy decisions.

In addition to these powers, the DE has been responsible for devising and delivering the range of employment subsidy schemes outlined in the previous chapter, e.g., the Small Firms Employment Subsidy and Young Workers' Scheme. Also, the Department has had responsibility for the more 'sophisticated' policies of trying to reduce the numbers seeking work – the Job Release Scheme and the Job Splitting Scheme.

The DE has interests in broader aspects of the government's policy in the unemployment field. For example, Branch A of the Economic Policy (Manpower Division) has responsibilities for

Regional and local employment questions; DE interest in regional policy; including boundaries of Assisted Areas and travel-to-work areas; inner cities and urban development corporations; Mergers Panel; dispersal. (Civil Service Year Book, 1983:239)

Most of these policy areas are, of course, within the ambit of the Department of Trade and Industry. Other branches deal specifically with the DE's interest in the work of the MSC, and another does agency work for the Department of Health and Social Security in the provision of unemployment benefit and supplementary allowances for the unemployed. As MSC staff are officially DE civil servants, the department also handles some personnel functions for the Commission.

In contrast to the MSC, the DE does not have a formal tripartite structure. However, it is at the centre of a policy community which overlaps with that of the MSC, and it thus invariably consults outside interests prior to launching initiatives. The normal pattern of policy making for DE employment subsidy schemes has been for officials and ministers to agree on some intermediate proposals, which are then discussed with officials from the Department of Industry (now Trade and Industry) and the Treasury. After some consensus has been reached, the DE consults CBI and TUC representatives, during which process the delivery mechanisms are 'fleshed up'. The business and trade union representatives often play an important role earlier, in presenting an issue to the DE, putting it on the government's agenda and broadly defining the nature of the problem.

Whilst this description of events is fairly typical, there are naturally some variations in style. In some cases, ministerial influence is greater than normal. The former Minister of State for Employment, John Golding has been accorded considerable responsibility for initiating the Job Release Scheme. Professor Alan Walters, of Mrs Thatcher's No. 10 office, was instrumental in the inception of the Young Workers' Scheme. The part-time variant of the Job Release Scheme emerged as a product of the DE's constant policy review process. Usually, the number of other government departments involved is greater than the three mentioned above. For instance, in the case of the Job Release Scheme, in addition to DE, Department of Industry and the Treasury, the DHSS, Department of Energy, Home Office, Inland Revenue, Civil Service Department and MSC all contributed to the policy-making process. Also, the role of non-governmental bodies varies. In the case of the Job Splitting Scheme, one business organisation – GEC – played a greater than usual role in setting the parameters of the programme, as it was one of the few companies already pioneering such a programme.

4.4 Local government

As has already been indicated, local authorities are represented on the Commission as well as on the lower-level MSC consultative bodies. This is in acknowledgement of their key role in the implementation of MSC schemes, and is manifest first in the role of local authorities as sponsors or managing agents of MSC projects. From the outset, the MSC has always looked to local authorities to provide and manage its schemes, especially in the years prior to the upsurge in the involvement of the private sector. For instance, until about 1977, local authorities were providing up to 80 per cent of the places under the Job Creation Scheme, since when they have continued to provide about half of the places on the other adult job creation schemes.

Similarly, from the outset local education authorities came to play a vital role in the TOPS programme. In 1973–4, almost half of the courses taken were provided by Colleges of Further Education, with a similar proportion in 1982–3. The courses ranged from clerical and commercial qualifications to technician and computer training. The provision of these courses meant that the local education authorities and colleges came to have an important say in the nature and design of MSC training courses, but became increasingly dependent on the MSC as the provider of a large, steady source of income.

Like their national counterpart, many local authorities have become particularly sensitive to high local levels of youth unemployment. This led to their generally very positive response to the Youth Opportunities Programme. For instance, the Strathclyde Regional Council set up a YOP committee under the Education Department, which became a focal point for other bodies in the area involved in delivering the programme. Representatives of the Social Work Department, Glasgow City Housing Department, MSC officials, local voluntary organisations and trade unions all participated in its activities. The Regional Authority itself (rather than the MSC) paid the wages of a senior administrative officer to head its YOP section. This was responsible for co-ordinating the activities of nine Community Service Agencies (CSAs) and four training workshops. The CSAs, whose running costs were totally funded by the MSC, undertook project work and community service tasks within the Glasgow area. These took the form of general environmental improvement, building projects, and a vast amount of painting, decorating and gardening work. Between 1978 and 1982, almost 1,000 young people per year took part in these CSA schemes alone. Whilst, on the other hand, YOP served the purposes of successive national governments, it was also adopted by the Strathclyde Region, in partnership with Glasgow City Council, for maintaining its credibility within its own hard-pressed local communities.

In addition to using the CSAs, the Regional Council also established special training workshops (and maintained others it had set up under the Job Creation Scheme), in its own surplus properties. These tended to offer training in a range of skills, e.g., metalwork, textiles, painting, and printing. The contribution of the Region was often extended if it was felt that the MSC's provision for equipment and furbishings in the workshops was inadequate, the Region drawing on its own resources to improve things (often through its Urban Aid finance). By 1983, the Region's workshops were catering for about 400 young people per year.

It was not just large Metropolitan Councils with higher than average youth unemployment which involved themselves in YOPs. Hounslow, a borough of West London, has had comparatively low levels of youth unemployment, yet, as Roy Gregory (1984) has shown, it too, realising that in September 1981 there would be 700 unemployed school leavers, was spurred into action. Like Strathclyde, Hounslow put together a package of community projects and training workshops, for which it had to find £62,200, 10 per cent of the total bill.

Not only have the local authorities become involved in the implementation of MSC schemes by way of these 'special' responses, but preexisting services of local authorities apart from the colleges have also been essential to the administration of YOP, and YTS particularly. The Careers Services have been the most obvious such resource for the MSC. They provide data on the likely size and profile of the future school-leaver cohorts, essential for overall MSC planning of regional and local needs to be met. Further, they constitute a most important intermediary between school leavers and the world of employment – or unemployment. Traditionally, they give advice on what sort of job or apprenticeship school leavers should enter. Now, greater attention is spent advising school leavers on the range of MSC schemes available. The confidence of the careers officers in the quality of the *individual* schemes, and their compliance with the overall system, is a foundation for the filling of places on YOPs and YTS.

We have already alluded to the fact that local authorities derive some local credibility benefits from participating within, and even contributing resources to, the MSC's policy responses to unemployment. It should also be said that local education authorities (incorporating colleges of further education and the careers service) have been particular victims of central government resource squeeze, from Anthony Crosland's announcement to local authorities in 1975, that 'the party's over', to the current attempts by the Thatcher Government to curb local authority spending. Thus, participation within the MSC schemes has provided a timely injection of additional resources, usually sufficient to keep the respective organisations ticking over and in some cases to expand them. In addition, small numbers of long-term jobs have been created within local unemployment industries, which also make some small, but welcome, contribution to increasing demand for local products and services.

The MSC has therefore brought benefits to local government, though at the same time there remains some suspicion within local government over the style of the MSC's operations, notably its desire to bring solutions to problems from outside, without seeking to change, youth training for instance, from within the existing system. In short, it is often felt that the MSC acts without sensitivity to established local government practice and without taking due account of existing local government expertise.

4.5 The voluntary sector
It is significant that the first job-creation scheme to operate during the UK's post-war recession – Community Industry – (albeit on a small scale

initially and with a narrowly prescribed target group) was devised and administered by a voluntary organisation, the National Association of Youth Clubs. The scheme is listed in the MSC's Annual Reports, as the MSC provides the finance, but it is the Association that actually continues to run the scheme. Although it caters for only about 7,000 people per year, this relieves the already burdened MSC machinery from having to worry about providing opportunities for this group. In fact, the voluntary sector has continued to play a significant role in the delivery of MSC programmes at the local level, and voluntary 'peak' or 'umbrella' organisations have, as a result, been able to make some policy input at the regional or national levels. In this sense, the policy community which 'processes' the unemployment issue has been continually expanded.

More and more organisations – public, private, mixed public/private- –have been sucked into the policy area, vacuum cleaner fashion, as the unemployment problem has worsened, spawning an unemployment industry. In acting as the agents of the MSC in youth opportunity and adult job-creation schemes, voluntary organisations have usually, at the same time, been able to realise some of their own organisational objectives. Thus, they have administered the establishment and running of community day centres, provided services for the elderly, and resource and information centres for the unemployed, set up training workshops (e.g., for the handicapped) and presided over the completion of environmental improvement projects.

The Community Task Force (CTF) illustrates the extent to which charitable organisations have become an essential feature of the practical delivery of MSC programmes. Having been established to offer outdoor adventure holidays to children from inner-cities, CTF currently provides almost 10,000 places on the Community Programme (the adult job-creation scheme introduced in October 1982) and has provided about 2,000 places on YTS. Indeed, CTF has completely reorganised its own management structure in order to match the delivery systems of the MSC. Moreover, like all YTS sponsors, it has contributed to the scheme by launching a major programme of induction and training to prepare its staff for the new youth scheme (see McGrath, 1983).

Community Service Volunteers (CSV) provides a further example to indicate the scale of the contribution of the voluntary sector to job-creation programmes. During 1981–2 the CSV was operating eleven youth employment schemes funded mainly by the MSC, offering community service opportunities for about 2,000 sixteen-to-eighteen-year-olds (through the Youth Opportunities Programme) and 55 adults (through the Community Enterprise Programme)– all who otherwise would have been unemployed (CSV, 1982). The reference to national organisations should not hide the extent of initiatives by *local* voluntary organisations in this field, which has also been crucial to the implementation of MSC programmes. For example, during 1981–2, organisations within the Glasgow Council for Voluntary Service provided just over 200 places within the Community Enterprise Programme, 12 per cent of the places within the Glasgow district (Glasgow Council for Voluntary Service, 1982). To give some idea of the number of groups operating at the local level, in 1981–2 the Glasgow Council for Voluntary Service had a membership of almost 200 organisations. Of these, 66 voluntary organisations and charities provided training opportunities through the local Community Project Agencies, set up to allocate MSC finance for such initiatives. If this level of group activity is roughly typical of the national pattern, we could expect over 3,000 locally based groups to be providing similar opportunities.

Voluntary organisations also provide specialised services within the unemployment industry. The Volunteer Centre contributes to the training of those involved in training and supervising participants in government schemes, and is provided with finance by the Home Office, as well as receiving MSC support to develop the Voluntary Projects Programme. Currently, the Centre's director chairs the consortium of national voluntary agencies which supports the Opportunities for Volunteering Scheme (funded by the DHSS) and houses a project exploring ways in which those in paid unemployment can become involved in local community activities. The Retired Executive Action Clearing House tries to find retired experts for voluntary organisations' training programmes and for YTS Managing Agencies.

In addition to the broader voluntary organisations, national youth organisations have increasingly directed their energies towards the problem of youth unemployment (e.g., National Association of Youth Clubs, British Youth Council and the National Youth Bureau). For instance, the Youth Opportunities Development Unit was set up within the National Youth Bureau with funds from the MSC. The unit provides information and advice to youth workers in general, including those responsible for the delivery of the YTS schemes.

More specialised voluntary groups have also become involved in the unemployment industry. In October 1983, the National Association for the Care and Resettlement of Offenders (NACRO) was running 48 projects in England and Wales under the YTS, providing about 2,300 places. Most of the young people participating are referred by the probation service and social services. NACRO is, in addition, a national agency for the delivery of the Community Programme, providing up to 8,000 long-term unemployed ex-offenders. NACRO's Employment Development Unit (for YTS schemes) is financed by the Home Office, the MSC, and the DHSS. The Community Programme section is funded by fees earned by acting as an MSC Managing Agency, and the Voluntary Projects Programme by a direct MSC grant.

Not only have voluntary organisations fulfilled their traditional role as providers for the disadvantaged, but they have, moreover, become an essential part of the MSC 'delivery system'. During 1981 – 2, 44 per cent of community project places and 25 per cent of training workshop places under YOP were provided by voluntary organisations (White, 1983). Indeed, the Secretary of State for Employment recently commented that

A great deal of credit for the success of Special Programmes must be attributed to the part played by voluntary organisation . . . it is vital . . . that voluntary organisations should continue to play a very important role (in the Youth Training Scheme). (MSC, 1982:17)

There are a number of reasons for the effectiveness of voluntary organisations in implementing public policies. In many cases they have provided opportunities for the unemployed *before* the MSC. Related to this, they usually have superior detailed knowledge of local conditions, and of local government, business and trade union personnel, and are thus well equipped to develop local schemes. Thus, they have developed considerable expertise in identifying what will 'work' at the grass roots level. Central policy-makers, and even locally based MSC personnel, inevitably lack this important skill to some degree.

Voluntary bodies, such as the Community Task Force, may adjust their own activities and internal structures according to the nature of governmental activity, in order to contribute to a recognised area of need, and also to enhance the standing of their own organisations in terms of finance accruing and increased responsibility within the delivery network. An entrepreneurial phenomenon is at work, with voluntary bodies being attracted to MSC programmes and the issues which surround them. Leaders of existing groups see the unemployment problem as not just a *problem* but also an *opportunity* for extending their own base. NACRO, for instance, views the MSC schemes as providing an opportunity to try a radical new approach to tackling the management of offenders in the community.

It should not be assumed from our description of the role of voluntary organisations that they share *identical* interests and views with the MSC. The Community Service Volunteers were recently critical of the MSC's termination of funding for the work preparation 'Springboard' scheme administered by CSV. Also, the proposal by the MSC to reduce the number of Youth Training Scheme places within BI mode (i.e., in community and training workshops) has been criticised by the voluntary sector who run them. This proposal prompted letters to *The Times* from the directors of the National Council of Voluntary Organisations and Christian Action. Our point is that the MSC and the voluntary sector have an interest in continuing to work with each other, and we expect the MSC to avoid totally alienating its voluntary partners over this issue.

4.6 Other specialist organisations

The unemployment industry has also become permeated with a whole range of other specialist organisations which have come to play important if varying roles in the policy process. The research and campaigning organisation Youthaid has conducted evaluation studies on behalf of the MSC on the YOP and CEP schemes, and was represented on the old Special Programmes Board (a precursor of the present Youth Training Board).

Other organisations have become essential to the MSC's delivery of schemes, and notably the YTS. The Link Organisation, for example, has become a major YTS managing agent, and initially planned to place about 15,000 school-leavers with sponsor companies, aiming to receive £1.5 million to cover overheads and running costs (*The Times,* 26.4.83). Similarly, Sight and Sound Education, the keyboard training company, run by ex-Liberal MP John Pardoe, aimed to act as a managing agent for just over 4,000 trainees.

As MSC schemes become more of a permanent feature of the British economy, we would expect a growth in the numbers of such organisations that are able to identify a gap in the delivery and provision systems and fill it themselves. Thus, the issue area is something like a 'market', with groups exploiting market opportunities through the identification of gaps in the market and through the development of new 'products' (schemes).

4.7 The business sector

Over the last decade, the role of the business sector within the unemployment industry has developed, from that of being a partner on the Commission and an interested active partner within ITBs to that of a major corner-stone of the delivery of many governmental responses to unemployment. As the economic crisis worsened, its role increased in providing facilities for the Training Opportunities Scheme courses, in sponsoring those on job creation courses, and in offering work experience and training opportunities under YOPs and YTS.

Under YOPs, employers' (business, voluntary or governmental) premises were used for work experience opportunities either within the premises or in firms' training workshops, as well as for work preparation, whether for short training courses or for assessment and employment induction training courses. Under the YTS, the MSC contracts out the responsibility (often to business organisations) to act as managing agents responsible for designing, managing and delivering the year-long package of training and work experience. In fact, the MSC have a preference for large business organisations as sponsors, not only because they may well have a training department which trainees can benefit from, but also because they provide the best opportunity for trainees to be kept on in full employment.

During 1980, the MSC recognised its own inability to provide opportunities for the growing number of YOPs participants following the sharp rise in youth unemployment. It asked the CBI whether it could assist by establishing what later became known as the CBI Special Programmes Unit (CBI SPU). The CBI SPU, which consists of about 50 secondees from business organisations, is entrusted with the task of securing the commitment of leading employers to provide places for YOPs participants.[1] This is done in two ways: by using board-level contacts to persuade large firms to make a commitment to take on a certain number of trainees nationally; and, secondly, using the regional structure of CBI SPU, by secondees encouraging smaller firms to participate and provide training opportunities. It claimed to have created 35,000 work-experience places under YOPs in 1981 – about 40 per cent of all new places for that year – and 10,000 twelve-month training places in 1982 (CBI SPU, 1983). These figures are slightly misleading in that they do not distinguish businesses who would have offered places anyway. However, it seems likely that the CBI SPU did act as a major catalyst for this shift in business attitudes.

In order to assist the MSC in preparing for the YTS launch in September 1983, the CBI SPU organised a huge number of lunch-time conferences to provide contacts between local MSC staff and high-level representatives of business and industry. Also, it approached individual firms to encourage them to consider taking on YTS trainees and conducted feasibility investigations where appropriate. CBI SPU secondees further acted as 'trouble shooters' if problems arose within individual schemes in their early stages.

In addition to the general reasons for business activity in this field (see Chapter 5), the YTS provides employers with, at worst, nine months' cheap labour per participant (discounting the off-the-job training period), though this should be counterbalanced with the administrative costs involved and the responsibility to provide some on-the-job training. At best, employers have the opportunity to give young potential recruits an 'extended interview', that is, they see them on the job for a comparatively long period.

4.8 Trade unions

The role of trade unions within the policy process is different from those

---

[1] In 1982, the Sponsoring Board of CBI SPU consisted of top level representatives of the following organisations: Metal Box PLC, the CBI, Z. Brierly PLC, International Thomson Organisation PLC, Thorn EMI PLC, Wimpey Construction UK PLC, BP Oil PLC, Guest Keen and Nettlefold PLC, United Biscuits (Holdings) PLC, Rank Xerox PLC, BAT Industries PLC, PA Management Consultant PLC, National Freight Consortium, British Railways Board, Barclays Bank PLC. The board is chaired by Lord Carr, Chairman of Prudential Assurance Co. PLC.

of the voluntary and business sectors, but it is similarly crucial. There are what could be described as two faces of TUC activity regarding the unemployment issue. Its 'political' policy has been to criticise the Thatcher Government and the MSC. For example, in 1983 the TUC called for a £10-billion spending package to fight unemployment (TUC, 1983a). Similarly, at the 1984 budget, Len Murray, then General Secretary, urged the government to change its economic policy in the interests of the unemployed – a plea backed by the CBI Director-General, Sir Terence Beckett. In 1983, the TUC also gave its backing (though with some reservations) to two organised protests against the government's policy on unemployment: the Jobs for Youth Campaign and the People's March for Jobs. The Jobs for Youth Campaign used the slogan 'Give us a future', and emerged in 1981 to transport unemployed teenagers around the country in the 'Jobs Express', and finally to London for a demonstration, with a delegation to meet the Prime Minister and other members of the government. After the Jobs Express, the Campaign lapsed, but efforts were made to revive it, in 1983, with the publication of a charter: 'A New Deal for Youth'. The People's March for Jobs first took place in 1981 and attracted considerable press attention. The second march from Glasgow, Liverpool, Keighley, Hull, Great Yarmouth and Lands End, converged on London in the week before the 1983 General Election, and so gained some publicity.

However, at the same time as involving itself in these activities, the TUC has remained a loyal, if sometimes critical, partner in the Manpower Services Commission, whilst in other spheres government – TUC relations have broken down. The wider role both of the TUC and of individual trade unions is in supporting the MSC schemes not only at the Area Board level, but more significantly, at plant level. In some localities, especially those of high youth unemployment, trade unionists have been especially keen to press their employers to participate in YOPs and YTS, as they see no other alternatives for their children. Similarly, the TUC has published a guide to the YTS, explaining that

the trade union movement has long campaigned for training opportunities for all young people. The Youth Training Scheme developed by the Manpower Services Commission is a mighty step in that direction. It will be introduced to many workplaces during 1983. The trade union movement needs to be ready to protect the interests of young people; ensure that the YTS is not a cheap labour scheme; develop trade union influence over the way it operates. Under the YTS there are large opportunities but also massive challenges. This leaflet aims to help trade unionists to understand them and face up to them. (TUC, 1983b)

The leaflet goes on to encourage local negotiators to urge their employers to take on trainees; to take part in negotiations over their status, pay and conditions, and trade union membership; and to become involved in the monitoring of the schemes. Warnings are given over the maintenance of national standards, but in practice this appears subsidiary to the main aim of co-operation. Indeed, there is evidence that trade unions have recognised potential benefits of YTS in providing new members to compensate for those lost in redundancies. Under the rubric of the scheme, employers are expected to give permanent employment to two out of every five trainees taken on, so unions are rushing to offer free or very cheap membership with many benefits to trainees in order to encourage those kept on to become full members.

In urging trade unions to participate in the scheme, the Assistant Secretary, Kenneth Graham told the 1983 TUC Youth Conference that

The scheme is entirely consistent with TUC policy on training for all, but we have to ensure that something which is consistent when written down is consistent in practice ... The more that schemes are established within the unionised sector, the greater our ability to ensure these young people are not treated as cheap labour. And if we can recruit them into the trade union movement the greater our ability to keep contact with them after their time on YTS, whether employed or unemployed (quoted in *The Times Higher Education Supplement*, 25.2.83).

Again it would be misleading to suggest that trade unions completely share the perspectives of either the MSC or the government on the issue. There have been disagreements over the operation of YTS, for example, some of which the TUC have won, and others which they have lost.

The importance of the union role was most forcefully illustrated in the case of the YTS, when the National Coal Board threw 240 school-leavers off a project in Staffordshire because the local National Union of Mineworkers refused to co-operate with it – reportedly on instructions from the national executive, which opposes it because of the low allowances and lack of permanent job opportunities. Whilst the MSC can tolerate some instances of trade unions preventing the operation of YTS, clearly it cannot afford for this to happen on too many occasions. Thus, the MSC must maintain a certain amount of goodwill from, at the very minimum, the trade union representatives on the Commission, and preferably other trade union leaders. For the successful implementation of certain schemes involving on-the-job training and work experience this must be complemented by winning the co-operation of the local trade union officials.

4.9 YTS: a case study of the policy process

As youth unemployment continued to rise dramatically during the early 1980s, calls were increasingly made within the unemployment industry for some government policy response to build upon the YOP scheme, which was proving inadequate both in training terms and as a vehicle for employment creation. But whilst there was a united call for something to be done about youth unemployment, there were sharply differing views as to exactly what that should consist of. The most significant cleavage was between those who favoured the creation of a national system of opportunities for work to benefit the community (e.g., Youth Call, an umbrella organisation including Community Service Volunteers and Help the Aged) and those advocating greater training opportunities, who included many trade unionist, youth and educational organisations.

Within the Commission itself the idea was raised by the trade union representatives, and in May 1981 the MSC sent proposals to the then Secretary of State for Employment, James Prior, for a new training scheme to replace YOPs. This document was published in May 1982 under the title of *A New Training Initiative: A Consultative Document*. It set out three general objectives: to provide employers with a more assured supply of key skills and a more versatile and productive labour force (which also required a positive response from the employers); for employees and their unions to offer a better start in working life for all young people (requiring greater flexibility by trade unions and the adult workforce); and for the education service to realise many of the hopes and aspirations of young people by adjusting its approach to these new demands (MSC, 1981b:5). It is significant that each of these objectives was posed in relation to the three interests most essential for the success of a new scheme. In a later section the paper argued that

The main instrument for change must be collective agreement at the level of the sector and the company . . . It is of prime importance to the achievement of the objectives that the country now has training institutions with considerable experience of setting standards and developing courses to meet the needs of employers. Such bodies as the City and Guilds of London Institute, the Royal Society of Arts, the Council for Technician Education and Business Education and their Scottish counterparts can make a valuable professional contribution in the area of testing standards of individual competence. Industry Training Boards and some employer organisations and research associations can also play a major part in terms of monitoring standards of industrial training provision. (MSC, 1981b:6)

Thus the MSC was already recognising the future participation of a wide range of organisations with functional relevance for the running of this new scheme. The document envisaged a scheme which would provide skill training for jobs available, which could eventually give the opportunity for all under-eighteen-year-olds either to continue in full-time education or to enter a period of planned work experience combining work-related training and education, and could also provide opportunities for adult retraining. At the end of the document an invitation was made for interested parties to comment on the scheme.

In the next MSC publication on the subject, it was reported that the MSC had received almost 1,000 submissions from employers, unions, trainers, local authorities and voluntary bodies expressing overwhelming support for the proposals contained in the earlier document (MSC, 1981b). This second document also highlighted areas of agreement in responses to the original proposal. These included a coherent approach to training (including the rationalisation of the MSC's own programme), the need for strong government and MSC support for securing change, and an emphasis on local planning and management of training: that training should begin in school and end in work, and that the education service should play a full role in the developments.

This MSC publication was swiftly followed by a government White Paper, under the same name, which broadly endorsed the MSC document and planned to commit £1,000 million for a full year's foundation training to those leaving school who were without a job (Cmnd. 8455). At this stage, it was planned that 300,000 places should be available from October 1983, providing places only for sixteen-year-olds and some unemployed and disabled seventeen-year-olds, as opposed to the recommendation for all under-eighteen-year-olds.

When introducing the White Paper to the House of Commons, the then Secretary of State for Employment, Norman Tebbit, announced that it was the government's intention that unemployed sixteen-year-olds who did not take part in the scheme would forfeit eligibility for supplementary benefit – thus a form of compulsion was envisaged. Tebbit proposed an allowance of about £750 per year for trainees, about £15 per week. The questions of compulsion and payment levels were to be issues of keen contention within the YTS policy community, and indeed were contested in Parliament by the Labour Party and Liberal Party spokesmen, who otherwise welcomed the scheme.

In January 1982, a Youth Task Group was set up to examine the proposals. The membership of the Task Group is set out in Table 4.2, which indicates the breadth of functional interests represented.

The Group considered that its proposals were concerned not with short-term measures to fight youth unemployment but with tackling the long-term challenge of providing a bridge between school and work. The report argued against a compulsory scheme, (either for sponsors or participants), and whilst it urged that the scheme should have massive government support (notably in terms of finance), it also stated a preference for local initiative in the details of scheme-content. Having gone into details as to the delivery and costs and implementation procedures (see Chapter 3.4), the Group concluded by stating that it was inconsistent to operate the Young Workers Scheme alongside the proposed YTS, as the former offered no training content.

The MSC fully endorsed the Youth Task Group's report, setting itself in opposition to the government's proposal to withhold benefits from non-participants, and also opposing the payments levels. The Task Group recommended a £28 per week payment. As the disagreement developed, the three TUC members of the Commission threatened to resign over the issue. Eventually, the government backed down on the compulsion

Table 4.2   Membership of the Youth Task Group

Mr G. Holland, Director, Manpower Services Commission	Chairman
Mr K. Court, Director, Personnel and Management Services, Blue Circle Industries Limited	Representing CBI
Mr P. J. Daly, Company Education and Training Manager, Thorn EMI Limited	Representing CBI
Mr D. Stanley, Deputy Director, Education and Training, Confederation of British Industry	Representing CBI
Mr C. D. Grieve, General Secretary, Tobacco Workers' Union	Representing TUC
Mr L. Wood, General Secretary, Union of Construction, Allied Trades and Technicians	Representing TUC
Mr R. Jackson, Secretary – Education Department, Trades Union Congress	Representing TUC
Mr G. Hainsworth, Director of Education, Gateshead Metropolitan Borough Council	Representing Association of Metropolitan Authorities
Mr W. Petty, CBE, County Education Officer, Kent County Council	Representing Association of County Councils
Mr G. S. Bain, Deputy Director of Education (FE), Strathclyde Regional Council	Representing Convention of Scottish Local Authorities
Mr J. Collins, Chairperson, British Youth Council	
Mr N. Hinton, Director, National Council for Voluntary Organisations	
Mrs P. White, President – Institute of Careers Officers	
Mr A. Colledge, Principal, Cranville College, Sheffield	Representing professional education interests
Official observers:	
Mr D. J. Hodgkins, Department of Employment	
Mr C. R. Walker, Department of Education and Science	

SOURCE: MSC, 1982e:22

question, and initially compromised on withholding 40 per cent of benefits for six weeks only. It also raised the initial allowances to £1,300 per year, or £25 per week. Thus, on these issues the government, when faced with firm, united opposition of all those parties essential to the delivery of the scheme, was reduced to becoming more like a partner in a bargaining process than the single focus of power. Tebbit told the Commons that

. . . the Government has noted the firmly-held and clearly expressed views of those on whom the operation of the scheme depends, that its launch could be seriously impaired by the withdrawal of supplementary benefits from sixteen year olds (*Hansard*, Vol. 26, Col. 23, 21.6.82).

Indeed, when the scheme actually came into operation, even the amended penalty to those not joining the scheme was withdrawn – a battle over which the MSC beat the DHSS.

The scheme was finally launched in September 1983, but the programme (described in Chapter 3.4) was not implemented as intended uniformly across the country. The role of individual unions nationally, and in particular localities/sectors, was to prove crucial to the implementation of individual schemes within YTS. Almost as soon as it was launched there was news of several instances of difficulties in securing union compliance. From the start, the TGWU refused to amalgamate the already existing agricultural apprenticeship scheme with YTS, fearing that employers would not retain young people for permanent employment but would take on new trainees each year to do the least skilled jobs. This, however, was not likely to have cost the MSC too many places, even if it did deprive young farm workers of opportunities under YTS, but in other instances the numbers involved were more considerable.

Initially, the Prime Minister had vetoed the proposition that the civil service should provide about 5,000 places under the scheme, presumably on account of her resolve to reduce the size of Britain's bureaucracy, but eventually she changed her mind. This was probably due more to the efforts of her close colleagues, especially Norman Tebbit, then Secretary of State for Employment, than to any other influences. However, the civil service unions have yet to agree to co-operate with the scheme. Initially, some unions were unhappy that government was unwilling to take on extra permanent staff in order to deal with the training of the young people, and were not satisfied with the amounts of training that would be available. Eventually, by November 1983, all the executives of the unions agreed to co-operate with the scheme. However, the annual conference of the Civil and Public Services Association ignored the advice of its executive and withdrew co-operation with the government because of its opposition to two young people working within the Cabinet Office at 10 Downing Street. At the time of writing, other instances of union non-co-operation with the scheme leading to failure to implement include the Union of Communication Workers (causing the Post Office to withdraw its proposal for 4,000 YTS places), and several unions preventing the Heating and Ventilating Contractors Association from launching a scheme to provide 750 places in the industry.

All this is not to suggest that unions have been the only obstacle to finding YTS places. Although it is not possible to quantify it, anecdotal evidence suggests reluctance – especially on the part of small firms – to take on trainees because of the amount of paperwork involved. There has also been some tension between the Construction Industry Training Board (the provider of the most YTS places) and the MSC over the nature of the training to be provided: although both wanted training provided, the former wanted to concentrate on industry-related skills whilst the latter was more concerned for the trainees to receive wider and transferable skills.

The implementation of policy is often very different from bold intentions stated at the outset. For instance, it was proposed by the Secretary of State for Defence, Michael Heseltine, that the three armed forces should take on 5,200 YTS trainees, despite the opposition of both the Ministry of Defence and the MSC. The initial quota of places was to be 1,900 in September, and although about 3,000 people showed interest in the scheme, only about 600 were considered suitable by the armed forces. Presumably, one problem was that most of those who were seriously interested in a military career would have gone in through the normal channels. The YTS recruits, recruited by the normal standards, had no obvious advantage over other entrants, but had disadvantages in pay, absence of long-term prospects, and the 'off-the-job training' to complete as well as meeting the training expectations within the forces.

Another instance of the scheme not matching policy-makers' intentions is that of the trainees' allowances. Although a national rate for the scheme has been agreed, in some cases this has been overridden, usually as a result of trade union action at the local level, with the object of raising allowances to match the normal rate for the job. Consequently, some local authorities have agreed with NALGO demands that trainees should be paid the negotiated rate of £52 per week, whilst others have not. Similarly, in some areas the AUEW has managed to secure the negotiated rate for trainees. The decision by the British Airports Authority to agree to union pressure to pay trainees £33 per week plus a travel allowance was particularly embarrassing for the MSC, as the Chairman of the Authority is one of the employers' representatives on the Commission.

Probably, the aspect of implementing YTS which has been of most concern to the MSC is the poor response rate to the scheme, not among potential sponsors but among the young people themselves. The shortfall for the first year of the scheme is expected to be about 100,000 on the initial target of 460,000. Table 4.3 indicates considerable regional disparity in the response to YTS, and, with the exception of Scotland, the level of take-up appears to bear a close relation to the extent of youth unemployment: Northern England, Wales, North West England, the Midlands and Yorkshire/Humberside all having worse youth unemployment levels than London or the South East and South West of England. Initially, the MSC spokesman put on a brave face at the increasing likelihood of problems here, and insisted that the target would be met, but by the autumn of 1983 they conceded that there would be a shortfall.

Table 4.3 Proportion of approved YTS places filled by 31.1.84

	%
Scotland	70.4
Northern England	84.4
Yorkshire/Humberside	75.4
North West England	77.1
Midlands	75.9
Wales	83.0
South West England	72.7
South East England	71.6
London	53.0
Great Britain	73.6

SOURCE: IDS, 1984:3

What explanations can be offered for this mismatch? A combination of factors seem to be significant. First, it now seems that the DES, in providing estimates to the MSC on the size of the sixteen-year-old school-leaver cohort, underestimated the number of sixteen-year-olds entering further education. This itself may be an instance of a number of the non-participants 'voting' against the YTS 'with their feet', although no adequate data is at hand to prove this. In addition, there were more school-leavers in employment in the autumn of 1983 than had been expected by the MSC. These factors should not disguise the fact that a House of Commons written answer from Sir Keith Joseph in March 1984 (see Table 4.4) indicated that, between January 1983 and January 1984, there had been a *decline* in the numbers of sixteen and seventeen-year-olds in full-time education, that the numbers unemployed had only decreased by about 7 per cent, and that the numbers employed had increased by under 2 per cent. The situation was complicated by the regional MSC offices inflating their target number of places in the fear that sponsors might drop out, and that demand for YTS places might be more in keeping with the figures for youth unemployment. A further contributory factor to the shortfall appears to be that more school-leavers have opted to take up employment under the Young Workers' Scheme, rather than join the YTS – presumably because of the higher immediate material rewards and the belief that the jobs will prove more secure than YTS placements. It was recommended by the Youth Task Group that some provision be made to avoid this conflict of policy responses, and whilst this course was not followed at the launching of YTS, it now appears that the government will withdraw the option of the YWS for sixteen-year-olds.

Table 4.4   *Education/labour market status of young people January 1983 and 1984 – Great Britain (in thousands)*

	Aged 16[1]		Aged 17	
	13 Jan 1983	12 Jan 1984 prov. est.	13 Jan 1983	12 Jan 1984 prov. est.
Total population	910	900	930	910
Full-time education	440	400	290	280
– Schools	290	280	180	170
– Further education[2]	150	120	110	110
YTS/YOP	170	220	70	50
Claimant unemployed	130	110	160	160
Other[3] (mainly employed outside YTS)	170	170	410	420

[1] Ages as at 31 August of preceding year.
[2] Excluding YTS/YOP.
[3] Mainly those in employment outside YTS but also includes some who are seeking work but not claiming benefit, some who are neither employed nor seeking work (e.g. because of domestic responsibilities) and net errors in the other estimates.

Estimates are rounded to the nearest 10,000.

SOURCE: *Hansard,* Vol. 55, Col. 597, 7.3.84

Within the MSC, it is also believed that they underestimated the incidence of frictional unemployment among the young, who tend to change jobs more frequently than adults and do not see themselves as potential YTS clients whilst unemployed for a short period between jobs. Given the haste in which the whole scheme was conceived and set up, it is likely that another of the problems was sheer lack of time in preparing school-leavers for the general concept of YTS. Furthermore, managing agents and sponsors had little time to conduct any serious recruitment (IDS, 1984). This situation was compounded by many schemes not receiving the MSC's contractual approval until a couple of months before they were due to begin. It appears that those managing agents who recruited trainees *prior* to receiving their MSC contract were relatively successful in filling places. This is a classic example of the nature of the policy process having crucial implications for policy implementation.

Whatever the precise combination of reasons for the shortfall, it has undoubtedly had some damaging effects on the future operation of the scheme. First, the confidence in the MSC of many of the 'providers' within the unemployment industry, and in the MSC's planning and co-ordination abilities, has been dented. In some cases, the lack of trainees has had serious financial implications. This has been especially true for managing agents and sponsors whose budgeting assumed that all places available would be filled. Technically, the MSC should not have made any payment for unfilled places, but in order to maintain the goodwill of large public managing agents especially, some payments of agents' fees have been made for the target number, as opposed to the real number, of trainees. Due to the high drop-out rate (nationally about 18 per cent), agents and sponsors have again suffered financial shortfalls, though they are at least able to claim the full training fee. However, there appears to be some disparity in the amounts which area offices of the MSC are prepared to reimburse sponsors and agents whose schemes are not completely filled. Similarly, many further education colleges have en-countered financial difficulties – ultimately to be borne by the local education authority – and such is the pressure on some colleges that they are having to consider closing some of their courses.

The manner in which the YTS has emerged has several important implications. First, the number of managing agents may well be reduced by the second year of YTS. Whilst this may reduce the extent of trainee choice, it may not be altogether a bad thing, as there was undoubtedly a minority of agents overly committed to the idea of making money out of the scheme and insufficiently mindful of the trainees' best interests. It is most likely that they will be the first to leave the industry after this shaky first year. Secondly, a smaller number of agents will certainly make the MSC's job of policing the scheme easier, enabling a closer check to be kept on any 'cowboys'. However, the financial hardships and practical com-plexities of the scheme are also likely to temper the enthusiasm for future participation on the part of the well-intentioned 'providers'.

Thus, despite being underpinned by a reasonably united unemploy-ment industry at the time of the YTS launch, the network has actually become considerably strained in the process of implementation. Aware of this problem, the MSC endeavoured to reinforce co-operation by setting up contact groups so as to enable regular communication between its own officers and representatives of various provider organisations. This has not succeeded in dispelling controversy, for – in addition to the problems outlined above – many providers have found the MSC a difficult organi-sation to deal with because of the relative inexperience of some MSC personnel and the different approaches of national and local officials to the implementation of the scheme. Most recently, problems have arisen over the government's proposal to reduce the number of Mode B places for 1984 – 5. This is not a simple response to the shortfall for 1983 – 4, as it was this mode which came closest to meeting its target for the first year. The MSC's view is that Mode A schemes offer the best prospects for permanent employment for young people. They are also the cheaper schemes. The proposal that Mode B schemes should be reduced has drawn considerable criticism from within the policy community – and especially from the scheme 'providers' – who argue that this mode caters for youth who are least attractive to employers, and who will otherwise remain on the dole. The merits of this argument aside, the case illustrates that once having involved non-governmental groups and organisations in the policy process, the MSC finds it more difficult to make policy changes without inviting the public criticism of those whose organisation and resources stand to lose most by such changes.

Perhaps the most important aspect of the YTS policy process, however, is its impact upon the employment prospects of school-leavers. Will the scheme significantly improve the potential of the individuals, and their attractiveness to employers? Or will it simply become a step on the way to prolonged unemployment, bringing with it not hope, but disillusion and cynicism? It is really too early to answer these questions. The formal course content of YTS is certainly an improvement upon YOP in terms of the training provided, but the government, and to a lesser extent the MSC, tend to paint too rosy a picture of the likely impact of the scheme upon the youth labour market over the next few years. On the other hand, those whose function it is to criticise the government by pointing to implementation difficulties, often fail to take account of the fact that the scheme was devised both under pressure and at speed. Most policies devised under these conditions are subject to teething problems and require some years of practice to iron them out. Further, one should not fall into the trap of making sweeping generalisations as to the success of YTS. In reality, it is not a scheme but a collection of a large number of schemes whose contribution to the trainees' future depends to a large extent on such factors as the skills taught, the type of organisation providing the place, the sectoral and geographical locations of the programme, and the individual motivations of the providers and the participants. This is perhaps most vividly illustrated by contrasting the likely job prospects of small numbers of YTS trainees in information technology centres with those on the community projects.

At the time of writing, no fully representative study of the opinions of youth concerning YTS has been conducted. As was the case with YOPs, we can expect some correlation between their having broadly positive views of the scheme and finding employment shortly after 'graduating'. There has been criticism of the low level of allowances paid under YOPs, (e.g., People and Work Unit, 1984:8), although this does of course considerably exceed the average amount the young people would otherwise receive from Social Security. Given that no government is likely to raise the real value of the allowance by very much, it is clear that the individual schemes will need to emphasise the training function in order to minimise the accusation from young people that YTS is slave labour.

A final consideration concerning the implementation of YTS is that of its effect on the employment chances of adults. Like the YWS, the YTS offers employers a considerable incentive to take on young people rather than older members of the workforce who can bring no wage subsidy. In the case of the Mode A of YTS, the employer can either derive benefit from a succession of trainees, who are subsidised yet contribute to the total work, or at worst receive a maximum subsidy for the first year's employment of five trainees, two of whom he can then take on permanently. Indeed, these two might already have been taken on as young workers, so that no additional jobs would have been created at all. This situation has led to fears – notably among trade unions – that it will bring about not only a fall in recruitment of adult workers but also lay offs. Again, the scheme has not been in operation long enough to verify these claims, but whilst the latter fear may be of dubious validity (employers preferring to keep on experienced and trusted workers), there may prove to be some substance in the former.

In summary, this case study has illustrated the role of provider groups in the emergence of the new programme. Whilst the government clearly had its own policy intentions for the YTS, some of these had to be sacrificed in order to get a 'working agreement' on its broad framework. The political costs of the government failing to get a scheme off the ground were considered sufficient to justify these compromises. As was illustrated in the previous sections on the 'provider' organisations, the scheme was heavily dependent upon specialised knowledge and the good-will/interest of non-governmental sponsors and managing agents. Like so many other cases, the design of the government's scheme did not neatly match the market, which was best illustrated by the shortfall in numbers. In reality, the policy-making process which began with the critical evaluation of YOPs and the MSC's document *A New Training Initiative,* has simply continued as the scheme has progressed. This is evident nationally, with the proposed rebalancing of the proportions of Mode A and Mode B schemes, and locally with the wide variety of conditions under which the trainees exist, and the levels and quality and training introduced into the individual schemes. Thus, YTS is not just a government pet scheme: it has emerged as a legitimate interest and responsibility of a diversity of other organisations. Despite the continued existence of differences within the peak of the policy community over the future development of YTS, we would expect these to be resolved through a negotiated process. Equally, we would expect local providers to continue to adapt YTS to their own needs and concerns.

This process of *sharing* in the devising and delivery of the scheme brings with it important broader political consequences. It reinforces the government's view that unemployment is not solely its own responsibility. The very fact that a diversity of local and national organisations have become involved in this central policy response serves to reinforce the view that this is a problem for the whole community. Thus, not only are more non-governmental organisations drawn into the unemployment industry, but the government is able to pursue its own broad economic strategy with the existence of 3 to 4 million unemployed, and – with reference to YTS – extremely high levels of youth unemployment, which does not, at least at the moment, pose an insuperable political threat.

4.10 Policy style and politics

In the light of our findings on the Conservatives' economic policies (Chapter 1), their other policies more specifically directed at unemployment (Chapter 3), and the nature of the policy process, we discover that a mixed style has emerged. In contrast to its predecessors, the Thatcher Government has pursued some quite radical economic policies, complemented by considerable departures in trade union law, although these still fall short of manifesto promises. In some of these cases the policies have been 'given', and have not been susceptible to the normal bargaining/consensual style. In the field of direct policy responses to alleviate the rise of unemployment levels, however, the government has not been able to make much change in the traditional patterns of policy formation and delivery, notwithstanding protestations to the contrary by some in the unemployment industry.

Obviously, the Conservative Government, like its predecessors, has had an impact over policy content, but this has had to be tempered by concessions to those who are essential for the success of policy responses. First, given that unemployment is a cross-sectoral problem, we find that even within Whitehall the policy area is not totally monopolised by the MSC and the Department of Employment. Rather, a 'manpower group' exists which is responsible for the overall mix and co-ordination of policies. Besides DE and MSC, the Departments of Trade and Industry, Education and Science, and Health and Social Security are also represented on this group, which has itself to deal with the Treasury. This peak-level inter-departmental network is duplicated at lower levels, in more specialised discussions of policy in this field, and, of course, less formal inter-departmental exchanges are endemic to the policy-making process. As has been illustrated, target figures set by the MSC for the Youth Training Scheme were based on assessments of the number of school-leavers in 1983 made by the DES.

Outside the immediate ambit of the MSC this picture is duplicated. For instance, the Department of Employment, prior to launching employment subsidy schemes, has engaged in discussions with other departments over the economic and industrial aspects and implications of the proposals. Illustrative of the policy impact of this system, and one of several explanations given for the de-radicalisation of Sir Geoffrey Howe's Enterprise Zone proposal was the following:

A regular series of interdepartmental discussions was held. Other departments (than the Treasury), such as DOE, Scottish Office, DHSS and Employment predictably resisted changes on matters directly concerning them – for example, DOE argued to retain local authority involvement; DHSS sought to maintain health protection; Employment did not agree to changes in employment legislation. (Jordan, 1984:131)

The dramatis personae, of course, extends much wider than this Whitehall network, into something which we have elsewhere described as an 'unemployment industry' (Moon and Richardson, 1984b), whereby a great variety of non-governmental organisations are involved in the making and implementation of policy. A system of 'exchange relationships' (Jordan and Richardson, 1982) exists and a genuine policy community appears to be evolving within the loose network of groups, and within the business, voluntary, local government and MSC spheres. As has been seen, the MSC prompted the formation of the CBI SPU. There are also examples of government stimulating the organisation of voluntary bodies in order that they should deliver schemes for the unemployed: for instance, the part played by the Social Work Services Group of the Scottish Office, in 1982, in inviting the Carnegie UK Trust to administer a £400,000 government grant-in-aid fund (£490,000 for 1983/4) to stimulate general voluntary activity, explicitly including unemployed people, for community benefit. In some cases, this also enabled various needs – from information to recreation – of the unemployed to be met. The Carnegie's Trustees decided to form a trust, the Unemployed Voluntary Action Fund (whose trustees could include representatives from the Scottish Office, the Carnegie UK Trust, and relevant voluntary organisations), which was made responsible for the allocation of the money to 44 different voluntary organisations, who supervised schemes within the framework outlined. Thus, the Trust relieved the government of the administration of this task and simultaneously created the opportunity for more flexibility in the use of grant-in-aid. The unemployment industry has at the same time further expanded.

Groups have not only come to play a significant part in the implementation of schemes for the unemployed, but they have also been invited to participate at policy-making and programme-evaluation levels, signifying their arrival as 'insider groups'. Whilst the existence of the CBI, TUC and local authority representatives on the MSC Commission and lower-level boards is now taken for granted, an interesting development has been the part played by the smaller specialist groups. The Chairman of the British Youth Council (BYC) and the Director of the National Council for Voluntary Organisations were both members of the MSC Youth Task Group, which produced the blueprint for the Youth Training Scheme. The Chairman of the BYC and the Director of NACRO are currently members of the Youth Training Board which monitors the Youth Training Scheme. Until recently, Youthaid enjoyed considerable status within MSC circles, having been commissioned by the MSC to conduct an evaluation of the Community Enterprise Programme, and being represented on the old Special Programmes Board. Youthaid blames the advent of Norman Tebbit as Secretary of State for Employment for the demise of its role as a 'constructive critic'. It is probably too early to say whether this heralds a new phase in which small group participation is reduced, or whether this is a hiccup in the general pattern of close contacts between these groups and the MSC. Certainly, other groups have continued to enjoy access to MSC, but perhaps these have been more careful to protect their image as partners of the MSC.

The current controversy over the government's proposal to reduce YTS-mode BI places (i.e., those in community and training workshops) for 1984–5 has provoked a sharp response from the voluntary sector in the issue community, though at the time of writing it is not known whether the government will alter its plans accordingly. Also, the CSV was publicly critical of the closure of its YTS pilot – the Springboard scheme in Kent. Certainly, some of the voluntary sector in the unemployment industry have publicly or privately expressed disquiet over a government style – mainly associated with Tebbit's term as Employment Secretary – which has taken less notice of their claims than was previously the case. Whilst there is some substance in these views, Tebbit certainly did not overturn the broad style of working in the unemployment industry, as witnessed by the continuing involvement of non-governmental interests.

This chapter was designed to provide an insight into the workings of the unemployment industry. This is characterised by a wide range of non-governmental organisations, which we have attempted to illustrate, though we have not been able to cover them exhaustively. They have come to play a vital part in the response of the government to the unemployment problem: in the testing of new initiatives, in the evaluation of existing schemes, and in the production of new ideas for coping with unemployment.

It is to be expected that as long as the unemployment problem is with us, so too the unemployment industry will remain, if not grow. This is likely to have several important consequences. For only the unemployment industry, by virtue of its specialised knowledge and experience, should enhance the quality of government responses to unemployment, bringing useful insights to bear on the profiles of future schemes. However, as the MSC increasingly depends on the business, local government and voluntary sectors, it will find it harder to introduce programmes towards which these groups might be unsympathetic.

Although we said earlier that the MSC was formally introduced as a tripartite body, it is in fact a 'multipartite' organisation, with a wide range of non-governmental actors impinging on various aspects of the policy-making process within the MSC. This is not simply a consequence of the predilections of the Heath Government who set it up: it reflects how far the MSC depends upon this variety of non-governmental and local governmental bodies for the very operation of its programmes. One broad policy consequence of this system is that many provider organisations, whether local authority, business or charity, have been able to pursue their own special objectives within MSC schemes while drawing upon the MSC's financial and organisational resources. Of course, there exists an intricate MSC staff field-level network, but this is quite incapable of delivering the programmes by itself. Whilst this system makes radical policy departures more difficult than the government might wish, it has ensured the maintenance of schemes in response to unemployment, something which, in our view, has enabled the Conservatives to escape the accusation that nothing has been done for the unemployed.

5 Regional, Local and Business Initiatives

One of the most significant features of the unemployment issue is that, not only have the activities of the MSC, the Department of Employment and other central government departments attracted the involvement of outside organisations, but also such bodies have engaged in their own policy responses to the problem. In terms of quantitative impact the most important such responses have been by local government and business organisations, both of which have adopted the twin aim of stimulating local economies and creating new employment. Of course, many of these organisations are simultaneously involved in delivering MSC programmes along the lines described in the previous chapter. However, we consider this phenomenon of activity *outside* the realm of central government policies to have sufficiently important consequences in terms of local employment prospects and in terms of the politics of the unemployment issue, as to merit separate consideration. Whilst the unemployment issue has been typical of other economic and social policy problems in attracting a constellation of groups into the making and implementation of government policies, the extent to which they have also struck out on their own initiative is possibly more distinct in the case of unemployment.

5.1 Local government involvement

The direct involvement of local government in attempting to reduce unemployment in its area of responsibility is not a new development. During the 1930s it became active in the development of industrial estates, factory building, and even went so far as to give financial aid to local industry as well as being involved in municipal enterprises. Whilst not new, such activities are, however, relatively novel in the post-war world given the absence of mass unemployment until the last decade. During this period, however, different local government initiatives have emerged alongside those of central government, though the extent of local responses may also reflect central government's added preoccupation with inflation. Of course, local government has also long been involved in efforts to attract industry to its area, but these policies too have taken a new turn with mass unemployment. The ability of local government to shift its mode of activity more towards fighting unemployment was significantly increased in 1977 by the Labour Government, who encouraged local government to give priority to industry in the exercise of many of its functions.

In his case study of the London borough of Hounslow's response to unemployment, Gregory (1984) records how, in 1977, following the Department of Environment and Department of Transport Joint Circular 71/77 'Local Government and the Industrial Strategy' suggesting ways in which local governments could improve the conditions for greater industrial confidence and growth, an inter-departmental Industrial Strategy Working Group was formed in Hounslow. The Group soon appointed an Industrial Liaison Officer, and set about trying to keep existing firms in the borough and attract new ones to it. This was born out of the realisation that so many central government policies were geared to attracting industry to inner-city areas, as opposed to suburban authorities like Hounslow. However, there was no immediate need for urgency, as unemployment in the area was still only half the national average. In 1980, when the local level of unemployment reached the emotive figure of 4,000 the political mood changed and the renamed Employment Strategy Working Group began to alert the Council to the possibility of providing industrial and warehouse units for small firms.

In Hounslow, as in the whole country, it was not simply rising unemployment, but rising unemployment among school-leavers which prompted action. In addition to providing more YOP places, the Council took a wider view of the problem, and the Environmental Planning Committee was urged to consider redevelopment plans to secure the 'maximum number and variety of jobs consistent with good planning practice' (Gregory, 1984:47). Thus, like many other councils, Hounslow has dovetailed other policy objectives to meet simultaneously the problem of unemployment.

In contrast to many councils which have established 'arms length' economic development units, Sheffield City Council claims to have been, in 1981, the first local authority to establish an Employment Committee and an Employment Department. From the outset, the Sheffield Employment Committee envisaged a co-ordinating role in

preventing further job losses in the City; to alleviate the worse effects of unemployment and to encourage effective training for new skills and jobs; to stimulate new investment, to create new kinds of employment and to diversify job opportunities in the City; and to explore new forms of industrial democracy and co-operative control over work. (Sheffield City Council, 1982)

The particular task facing the Sheffield Council has been to minimise and compensate for the high number of redundancies in the steel industry, and the model chosen is one of 'municipalisation' of local industry, either through direct ownership, or regulation and planning agreements. Policies pursued include the provision of special aids to businessmen and to co-operatives, such as loans, grants, premises, and advice. In contrast to many other such local government assistance, Sheffield lays down strict terms under which assistance is available such that firms must comply with aspects of the Council's social and political policy, e.g. no trading links with South Africa. Special emphasis is also given to the support of local co-operatives. This assistance has mainly been given to maintaining jobs in organisations which had been threatened with closure, and in some cases has led to complaints of unfair competition from other competing concerns. In addition, the Council has bought shares in a new computer company, and provided initial grants and low interest loans which add up to a further £71,000 commitment, for which six new jobs have been created in the first year of operation and a further six promised in the third year, with sub-contracting guaranteed for local firms 'where possible'.

Although the Council itself has refrained from estimating how many jobs have been affected, some observers estimate that, in the first eighteen months, about 1,000 had been saved or created as a result of the Council's strategy (Grayson, 1983:24). Despite this sign of success, there are fears that the Council's activities may actually act as a disincentive to prospective new firms who might be wary of the high level of intervention which might occur. Also, the preservation-of-jobs-at-all-costs approach might hinder future growth unless the firms receiving assistance are encouraged to diversify and seek new products and markets. More generally, there might also be costs to existing firms, of this level of local government activity, in the form of higher levels of rates than would otherwise pertain.

Glasgow District Council is more typical of other local government involvement, providing business assistance schemes but without the extent of intervention and regulation seen in Sheffield. Glasgow provides discretionary help to cover costs incurred in enforced relocation within the city, for marketing assistance, and for plant and machinery purchase where other forms of public sector assistance are not available. In addition, like Sheffield it provides grants for co-operatives or common ownership enterprises – though greater emphasis is put on the creation of new concerns. With more specific emphasis on jobs in particular areas of the Council's jurisdiction, grants are available for any firm planning any works which would benefit the local area, with an additional £1,000 per job created or preserved thereby. One noteworthy success for the Glasgow District Council was the expansion of major car showroom and workshop complex by a local company, for which the Council provided the land. Fifty new jobs were created as a result of this, and a further 100 are expected within three years.

It was reported in June 1984 that the Council's business advice centre had provided advice for over 2,000 city businesses in the previous eighteen months. A survey was conducted of 50 such firms, and 34 of these responded, of which 32 had found the service useful. Most had wanted general guidance in how to secure more orders. Others asked for direct financial aid and advice on starting a new business or moving to different premises. Of these 34 companies eleven were helped in winning new orders, which led to the creation of 81 jobs, and a further nine companies were able to safeguard at least 56 jobs as a result of advice given.

Glasgow is an interesting example of the phenomenon that policies to combat unemployment may sometimes have the effect of advantaging one area at the cost of another. Thus Glasgow has been critical of the Locate in Scotland Policy, which it sees as favouring new towns. As a result, Glasgow is now trying hard to attract service industries to the city (having lost 10,000 manufacturing jobs in the last three years). It had a recent success, in June 1984, in attracting an American company of consulting engineers. Part of the help that the city was prepared to give was a rental for office space of £5.00 per square foot, considerably below current levels. The company's Vice President explained that the City's Estates Department made strenuous efforts to smooth the company's path – this, apparently, included not only financial inducements, but also helping him to choose a house in the city and finding a good local source for suits! (*The Scotsman* 27.6.84).

The Glasgow City Council has attempted to utilise its policy priorities in related areas to combat local unemployment. For instance, in 1983 – 4 about £50 million was made available in the form of repair and improvement grants for housing, but it was emphasised that benefiting firms would be expected to increase their workforce. The convenor on housing commented that, 'It's the No. 1 priority of this Administration to assist wherever possible in the creation of new jobs. We're looking to one of the hardest hit industries to play their part'(*Bulletin,* February 1983, No. 22).

Initiatives on the scale of the Hounslow and even the Glasgow responses, whilst important on the micro level both politically and possibly in terms of local employment and economic growth, make only a tiny dent in the overall problem of unemployment. Between national government policies and responses at the district level come initiatives on the part of the metropolitan authorities. Indeed, the ability of this level of local government to respond to the problem of unemployment in urban areas has, of course, been considerably increased since the reorganisation of local government in 1972. This reorganisation created the larger metropolitan authorities, which are possibly more capable than their predecessors of tackling such problems (by virtue of their greater budgets and powers), and which in many instances embrace areas of particularly high unemployment. It remains to be seen what impact current government legislative proposals to abolish the GLC and the other metropolitan authorities (even if the envisaged package became law unamended) would have on the unemployment field.

Like the TUC (see Chapter 4), most of the metropolitan authorities, and indeed many district authorities, are politically opposed to the Thatcher Government's economic strategy, yet have ironically become part and parcel of the cushioning response to unemployment, giving the government greater *political* leeway to pursue its own economic objectives. This dilemma is well illustrated in a recent GLC publication, a booklet containing a record of the GLC's achievement, an alternative strategy for jobs, and an attack on Conservative policy in this field. It states that 'The GLC cannot reverse these national trends on its own but it can set a good example of what *should* be done. And it can give working people support in their action to get something done' (GLC, 1983:5). In addition to providing a rationale for greater government intervention and expenditure for creating jobs of community value, the booklet details some of the intended activities of its own Greater London Enterprise Board, which was launched in order to implement the GLC's economic policies. These would follow the initiative previously taken by the GLC in purchasing a furniture factory for £1.4 million, investing in it a further £150,000, and preserving the jobs of 120 of the 400 workers.

In Scotland the regional authorities have greater powers than their counterparts in England and Wales, and have thus greater resources for tackling unemployment. By far the largest of these authorities is the Strathclyde Regional Council, accounting for about half of the population of Scotland. A recent report for the authority identified 75 areas within the region requiring priority treatment due to various forms of 'multiple' deprivation. In thirteen of these cases unemployment was described as 'more deeply ingrained and the population seems doomed to live in deserts of permanent unemployment and deteriorating housing and environment' (Strathclyde Regional Council, 1983). In short, the magnitude of the problem facing the Council is massive by any standards: an average level of unemployment of 18.6 per cent, with more than 200,000 people without work, including, in one area, more than 49 per cent of the workforce.

The region has responded to this problem with a range of its own initiatives, and others drawing on business and EEC support. Strathclyde Region has pioneered an employment subsidy – now followed by other Scottish regional councils – the Employment Grants Scheme. It subsidises wages of employees who have been recruited from off the dole by up to 30 per cent, up to a maximum of £39 per week. In its first year of operation, 1982–3, the scheme helped to create 2,350 jobs in small firms (mainly construction, engineering, and textiles). In 1984–5, the scheme will cost £2 million, £1 million of which the Council hopes will be financed by the European Social Fund. It is intended to create 1,250 jobs for the under-25-year-olds, who are eligible after three months of unemployment and are subsidised for six months, and 625 jobs for the over-25-year-olds, who are eligible after a year on the dole and are subsidised for the first year of employment. Previous schemes for which the Council shared the costs with the EEC provided £2.9 million, contributing to the creation of about 6,500 jobs. After twelve months, 75 per cent of the subsidised workers were still in their jobs. In addition, other expenditures have been provided to improve the quality of life in areas of particular deprivation, which has itself led to the creation of a small number of jobs. These not only include environmental and social service projects, but also such initiatives as a computer training centre for the unemployed.

Under the auspices of the Strathclyde Department of Education, the Community Service Agencies authorise projects at the community level which normally provide temporary employment for a small team, consisting of one or two adults and groups of between about four and twenty trainees. Projects include the removal of graffiti, provision of meals for OAPs, landscaping, and the renovation of derelict properties for community use. The CSAs not only provide regional finance for such schemes but look to other bodies such as MSC for subsidies.

On the industrial front, the Industrial Development Unit is designed to 'promote industry and commerce within the Region and thereby to create new jobs and to preserve existing jobs within a viable environment'. The Unit has three main sections. The first is concerned with the promotion of local industry by means of advertising, exhibitions and general publicity, and especially with attracting new business from outside the region, as well as encouraging the growth of indigenous industry. The second section deals mainly with how best to utilise the stock of land and buildings in the region, whether publicly or privately owned, and with building new factories. The third section provides management advice to existing companies thinking of expansion, and individuals hoping to start new businesses.

The Unit also runs New Enterprise Workshops with a range of modern machinery and available technical expertise, with the aim of helping individuals with ideas for products and processes. This help is to enable them to develop a prototype which can be used as the basis for starting a new company, or can be sold to an existing company to market. The Unit also operates a group of Nursery Factory Units, which are available for low-cost, short-term rental, to allow new products to be tested on the market with relatively small capital investment costs. More specific attention is paid to unemployment under the Integrated Workforce concept (pioneered in Northern Ireland), which involves the Unit in training groups of the unemployed for specific new companies emerging from the New Enterprise Workshops.

Whilst the Strathclyde Region has a comparatively large resource capacity to respond to unemployment, it is of course faced with a considerably larger problem, and, like all authorities, simultaneously facing real cutbacks in the Rate Support Grant. Also, the advantages of economies of scale which the Region brings must be balanced against the difficulties of size. As shall be seen later in this chapter, a small and comparatively homogeneous area can often provide a more practical focus for resisting rises in unemployment, chiefly because of the relative ease of communications, greater extent of personal contact between providers, and the advantages of a community commitment. It is thus instructive that, in its strategy for the 1980s, the Strathclyde Region has not only picked out special areas for priority treatment, but also committed itself to back up communities which want to plan and run their own projects to help their own areas. The Regional Council has recently devised a new means of counting the unemployed. Instead of producing unemployment reports on Jobcentre areas (which contained both high and low unemployment levels), they now produce reports on areas which group the 383 postcode sectors into 79 'community areas'. This provides information based on recognised communities rather than MSC administration boundaries (Strathclyde Digest, No. 44, 1984), offering the chance for more effective targetting of assistance.

5.2 The business response to unemployment

Perhaps one of the most surprising developments within the unemployment industry has been the emergence among business organisations of a sense of corporate responsibility. The most significant national development to this end was probably the conference at Sunningdale, in 1980, where large US and UK firms discussed community involvement and set up a new organisation, Business in the Community, to stimulate the formation of local enterprise trusts. Enterprise trusts are independent local agencies whose boards normally consist of business and local government interests, and which aim to give advice and often practical assistance to existing and new small firms on questions of finance, market research and premises. The trusts are usually staffed by businessmen on secondment from their own employer, often a national or multi-national company. Sometimes the secondees are young 'high flyers', sometimes they are approaching retirement.

This new type of organisation was pioneered by the Community of St Helen's Trust, which has operated (with particular support from Pilkington Brothers) since the early 1970s in the St Helen's area of Merseyside, with the object of stimulating growth so as to ease job losses caused by structural changes in traditional local industry. As well as the support from Pilkington's, the Trust has received financial help, practical assistance, or support in the form of secondees, from all of the major banks and other national and local firms. Between 1978 and the end of 1983 alone, the Trust claimed to have been involved in 262 new business starts (of which only fifteen are known to have failed) and 148 business expansions by its clients.

The Trust has given particular emphasis to building up engineering industries capable of providing a range of subcontractor services, deemed to be of great value in attracting further new companies to the St Helen's area. The Trust did not claim to be the only organisation for creating new jobs in the area, and has had to acknowledge that local unemployment has continued to rise. However, in 1982 and 1983 the rate of increase in unemployment was lower than the national average rise or that of north-west England and Merseyside (Community of St Helen's Trust, 1984). Pilkington has also been running its own youth training scheme, Index (Industrial Experience), for sixteen to eighteen-year-olds. This is a two-year scheme, whose first year is financed by the MSC under YTS (and formerly YOP), and the second year funded by Pilkingtons, other local firms, individual contributions, and the EEC.

The idea of local enterprise trusts has been quick to catch on. Since 1981, the CBI Special Programmes Unit (see Chapter 4) has been keen to stimulate their creation, under its Community Action Programmes (CAPs). By the middle of 1983, CAPs were in operation in 21 towns (primarily in England and Wales) and a further 20 towns were under consideration for 1983, with the aim of establishing a CAP in all those 'travel to work areas' with an unemployment rate of over 12 per cent and an employee population of more than 100,000 (CBI SPU, 1983). The normal pattern of events has been for individual firms to conduct or commission (usually from universities or commercial research organisations) 'town studies' of areas thought ripe for enterprise trust activity. These studies, typically, would give broad details of the local economy and its structure, and then proceed to outline constraints on the performance of local firms, the assistance already available and any relevant assistance 'gaps', and opportunities for the creation or expansion of businesses. Also included, would be suggestions of possible sources of practical assistance for an enterprise trust. On the basis of all this, a decision would be made by one or a group of companies whether to nurture an enterprise trust and provide secondees to act as their managing directors.

The Chief Executive of the CBI SPU revealed recently that the organisation has also been thinking about meeting the problem of what to do with the thousands of youngsters who finish their YTS training period and face the prospect of unemployment. The alternatives includes job-sharing and value-added training, and the stimulation of more locally based small firms. At the time of writing, Business in the Community and CBI SPU are in the process of merging to form a single national umbrella organisation. Whilst there is an obvious logic here, to avoid duplication of effort and maximise expertise and resources, our own investigations suggest that the medium-to-long-term success of enterprise trusts is very much more dependent on local efforts than on national co-ordination. A combined Business in the Community and CBI SPU might, however, serve to attract further business attention to the social consequences of unemployment, and the opportunities open to business organisations to relieve some of the attendant problems.

Among the crop of new enterprise trusts is GO, the Glasgow Opportunities Agency, set up under the auspices of Scottish Business in the Community. Its main specified aim is to create jobs by offering a free confidential business advisory service in order to establish new business, help expanding businesses and those in difficulty, and to aid management 'buy outs'. Specialist advice is given in the areas of finance, administration, marketing, personnel, property, planning and grants. In its first three months of operation, it claimed to have provided assistance to over 200 clients, and expected to have had a hand in the creation of about 160 new firms during 1984. It also considered one of its main achievements, during a time of recession, to be saving jobs in existing companies which, but for GO's intervention, might well have gone to the wall. Two-thirds of the initial financing of GO (just over £300,000) was provided by donations from the private sector, and this was supplemented by about £42,000 from the Scottish Development Agency and about £120,000 from the EEC, via the Scottish Industry Department. This balance of income is broadly typical of other enterprise trusts.

It should be added that the ability of the individual trusts to manage their finances and supplement these by attracting additional resources in cash or kind, can often prove to be a vital factor in their capacity to have an impact on the local economy. Our preliminary studies of the Neath Development Partnership[1] have indicated that one of the factors in its success has been the involvement of highly motivated and entrepreneurially minded individuals with a wide range of local contacts, capable of 'winning' the co-operation of those with resources, be they finance, physical resources, equipment or expertise.

Although locally based business initiatives generally seem to produce an effective use of resources, some national projects have also been successfully started. Practical Action, for example, was set up in 1978 by Sir Kenneth Cork (then Lord Mayor of London), and acts as a link organisation raising unused resources from the business sector and directing these to youth employment schemes which would benefit by them – whether run under MSC auspices or not. About half of Practical Action's costs are met by the MSC and the rest by about thirty companies. It has no overt campaigning or information provision role whatsoever, but prefers to live up to its name and get on with the job of matching needs with resources (usually equipment and expertise). It is estimated that, during 1982, £0.25 million worth of resources were raised from about 400 companies. Practical Action also runs a national

---

[1] We are currently preparing a book length comparative study of local responses to unemployment in several selected British localities.

discount scheme for the hire and purchase of equipment for youth unemployment projects.

It is not only private business which has joined the fight against unemployment. A notable public sector example was the creation, in 1975, of the British Steel Corporation (Industry) Ltd by the BSC, as it was about to embark on a major reduction in its steel-making capacity. The impact of the 150,000 job losses was of course highly localised, so the main aim of BSC (I) was to create as many jobs as possible in these dozen or so areas.

Like the enterprise trusts discussed above, BSC (I)'s team have been characterised by an entrepreneurial style, in raising local finance for firms wishing to set up or expand; in giving very detailed, careful and above all personal advice and assistance to those wishing to establish their own businesses; and in providing suitable – usually small – premises from which small businesses could begin to operate. This concept of provision of workshops was pioneered in the late 1970s at the former Clyde Ironworks, which was scheduled for demolition as part of BSC's restructuring. Instead, it was gradually converted into 82 units which local businesses could rent. Within four years 34 businesses set up in the Clyde Workshops were still operating, a further 27 small businesses had moved to the site, and 316 people worked there. Because of its success, the model has been followed throughout the country by private and public sector bodies alike.

Two special consultancy organisations have emerged from the BSC (I) staff, which are preoccupied with the question of finding jobs. PA Creating Employment (PACE) is backed by PA Management Consultants (early sponsors of the CBI SPU), and acts in a consultancy role to companies with spare capacity which they would like to expand. PACE attempts to persuade them to take on more labour at the same time as expanding. Job Creation Ltd (JCL) works differently, by actually moving into areas and operating on a similar basis to the enterprise trusts. It attempts to find openings for employment on behalf of its clients (e.g., local authorities or companies) and charges the client accordingly.

One obvious question that arises in the light of this growing sense of corporate responsibility is, *Why* are firms extending themselves in such ways when the recession has presented them with enough of their own problems? It is difficult to settle on a single answer, and the different organisations involved will no doubt attest to varying motivations. The desire for certain company directors and executives to receive public decoration for such efforts does not seem to be a sufficient explanation! The 1981 riots in Liverpool and London, particularly, are certainly thought to have made some impact on business attitudes, in a combination of self-interest and community responsibility. As *The Economist* (20.2.82) observed, companies like Marks & Spencer have come to recognise that a healthy high street depends on healthy back streets. By spending some £1.25 million on community work and charities, this firm was 'making a sensible long term investment in its market place. If urban disorders become a regular fact of life, many of its 260 stores would not survive.'

The decision of firms to provide secondments of their staff to enterprise trusts is probably a mixture of social conscience and a desire to be seen to be doing the 'right thing' by local and national decision-makers. In addition, the younger staff seconded are given a very practical training, with experience in dealing with a wide range of individuals, organisations and problem areas, equipping them better for future work in their parent companies. In the case of some older personnel nearer retirement, secondment provides an easier option for their employers than enforcing redundancy or early retirement, at the same time as meeting the other objectives listed.

A broader factor in explaining this trend should also be mentioned. In a revealing statement, the CBI commented that

. . . companies fear that if they make no attempt to find solutions to community problems, the government may increasingly take on the responsibility itself. This might prove costly to employers both in terms of new obligations and greater intervention in the labour market. Many companies prefer to be one step ahead of government legislation or intervention, to anticipate social pressure themselves and hence be able to develop their own policies in response to them. (CBI, 1981)

This does not of course apply only to central government and, as we have already suggested, some local authorities who require high business rates and high levels of regulation in order to achieve their policy objectives may alienate business.

5.3 The unemployment industry network

Despite the areas of differences between local government and business organisations, a further significant feature of the wider responses to unemployment is the extent of co-operation between these two 'worlds'. Indeed, even the illustrations we have already provided, of initiatives by one type of body or the other, have usually involved some form of co-operation. Further, although local government and business provide the main pillars of this network, other governmental (e.g., development agencies) and non-governmental (e.g., charities) organisations also play their part in the exchange of ideas and provision of resources in local and regional policies to reduce unemployment. The networks are underpinned by numerous formal and informal contacts as well as overlapping memberships of relevant boards and committees. For instance, the Chairman of Scottish Business in the Community stated that

One of our objectives has been to work with existing organisations with similar aims. I have already outlined the close working relationship we have achieved with the Scottish Development Agency and other public bodies. The Executive Unit has now developed working relationships with many other organisations such as the Scottish Council (Development and Industry), CBI SPU, the Scottish Enterprise Foundation, the Scottish Action Resource Centre, the North British Industrial Association, the Planning Exchange and the Chambers of Commerce – to name but a few.

It is a mark of the progress made in the field that the Executive Unit is now a focal point for requests for many groups and organisations about mobilising private sector interest and resources. (Scottish Business in the Community, 1983)

It is also significant that representatives of the Scottish Office, the Scottish Council of Social Service, the Convention of Scottish Local Authorities (two), and the Scottish Trades Union Council, sit on ScotBIC's governing council, and representatives of the Convention of Scottish Local Authorities, the Scottish Development Agency, the Scottish Council of Social Service, and the Manpower Services Commission, sit on the executive council. This gives an indication of the interplay between a range of interested parties in the unemployment industry and illustrates the difficulty of trying to classify these bodies as public, private or quango.

The size and impact of the business response is difficult to gauge. In some cases, much publicity is gained from what is very little investment. For instance, the Shell Livewire scheme, described as a 'Positive Approach to Youth Employment', has been extremely widely and professionally publicised in the Strathclyde Region, with such slogans as 'everyone can be a winner'. Livewire is a competition for the best young person's idea for their own business, and although all entrants are told that they will receive the benefit of assistance from Shell's special business advisers, the only financial commitment, apart from running the competition, which generates £46,000 worth of advertising, is the first prize of £500 worth of equipment or services, and second and third prizes of £250 and £150 respectively. In other cases, such as Neath (considered later), the commitment and resources provided appear more substantial.

Another aspect of local government and business partnership is in the process of attracting more companies to the area. Glasgow District Council and the enterprise trust Glasgow Opportunities have worked together to hold several exhibitions to enable Glasgow companies to display their products and services, and to advertise the business services offered by themselves and such other bodies as the Scottish Development Agency, Strathclyde Regional Council and the Scottish Co-operatives Development Committee. Such events also afford the opportunity to inform businessmen of the purchasing policies and needs of councils, thus improving the possibilities of local firms providing the goods and services required. For example, a Glasgow building services firm was expanded, following its managing director's attendance at such an exhibition, with the help and advice of one of the District Council's Business Development

Officers. The firm was given a contract to supply plastic window frames to some of the local authority's housing development scheme. As a consequence, the firm set up a small factory to assemble the window frames in Glasgow and twenty-five jobs were created immediately, with the promise of a further twenty-five in the future.

Again, we should note the possible 'displacement' effect of these local initiatives. Glasgow's success in encouraging the local manufacture of plastic window frames is possibly a new problem for another local authority as 'their' window manufacturer loses orders. On a much larger scale, local authorities are obviously outbidding each other to attract inward investment, with no firm evidence that there is a net increase in employment as a result. (The Glasgow 'success' cited earlier, of attracting a firm of engineering consultants, was in fact at the expense of Ireland, which had also 'bid' for the firm.)

The fight against unemployment has prompted joint responses by different types of governmental bodies. For instance, in 1983, Strathclyde Regional Council, Monklands District Council and the Scottish Development Agency agreed to provide £22 million over three years for job-creation projects in Coatbridge, where unemployment among young people had reached a staggering 80 per cent. The money is being used to improve roads, water and sewerage systems, and to develop a 500-acre area of the town in an attempt to attract new employers. Similarly, the Strathclyde Regional Council, Glasgow District Council and the SDA committed £2 million over three years to the Port Dundas Project. The aim is to promote the improvement and economic development of the area. The money will be used to help existing companies to diversify and expand, to provide low-cost industrial premises by renovating existing surplus property (another example of the propagation of the Clyde Workshops model), and to give special forms of assistance to new firms. The Port Dundas location was not selected as a recipient of public funds simply because of its deprivation (though it has been particularly badly hit by Glasgow's recession), but also because of its proximity to a motorway, enabling good transport links, and to the Forth and Clyde canal, providing the possibility of recreational ventures. In other words, its potential for growth was an important factor in this decision.

Most recently, in Glasgow, has come the announcement of another joint venture, funded by the SDA but to be administered by Glasgow Opportunities (GO). The Enterprise Funds for Youth (EFFY), also to be piloted in two other Scottish areas, provides loans of up to £3,000 to 16 – 25 year olds wishing to be self-employed or to set up small new enterprises. The loans are repayable over five years at favourable rates of interest. The purpose of asking GO to administer EFFY is that it will not only provide the most-informed vetting and screening procedures for applications, but also will be able to offer a continuing service of business advice.

The increase in the activity of co-operatives within local economies has become another feature of the wider response to unemployment. The concept of co-operative ownership is no longer solely within the political armoury of the left. It has become part and parcel of the general economic drift towards self-help and independence, and the encouragement of small firms. Thus, whereas in 1976 there was only one co-operative with worker-membership in Scotland, by 1983 there were more than 50 registered co-operatives, employing over 500 people and with a total annual turnover of £4 million plus. These are active in a wide variety of fields, from carpet manufacture to wholefood shops, from heat-pump manufacture to sound recording companies. The Scottish Co-operatives Development Committee, which acts as an umbrella organisation and source of advice and financial assistance, has become part of the Scottish unemployment industry network, receiving funds primarily from development agencies, and from regional and district councils. The Committee places a great stress on marketing, and has a Sales Division to assist co-operatives to identify additional 'high margin markets'. Indicative of the business orientation of the Committee is the fact that two of its members are representatives of the CBI.

One associated development in Scotland has been the community business idea, whereby members of a local community buy shares (usually costing between £1 and £5) within small local firms (which is initially supplemented by SDA funding) and then control them. The intention is that the community businesses should aim to create jobs for local people, to perform tasks of local benefit, and to reinvest profits to create more jobs. Other than these characteristics, community businesses vary enormously, especially in the degree of their commerciality, in the numbers of people involved in their establishment, and in the extent of concentration on specific types of work. The most common areas of activity include home production, retailing, environmental improvement and stone-cleaning. As in the case of enterprise trusts, a clear emphasis is placed upon finding the 'right' people for setting up and working within the community businesses, in terms of appropriate skills, commitment to the community company, and willingness to become involved in the widest aspects of running a community company. A good example of community business in the Strathclyde Region is Govan Workspace, a property management company with the special aim of increasing the provision of small commercial and industrial premises, which attracted 85 jobs and 12 new companies to the area in about two years. Other examples, however, still only hold out the promise of jobs in the future.

Recently, the Strathclyde Regional Council instigated the formation of the Strathclyde Community Business Unit to provide a 'one door' approach to getting advice and assistance, in view of the emergent web of competing agencies offering such services. The Strathclyde Community

Business Unit operates as an umbrella organisation and is supported not only by the Regional Council, but also by district councils, the Scottish Development Agency, the MSC, CBI and TUC. The Regional Council provided the initial finance but this is supplemented by Scottish Office, SDA and EEC support. The aims of the Unit are to create long-term jobs especially in areas of very high unemployment, to enable people to acquire new skills, to develop new services, and to contribute to community stability and development.

Voluntary and charitable organisations have also become part and parcel of the wider response to unemployment, either autonomously, or more usually in partnership with local government and local development and enterprise agencies. In some cases voluntary organisations are even responsible for the creation of 'community companies' and 'community co-operatives', which were first established to provide jobs but have prospered to provide profits and some job security for participants. In addition to its involvement in MSC-sponsored programmes, the Glasgow Council for Voluntary Service (GCVS) has played a major part in the founding and development of two such Community Businesses. The first of these, Goodwill Trading Inc., provides employment for those capable of repairing furniture and other household goods, which are then re-sold through the company's shops. The second, Poldrait Service and Industry Ltd, which, in addition to the help received from GCVS and the Council, has also used property provided by the Scottish Development Agency. Poldrait offers a range of services including electronic subcontracting, contract cleaning and office services, and seeks to create self-supporting and viable jobs for local people who serve the local community.

Churches have also acted as sponsors on MSC schemes, launching their own job creation projects, and have provided leisure and counselling centres for the unemployed. Church Action with the Unemployed was formed in 1982 to encourage more churches to respond to the unemployment problem, (especially long-term adult unemployment in inner cities), not only through pastoral work, but also with information on job-creation opportunities and advice on employment openings under MSC schemes. In his 1984 Dimbleby lecture the Bishop of Liverpool, David Shepherd, not only took the government to task for its inner-city policies, but also suggested that the Church should play a greater role in this respect.

One of the key elements of the wider response to unemployment is, of course, money. As intimated, the private sector is sometimes responsible for the provision of significant finance for enterprise trusts and partnerships. For example, the International Thomson Organisation has estimated that it has injected about £350,000 into the Neath Development Partnership over a period of three years. However, the remainder comes from public-sector sources such as grants from the District and Regional Councils. They are currently undergoing financial cutbacks from central government and face the possibility of rate capping, which will restrict their expenditure even further. At the same time, their other traditional spending priorities have had to be maintained, and in some cases increased, during the recession. Thus, despite appearances to the contrary, in many cases money is not being *especially* directed to tackling unemployment. Instead, small shifts in targetting are made, but there have been big shifts in the 'public packaging' of expenditure. No longer are housing, road and environmental improvements presented as initiatives for their own intrinsic worth, but as contributions to the fight for jobs. Alternatively, in as much as councils do appear to be making new expenditures in the unemployment field, the financing of these is often supplemented from other sources, viz., central government or European Communities.

Central government finance is available through several sources. First, the various regional development grants available from the Department of Trade and Industry (see Chapter 3) are used for projects which involve the creation or maintenance of jobs. In addition, the various development agencies in operation are a major source of finance for initiatives within their areas of competence. On some occasions they provide direct assistance, but on others they make use of councils and enterprise agencies to act as intermediaries. Indeed, development agencies have tended to play an important role in sustaining and indeed strengthening the partnership aspects of the wider response to unemployment. In 1981, the Scottish Development Agency claimed that it had 'developed its emphasis on partnership towards even closer relationships internally and externally'. Similarly, the Urban Aid programme, designed to upgrade the conditions of inner city areas, has been a source of finance for programmes involving the creation of work, usually either in environmental projects or in community services. The community business schemes in Glasgow considered earlier were initially funded and advised by the Local Enterprise Advisory Project, which was itself funded by Urban Aid, with Strathclyde Regional Council acting as the sponsoring intermediary!

The European Communities have constituted a major source of supplementary finance for responses to unemployment. Often this is provided through intermediary organisations who then redeploy funds. For instance, in 1981–2 the Welsh Development Agency received £0.5 million in loan capital, to be deployed in areas affected by steel closures. Indeed, in many cases EC money goes straight to central government, who pass it on to intermediary organisations who gain no extra income as a result – it simply forms part of the central government expenditure. The Welsh Development Agency in 1981–2 received a European Social Fund grant of £284,000, but this came through government accounts. In other cases, the Social Fund is applied directly to the policy implementor. In 1981, Bradford City Council received a subsidy of £229,000 for three years to enable it to recruit 72 unemployed people, and in 1982 a further £197,500 (for three years) to train and employ a further 57 individuals. In 1983, £321 million was spent by the Social Fund on training and employment schemes in the UK, almost half of which went to the under 25-year-olds. The Social Fund matches expenditure on the projects of the national public authorities.

Finance from the European Regional Development Fund is also available to designated areas of the country, and the first allocation of 1984 provided £68 million. This was granted to individual industrial and service sector projects, and is intended to have the immediate effect of creating or maintaining some 960 jobs. The £2.2 million investment project in Motorola Ltd, a semiconductor manufacturer outside Glasgow, is intended to lead to the eventual creation of 514 new jobs. Such is the importance of finance from the ECs that the Greater Manchester and Strathclyde Councils have taken the step of appointing Brussels-based liaison officers to process project applications to the various funds.

The web of sources of finance for the wider responses to unemployment has brought with it other implications beyond enabling certain activities which might otherwise have been prohibited. Perhaps most importantly, the fusion of public and private money in this field has accelerated the process of increased partnership between business organisations and public bodies. In the case of the Ardrossan, Saltcoats and Stevenston Enterprise Trust, the commitment of the two private-sector sponsors (ICI and Shell) gave the public bodies concerned (Strathclyde Region, Cunninghame District and the SDA) the confidence that vital entrepreneurial skills, which they are learning, but are not yet proficient in, and business advice, contacts and resources would be available. But ICI and Shell would probably not have gone ahead without some commitment, expressed in the form of investment, on the part of the public agencies. Having got this commitment, the private agencies are assured that the bureaucracies of the public agencies will be broadly co-operative over such issues as planning and land use, and that their resources, such as premises, and even contracts will be forthcoming.

The second major consequence of the financing of this unemployment industry is that a variety of financial providers and intermediaries come to populate the local and regional networks. This has caused some instances of duplication of provision, and these should be looked at closely with a view to improved co-ordination, as has been the case in the creation of the Strathclyde Community Business Unit. On the other hand, there are distinct advantages to a diversity of financial sources, in that a wide range of different strategies to reduce unemployment has been permitted. Further, there has been a definite learning process, not just between private and public organisations but also among the different types of public bodies, as they have co-operated to combat unemployment.

The development of local networks has been founded upon a growing realisation of mutual dependence on the part of the organisations involved. Although differences exist – particularly in some Labour-held councils which wish for high degrees of municipalisation – successful co-operative responses are still possible when participating parties put employment and the economic strength of the local community above their other differences. This is not, of course, to say that successful co-operation is always possible, as in some cases preferred routes to these goals will be just too divergent.

The main response of the government to the Toxteth riots in 1981 was to set up the Merseyside Task Force. This was designed to facilitate a partnership between civil servants dispatched to the area by the then Secretary of State Michael Heseltine (dubbed 'Minister for Merseyside') and local businessmen. The very fact that it took central government to intervene to create a sense of partnership there is perhaps indicative of the organisational and political difficulties which have added to Merseyside's economic problems over the past twenty years (see Parkinson and Duffy, 1984). It indicates that the emergence of co-operative frameworks among different levels of government, business representatives and the voluntary sector by no means follows automatically from economic recession and unemployment. The Task Force's Chief Executive commented that its major influence has been in 'actually getting discussion, getting meetings with different elements of the community and almost knocking heads together' (quoted in Parkinson and Duffy, 1984:90).

5.4 Local government – business partnership: a case study of Neath

The importance of a good working partnership between local government and business organisations is not just in individual project successes, and in attracting business in the area; it is also a vital factor in the efficient exploitation of any possible job opportunities within the locality, and in building up a climate of mutual trust and endeavour among the community at large, the workforce, and businesses. The comparative success of this type of partnership in Neath seems to illustrate this point. Neath had experienced about average levels of unemployment until the 1977–81 period, when a series of closures, especially in the steel, engineering and mining industries, provoked a rapid rise in job losses. It seems likely that the shock of moving, in a short period of time, from being about average to becoming well above average in the unemployment league acted as a considerable stimulus to members and officers of the borough council, and contributed a sense of urgency to the situation. This contrasts with other localities where high levels of unemployment have crept up at a comparatively steady pace, creating the illusion among numerous other councils of the inevitability of high unemployment and perhaps stunting their policy responses.

At the same time, the International Thomson Organisation (ITO) sponsored a town study of Neath, in 1981, under the aegis of the CBI SPU. Even at this stage ITO invited an officer of the council to share in their efforts by participating in the study. The findings of the study were initially gloomy, suggesting that the rate of unemployment would continue to rise, with no apparent prospect for new jobs either by attracting new manufacturing investment or by expanding the existing industrial base – a prospect shared by many other areas of the country overly dependent on traditional industries. The study team thus recommended the creation of a small task force consisting of representatives of the council, local industry and trade unions, to be called the Neath Development Partnership (in 1983, this was changed to Neath Partnership Enterprise Limited). The objectives of the Partnership were to be to stimulate job-attraction, job-regeneration and tourism in the Neath area. The Thomson Organisation committed itself to the area, and provided, in addition to secretarial and financial resources and the services of its own company, a secondee to act as managing director of the Partnership. This has been supplemented by other private-sector support from BP and PA Consultants.

The Neath Borough Council, which although it had no tradition of promoting the area to attract new industry, was, however, a willing partner, and was probably further motivated into action by the withdrawal of the Special Development status from Neath. The members and officers of the Council were becoming aware, not only of the scale of the problems, but also that it was incumbent upon themselves to become active in the fight against local unemployment. Thus the Industry and Development Committee formed a special link with the Partnership to facilitate greater working co-operation.

The initial members of the Partnership consisted of the ITO secondee, an ex-Welsh Office official, one borough councillor, one county councillor, representatives of BSC (industry), PA Management Consultants (who had been involved in the setting up of the original study) and Metal Box Ltd, and a trade union official. Since then, the representation of the Borough Council on the Partnership has actually increased, such that it provides two directors (the Borough Engineer and the Chief Executive) and the co-Secretary and Treasurer (the Borough Treasurer). The Borough Planning Officer is also active on the Board, but is not a director. One borough councillor who is a director of the Partnership has the unusual distinction of being a CBI SPU secondee and a trade unionist. The other members of the Partnership are the General Manager of Metal Box (Neath), a West Glamorgan County Councillor, representatives of BP, PA Management Consultants, the Welsh Development Agency, and the Wales TUC. Borough councillors and officers are further represented on the three committees of the Partnership: the ITEC Committee, the Estates Management Committee, and the Tourist Development Group.

It is, of course, possible for local government to have this level of representation within an enterprise partnership without actually engaging in active co-operation. This has not, however, been the case in Neath, where the council members and officers have been quick to respond to the situation and make the most of their new role. This is well illustrated in the establishment of the ITEC in Neath. The proposal, having been approved by the Welsh Office and the Department of Industry, was realised by means of co-operative action typifying the 'Neath style'. Metal Box were persuaded to provide the premises for the ITEC, and the Partnership acted as sponsors for an MSC Community Programme in order to acquire the labour to carry out the necessary conversions to the building. However, £40,000 was still needed to enable the ITEC to get off the ground, and the Borough Council was approached to provide it, having already provided a considerable amount of vacant property for the Partnership. Not only did the Council approve the expenditure, but it did so in only three days, going against normal patterns and responding to the urgency of the situation. It has continued to provide financial support for the ITEC with the hope of making it the best in Wales.

The Borough also pays for a Business Development Director and a Tourism Development Manager, who do not operate through a department of the Council (as is most common), but as part of the Development Partnership team. It has also made a major contribution to the Village Workshops (similar to the Clydeside model) by providing land, money for building the workshops and the salary of a manager (both supplemented by Urban Aid). The Workshops now provide work for over 100 people. The Council has bought land for the Enterprise Partnership to develop an artificial ski slope, and pays the considerable marketing costs of the Business Development Officer. All in all, the contribution which the Neath Borough Council makes to the success of the Partnership is very considerable, especially in terms of finance, land and property resources, and staff time, most notably that of senior officers.

The co-operation of the Council with the activities of the Partnership has not only brought with it the distinct advantages of more jobs to the area, but also led to changes in its own style of operation, making it more confident in entrepreneurial activities, which is especially impressive given the long-standing Labour orientation of the Council. This co-operative spirit has been contagious in Neath, leading, for example, to a positive response by the Metal Box labour force to restructuring plans involving changes in working practices and a small number of redundancies. At the same time, the commitment of the Metal Box company and other local employers to the town has increased.

One of the advantages Neath has enjoyed which is difficult to replicate in other localities is a 'team which clicked'. Furthermore, the team had connections with a wide range of functionally relevant organisations in local government, the trade union movement and local business, which considerably eased the task of making swift progress in particular initiatives and acquiring resources to expedite these. Indeed, one of the slogans of the Partnership is that it will only involve those who will 'bring something to the picnic'; it will not tolerate inactive partners who join for the sake of prestige alone.

The employment impact of the Partnership upon Neath has been impressive. At the beginning of 1983, unemployment in the borough had been 16.1 per cent, but by July of the same year this had already been reduced to 14.5 per cent – a fall of nearly 500. Between 1981 and September 1983 the Partnership itself had created 258 jobs, and projected another 550–630. As mentioned previously, it had carefully exploited opportunities provided under MSC schemes to develop its own projects (e.g., ITEC) and to contribute to the infrastructure of the area (e.g., by building a yachting marina) in the hope that this would lead to further *permanent* employment. It has also set up its own information technology firm projected to employ a further fifteen people. James Cooke, then managing director of CBI SPU, has estimated that if the Neath record could be duplicated nationally, there would be about three-quarters of a million more jobs across the country.

5.5 Discussion

What, then, has been the overall impact of these wider responses to unemployment? Whilst an aggregation of their national impact upon the economic strength and labour-market conditions is elusive, it is pertinent to raise some more general observations as to the role of these disparate initiatives.

First, the emphasis upon local-level policy formation and the theme of public and private sector partnership at this level seems very widespread. This reflects the growing strength of the 'self reliance' and 'initiative' themes popularly identified with, though in reality not exclusively advanced by, the Conservative Party. The government's critics would argue that this has come about as a result of the negligence of central government in the question of unemployment; others would say that decentralisation of responsibility is the only way to devise successful responses. Although neither the Labour nor Conservative Governments totally abandoned responsibility for the issue, we have seen that, at times, they have both pursued other policy objectives – notably the reduction of public expenditure and inflation and the increase of competitiveness – which have qualified their willingness to reduce unemployment at all costs. Moreover, the capacity of central government to *create* employment is hampered not simply by financial constraints, but also by insufficient expertise.

It appears that the combination of local government and local business partnerships, constituting a 'local mafia' with contacts throughout the community, can be quite adept at identifying local employment opportunities and business openings which might, in turn, lead to the creation of more jobs. Nevertheless, despite the flush of local initiatives in recent years, unemployment levels remain between three and four million. It is, of course, true to say that without these initiatives things would have been very much worse, but – looking forward – it suggests that the prospects for a greater impact upon unemployment are by no means certain.

As has already been pointed out, local authorities are currently undergoing considerable financial strain, and their capacity even to sustain current levels of financial support specifically to anti-unemployment initiatives must remain in some doubt. Similarly, in real terms, the amount of corporate finance provided in 1983 – 4 is lower than in 1979 – 80. Indeed corporate donation in 1982 amounted to only 0.1 per cent of UK pre-tax profits, compared with 0.8 per cent in the USA. Thus the future financial support of wider responses is uncertain.

There are probably about 300 enterprise agencies currently operating in the UK, but their permanence is not guaranteed. Indeed, the comparatively rosy picture painted in the case of the Neath Enterprise Partnership is not typical. Whilst it has achieved a certain degree of independent financial capability, others are still heavily dependent upon their parent companies. In many cases, there is also evidence of a fragmented community network, with different agencies often ignorant of the activities of other organisations. Sometimes there is too much emphasis on the 'numbers game', without due attention to the creation of *durable* employment. Clearly a balance needs to be struck between co-ordination and individual initiative within communities. This is especially important in large urban areas, where it is often difficult to localise the impact of labour-creating measures. Often, the reality of 'partnership' is lacking, and in some cases enterprise agencies view local government as obstructive, while local government may be sceptical about the real commitment of the agencies to the serious structural social and economic problems of their areas of responsibility.

There is also the question of the overall impact of the range of responses. Are mobile firms simply being drawn from one area to another, depending on the comparative advantage of local aids and incentives, with no *additional* jobs being created at all? Evidence would suggest that this is not uniformly the case, as new employment openings have undoubtedly been found in 'the new climate of enterprise'. Still, the nagging doubts expressed by some observers that many firms and jobs are simply being moved around (see Gregory, 1984) have not been quelled. Further, to what extent is the range of local initiatives hindering the government's aim of creating a climate of enterprise? The familiar conundrum of whether this support to industry is paying for firms who could survive without the aid, or who are not really commercially viable, or both, applies here. It should be added, however, that for many local authorities with especially high levels of concentrated unemployment make-work schemes, as opposed to stimulating enterprises of tomorrow, constitute a reasonable policy objective.

The political implications of these developments have so far assisted the Conservative Government in two main ways. First, the initial enthusiasm and well publicised instances of success have validated the government's view that it cannot be seen as the main provider of jobs. We would argue however that the Conservative Party should not be too confident of this trend being sustained. If the phase of corporate responsibility should peter out, and enterprise agency activity be publicly associated with too many failures, the initial policy success may yet backfire and the state be once again identified as the only source of finance and co-ordination capable of tackling the unemployment problem.

The second way in which these trends have assisted the government has been in providing palliatives for the unemployment crisis, thus putting some brake on the rapid increases in unemployment between 1981 and 1982. Indeed, they have also provided the symbolically important phenomenon of new jobs. The credibility of the government's overall strategy is dependent on new jobs being created, as the country's industrial and service sectors undergo restructuring. Once again, the Conservative Party cannot be too sanguine about this situation continuing: they cannot afford to allow the pace of new job-creation to slacken too much.

6 A Comparative Perspective

6.1 Introduction

There is no doubt that every Western nation has come to recognise the sheer enormity of the unemployment problem and has accepted that 'the crisis', and the continuing changes in the industrial structure, require governmental intervention. A central theme of this book has been that, whatever the political complexion of British governments, they have seen fit to spend public money on measures to reduce or ameliorate unemployment. We have also suggested that unemployment is an international problem. In the British case there has been much debate on how far Mrs Thatcher's own policies have exacerbated the international causes of the unemployment problem. Indeed, as we pointed out in Chapter 2, the House of Commons Treasury and Civil Service Committee appeared to be coming to the conclusion, in 1983, that the government's own policies were partly responsible for Britain's above-average levels of unemployment.

However, consideration of unemployment as an issue has been rather like 'the environment' as an issue – it has become internationalised. The political effects of, and policy responses to, unemployment are not confined to national boundaries. In particular, there is much international interchange of ideas in discussions of what policy responses are available. The market for policy ideas is, therefore, a genuinely international market with policy-makers in any one country very conscious of policy initiatives in other countries. For example, when the role of the private sector in Britain is being discussed, it is not long before Baltimore, in the USA, is quoted as a successful example of public/private partnerships responding to the local unemployment problem. The British job-creation scheme was consciously modelled on a Canadian one; the Job Splitting Scheme was devised after consideration of a similar Belgian scheme; and the French and German vocational preparation projects were examined prior to the design of YTS. Similarly, within the UK, the town of Neath is increasingly held up as a 'model' for local unemployment initiatives (Moon and Richardson, forthcoming).

The wide range of job-creation and marginal employment subsidy schemes have been judged reasonably successfully by OECD, in that they have some advantages, producing more work for less inflation, in contrast to income tax cuts which could otherwise be made. However, the OECD noted that in many such schemes there were problems of efficiency and monitoring that could be converted by more careful programme design (OECD, 1983).

Having noted the common existence of such schemes throughout the western world, we should not forget that they vary in their application (e.g., in the extent that they are directed at special groups or particular age groups). The Belgian and West German job-creation schemes have a much broader scope than their counterparts in Denmark, the Netherlands or the UK, for example. They may also vary in their size and duration. Table 6.1 indicates variations in expenditure on active labour market policies (excluding early retirement schemes) of four countries. The different levels of expenditure on these policies reflect national employment conditions and policy priorities. For instance, Austria had little need for such policy instruments, because of her successful economic and industrial restructuring policies. On the other hand, during the mid-to-late 1970s France and the USA were both experiencing relatively high unemployment levels, yet chose to spend modest amounts on active labour market measures, in contrast to Sweden, who by most standards had only a small unemployment problem.

Table 6.1   *Comparisons of expenditure on active labour market policies as % of GDP 1973–1980*

	1973/74	1974	1976	1977/78	1978	1980
Austria	—	0.12	0.12	—	0.11	0.11
France	—	—	0.32	—	—	0.46
Sweden	0.85	—	—	2.25	—	—
USA	—	0.21	—	—	0.65	—

SOURCE: Casey, 1983

In addition to having similar national government schemes, each country is characterised by attempts at the local level to stimulate unemployment in particular, and industrial and economic development in general. Comparable to the Scottish and Welsh Department Agencies, in West Germany, each *Land* has a semi-public body acting as a focus for inward investment and an instigator of promotional activities.

Todd (1984) suggests that the response of business organisations in the Netherlands to unemployment has been more positive than in any other EC country, and he provided the illustration of the Philips Job Creation Project in The Hague. Here, a bold commitment was made in the form of finance and a management team to create between 300 and 400 jobs in the area within two years. Further, the management team was the responsibility of the British consultants Job Creation Ltd (see Chapter 5) which was given a financial inducement by Philips to meet the target of commercially viable jobs. Thus, the act of creating the jobs was itself turned into a business proposition. The main objectives otherwise were similar to those found in Britain: encouraging local investment, strengthening existing business, and creating new business. The experience of this project confirms the findings from Neath, that a bold local initiative by a private sector organisation acts as an inducement to co-operative positive action on the part of local government and other local businesses.

There is also a great contrast between differences in broad economic strategies (in which one country may differ markedly from another, e.g., Britain and Sweden) and the similarities of practical policy responses to unemployment that may be adopted. Thus, in the USA, with its long tradition of a greater level of toleration of unemployment, poverty and temporary 'lay-offs' – and with a comparatively weak tradition of intervention – the National Commission for Employment Policy has, nevertheless, highlighted basic problems which may demand some form of government intervention. For example, it has pointed out that the USA 'has entered a period of profound change, not only in the characteristics of its worker population but in the jobs that will be available in the 1980s and beyond' (NCEP, 8th Annual Report, December 1982: 12). The changes have been likened to the industrial revolution. On the 'benefits' side, demographic trends are seen as encouraging, with a slower population growth in the 1980s leading to a more mature and stable labour force and to an easing of the competition for jobs. An additional (and probably more important) 'benefit' is that the service sector is expected to grow alongside what the Commission describes as the 'explosive' growth in the computer and telecommunication fields, and advances in robotics and other high-technology fields. On the 'costs' side, the economic and industrial changes will require a different labour force, with quite different skills and at generally higher levels of skills.

The Commission appears to recognise that the USA might be at a disadvantage in trying to produce a more appropriate labour force because of its decentralised system, lacking comprehensive national, State, or local employment policies. In typical bureaucratic language, the Commission suggests that ' . . . a basic question that policymakers might address is whether these various programs and policies should be integrated into a more coherent approach to solving employment problems and how this might be done most effectively, if such a goal is, indeed, desirable'. Within this apparently neutral question is posed the central issue of how far the US Federal Government should intervene in the workings of the labour market. In practice, the Federal Government has found some intervention unavoidable (as we shall see, later).

The purpose of this chapter is to draw attention to some of the more interesting and significant comparative examples of political and policy responses to unemployment, rather than to provide a very detailed catalogue of what, say, all OECD countries have been doing in the unemployment field. In principle, it should be possible to classify countries in terms of a general framework of responses. Thus, in terms of broad economic policies, countries might be classified along a scale from traditional Keynesian economic and fiscal policies, notably of high public expenditure and budget deficiting, to the currently more fashionable liberal economic and fiscal policies – as loosely typified by the policies advocated by Hayek and Friedman (see Chapter 2.1).

Countries might also be placed within a spectrum of labour market policies, with, at one end, a policy of very low governmental intervention in the workings of the labour market, and very high intervention at the other. In practice, each country has produced such a complex matrix of economic and labour market policies that it is exceedingly difficult to illustrate clearly the comparative cleavages. Moreover, the position of each country, in terms of either broad economic strategies or labour market policies, will change over time, sometimes, though not always, influenced by changes in government, e.g., France. The USA, despite the liberal economic rhetoric, is currently running a fairly large deficit, while many of the 'social democracies' are now very anxious to curb the growth in public expenditure and to reduce personal taxation. Our view is, therefore, that very great caution is needed in classifying countries because of the divergence between the public rhetoric and the reality of policy responses. We turn, firstly, to the USA, as the dominant economy in the western world, and as the economy which has clearly been the most effective in producing new jobs rather than being particularly successful at protecting existing jobs by means of subsidies.

6.2 The USA

A starting point for any consideration of the US case is the fact that its economy appears to possess what might be termed a 'jobs engine', which has been creating new jobs at a phenomenal rate by European standards. As the *Sunday Times* put it, there appears to be a great American 'job-burger' across the Atlantic (*Sunday Times* 'Business News', 24.4.84). The US economy has produced a net increase of 24.5 million jobs over the period 1970 – 84 while over the same period the Western European economies have suffered a net loss of 1.5 million jobs. The US economy generated more new jobs in 1983 alone than Europe generated in the decade prior to the recession in 1970. It is vitally important to remember this fact, of the USA's superior 'restructuring dynamic', when considering the unemployment problem in perspective. Although many of the attendant features of the US experience, such as the extreme differences in wealth and the existence of severe poverty, may not be politically acceptable in most of Western Europe, it does not detract from this feature of the relative dynamic of the US economy. This dynamic is, of course, in the service and small business sectors rather than in the traditional manufacturing sector. Some 90 per cent of all new jobs between 1969 and 1976 were in service occupations and it is estimated that, by 1990, 70 per cent of the labour force will be in service occupations (National Commission for Employment Policy, 8th Annual Report, 1982, 9). Just as in the UK, the USA has seen a large cutback in employment in some of its traditional manufacturing industries. For example, Chrysler cut its labour force by two thirds in a decade. Indeed, the US growth rate over the past ten years is inferior to some Western European economies and to Japan (see Table 1.4).

The task facing a government is quite different if it is running an economy which has some in-built 'jobs' dynamic, compared with running an economy, like the UK, which appears to be in a long-term decline, presenting a vast and complex package of policy problems. There are observers who see the whole of Western Europe as a great dinosaur when compared with the USA and Japan (see John Naisbitt, 'Last Days of a Dinosaur', *Sunday Times*, 22.4.84). Of course, this is not to suggest that the US economy is without problems. For example, there appears to be a fairly long-run decline in the growth of productivity in the US. Thus, in 1960, US productivity increased by 7.9 per cent compared with an increase of only 0.8 per cent in 1970, and a decrease of 0.7 per cent in 1980 (see Figure 6.1). In terms of 'measured skills' of its labour force, the US ranked second in the industrial nations in 1963 but had dropped to seventh place by 1981 (National Commission on Employment Policy, 1982, 12). This 'skill problem' produced a truly remarkable statistic for 1981, when, with 10 million people unemployed in the USA, there were nearly one million unfilled skilled jobs. The issue of the 'stock of human capital' is, therefore, likely to be a central one in the USA over the coming decades.

It is, however, surprising (in the context of our present 'gloom' over unemployment) that the US Department of Labor is actually predicting '. . . tighter labor markets, including higher wage rates and less unemployment', with a likely *increase* in the average retirement age as older workers are persuaded to stay on in jobs in the absence of a flood of young workers entering the labour market. The demographic changes will in turn produce changes in the supply of goods and services, with an increased emphasis on those goods and services needed by old people, rather than on the currently popular youth markets.

The practical situation today, is, however, rather different, with 7.5 per cent unemployment in the USA, (representing more than 9 million people out of work, over 2 million less than at the peak of unemployment in 1982). Although this is still high compared with some West European countries, e.g. Sweden, Switzerland and Austria, the most significant point is the rate of fall in US unemployment. The question now is whether this achievement is sustainable given the trade and budget deficits.

The problem 'here and now' has, of course, produced specific policy responses at federal, state and local levels. As Janet W. Johnston has

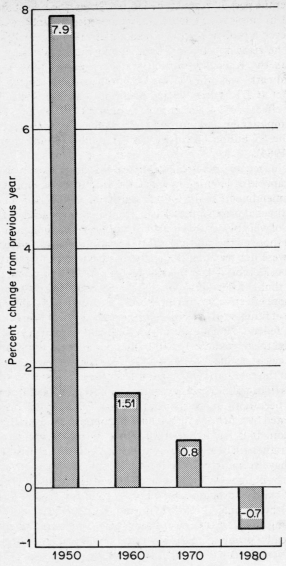

Output per hour of all persons in the private business sector

Source: US Department of Labor, Bureau of Labor Statistics

Figure 6.1   US productivity growth

argued, 'over the past 50 years in the United States, the role of the federal government in employment and training activities has increased dramatically, to reach a peak in the two decades from 1960 to 1980 (Johnston, 1984:57). The great impetus to federal employment and training efforts originated in the Kennedy/Johnson era. Perhaps the most significant federal landmark was the 1973 Comprehensive Employment and Training Act (CETA) (see Richardson and Lawther 1981:73–103). CETA took effect in 1974, and during the period 1974–9 the expenditure on federal employment and training programmes tripled to reach over $9 billion–some $5 billion of which was for public service employment (Johnston, 1984).

CETA is, in fact, an interesting example of the degree to which societies have been capable of learning how to cope with unemployment–in that successive amendments to the CETA legislation produced a much more effectively directed programme. When originally introduced, CETA was the subject of very widespread criticism (especially, though not exclusively, from those on the political right) for various abuses and for the fact that funds were not reaching the really disadvantaged in society. There was also a considerable degree of substitution of federal funds for state and local funds, thus considerably reducing the *net* increase in jobs per dollar. Despite a more effective re-steering of CETA (in terms of tighter controls over the use of funds and better targetting), and despite the fact that by the early 1980s federal expenditure on training and employment measures had stabilised to approximately $10 billion per annum (Johnston, 1984), President Reagan decided to end the CETA programme.

As is often the case in political life, it has proved difficult to kill public programmes (like old soldiers they seemingly never die!) and a new 'son of CETA' has been born in the shape of the Job Training Partnership Act (JTPA), created by Congress in 1982 despite opposition from the Reagan administration. It is fair to see the JTPA as a good example of policy succession, rather than as policy innovation. As in the British case, the Americans have seemingly found it difficult to be really innovative, and instead have built upon past experience – as well as responding to political criticisms of existing programmes. Thus, as Johnston argues, JTPA tries to return to the original objectives of the CETA with its concentration upon directing funds at the most disadvantaged members of society. It also specifically prohibits public service employment (reflecting the current political climate of opinion hostile to the public sector). There is a great emphasis on the contribution to be made by the private sector, with administrative responsibility devolved to the states and at the local level to a partnership of local government and Private Industry Councils (PICs). The emphasis on the private sector is not new – PICs were part of the re-created CETA before its final demise. Before discussing the recent development of JTPA, however, it is useful to note that US responses have in fact shown surprising similarities to those in Western Europe.

As Johnston's detailed review demonstrates, resorting to public job-creation programmes both in the USA and in Europe dates back to the 1930s. Thus, it is not the case that it is only the social democracies that feel that when the economy is in a downturn public funds should be used to create jobs for the unemployed. This philosophy was as evident in the 1970s as it was in the 1930s. Similarly, the USA has been willing to resort to 'targetted' anti-unemployment policies. As Johnston argues, 'counter-structural job creation programmes were politically viable in the 1970s, even though public sector jobs programmes have not proved very effective' (Johnston, 1984). Other programmes – such as work-experience programmes – sound very familiar to British ears, as do the programmes to improve the training and skills of the labour force as well as various hiring subsidy programmes. (In the USA these have usually taken the form of tax credits, with several Congressional Acts to this end. For example, between 300,000 and 500,000 jobs were said to have been created by the New Jobs Tax Credit Act of 1977.)

Johnston's description of the range and number of policy initiatives in the USA sounds more like a Scandinavian democracy than a country whose image is one of hard-nosed competition and private enterprise, although, as noted earlier, these schemes do differ in scale and application. Johnston's view that the many federal training and employment programmes do not constitute a 'carefully planned, comprehensive national employment and training policy' and that there has been no consistent, long-range approach to employment and training is no doubt true. But this would be equally true of the UK and most Western European nations. Whilst the JTPA, according to Johnston, accounts for less than 10 per cent of the total funds spent annually in the USA on employment preparation, it does remain the main thrust for federal programmes.

The Act was signed by the President in October 1982, to become operational in October 1983. The objective of JTPA is to 'establish programs to prepare youth and unskilled adults for entry into the labour force and to afford job training to those economically disadvantaged individuals and other individuals facing serious barriers to employment, who are in special need of such training to achieve productive employment.' 'Most in need' is not defined, and it is stated that the Act is intended to meet specific labour market needs, rather than simply raise skill levels in general. There is thus a potential incompatibility between helping the most disadvantaged and meeting local labour market needs. It is expected that the Act could serve up to 900,000 people each year (compared with an estimated two to eleven million most in need – see Auletta, 1982).

So far, it is too early to evaluate the JTPA's likely impact. There has been, however, a preliminary report on the transition from CETA-type programmes to JTPA programmes (see, An Independent Sector Assessment of the Job Training and Partnership Act. Phase 1: The Initial Transition, MDC Inc. March 1984, Reproduced by the National Employment Commission). There are a few indications of how JTPA will develop. Firstly, it is clear that federal funding has indeed been reduced, with a budget for 1983 of $3.6 billion compared with the 1979 CETA budget of $9.4 bn. The Phase 1 Assessment cites the case of Chicago, with an estimated 500,000 people eligible under JTPA but with funds sufficient for only 13,000. Secondly, labour market considerations look like being of primary importance, rather than the degree to which individuals need help. As one PIC chairman is reported to have said, 'There are plenty of poor people to deal with without worrying about the really difficult to employ.'

Although funding for JTPA is drastically reduced when compared with CETA, and although unemployment has been reduced, there have still been pressures to spend public money on creating jobs in the traditional manner. Thus, a new package of legislation designed to combat unemployment was proposed in February 1983. President Reagan had proposed a $4.3 billion 'emergency' jobs programme, plus almost $3 billion in extended unemployment benefits in the worst-hit areas. Democrats tried to increase these funds for what they argued was a 'make work' programme. The President objected to this description, but the funds were designed to create jobs by employing people on federally funded projects. In the event, some $4.6 billion was appropriated, with an additional $3.9 billion for unemployment insurance programmes in certain States.

What then do we conclude about the USA? It remains an economy of strange contrasts. President Reagan ensured that CETA was ended and that its 'replacement' JTPA received much-reduced funding. Yet, he has been willing to see a large deficit on the US budget and could be seen as Keynesian in practice, in contrast to his liberal economic rhetoric. It is interesting to note that, although Mrs Thatcher has publicly ticked off President Reagan for maintaining trade deficits, as it contravenes shared liberal economic principles, this has actually softened the impact of unemployment in Western Europe since high US demand has enabled Europeans to continue to export to US markets. There is also the huge contrast between the rapid increase in the total number of jobs and the very small rise (compared with Europe) in the rise in US productivity. Within these broad developments, we have seen a range of conventional policy responses, well tried in the so-called social democracies, which we consider next.

6.3 Sweden

Webber (1984) has suggested that, 'There is possibly no single political aspiration with which the social democratic parties in the advanced industrial democratic states have identified themselves more closely than the achievement or maintenance of full employment.' Schmidt has argued that there are certain features of social democracies – particularly their reliance on corporatist structures – which have enabled them to achieve much lower rates of unemployment than Britain and the USA. Thus, Schmidt claims, 'Corporatism is the best single predictor for differential rates of unemployment . . . All the countries with low rates of unemployment during the crisis in the seventies are characterised by either very strong or moderately strong models of regulating the class conflict' (Schmidt, 1981:19). He further argues that the contribution of corporatism, and a distribution of power which is skewed towards the left, tends to guarantee low rates of unemployment even during periods of economic crisis (Schmidt, 1981:21).

Webber suggests that two variables exercise a particularly strong influence on the capacity of 'social democratic' governments to combat unemployment.

The first of these is the closeness of the Social Democratic parties' relationships with the respective national trade union movements *and* the character of these unions. Where these relationships are close and the unions are highly centralised . . ., the conditions for maintenance of a comparatively low level of unemployment are favourable. This was, or has been, the case in West Germany and Austria . . . The second variable which seems to exercise a powerful influence on the capacity, or *will,* of such governments to maintain low unemployment levels is the strength of the Social Democratic *culture* in society – which shapes what levels of unemployment are, or are perceived to be, electorally acceptable or undamaging. (Webber, 1984)

It is beyond dispute that a number of social democratic countries have achieved remarkably low levels of unemployment. For example, the Swedish rate of unemployment (at May 1984) was a mere 2.7 per cent, compared with the UK rate for the month of 12.7 per cent. Sweden, in fact, is a good 'social democratic' case to examine in a little more detail. As Henning suggests, Sweden is often seen as the founder and pioneer of active labour market policies (Henning, 1984b:193). He classifies Swedish responses as: (a) influencing the *supply* of labour, e.g., through measures to stimulate occupational and geographical mobility; (b) influencing the *demand* for labour, e.g., through subsidies to retain or increase employment in companies, by creating opportunities for youth and other disadvantaged groups, and (c) influencing the process by which demand and supply are brought together – what are termed 'matching measures'.

He notes that the expenditure on labour market policy has now risen to approximately three per cent of GNP; and that there has been a continuous increase in the share of expenditure on measures designed to influence the supply of labour, at the expense of measures to influence the demand for labour, from 20.5 per cent of total expenditure on labour market measures in 1965 to 37.9 per cent in 1981–2. Over the same period expenditure on labour market measures as a percentage of total government expenditure rose from 3.2 per cent to 6.1 per cent (Henning, 1984:99). Of particular significance for the British case, is that Sweden has placed increased emphasis on policy instruments very familiar to British eyes – namely subsidies to companies facing closure or proposing large-scale redundancies. In the category of measures which he describes as designed to influence the demand for labour, Henning argues that '. . . there has been a marked change in composition, because aid programmes aimed directly at companies, in order to maintain employment or influence hiring, have increased in importance' (Henning, 1984:197).

In effect, the Swedes, during the crisis, have supplemented their traditional – and much admired – labour market policies (e.g., concern with training and re-training) with a policy of giving loans, subsidies and guarantees to companies in difficulties. It is, of course, difficult to establish, at the moment, whether these companies are experiencing temporary problems due to the international recession, or whether they are now virtual 'lame ducks'. Lundgren and Stahl estimate that public support for industry escalated very considerably in the 1970s: in the period 1976/7 to 1980/1 it amounted to 50 billion Swedish crowns, compared with the preceding five-year period when it was a mere 9 billion Swedish crowns (Lundgren and Stahl, 1980:55). Lundberg has calculated that total subsidies for private enterprise were 90 times greater in 1976 than in 1960 (Lundberg, 1979:26). Henning's conclusion is that Sweden has seen a radical change in its response to the unemployment crisis. He argues that

the hitherto much admired traditional labour market policy, based upon the accepted need for restructuring, flexibility and occupational mobility, has been retained; but increasingly, governments are forced to look at the short-term situation, bearing in mind changed attitudes on the part of the electorate. The Swedish worker is now possibly more like his European fellow workers in demanding secure employment in his existing locality. In this sense the scope for a rather rationalistic and technical employment policy is greatly reduced. (Henning, 214)

The explanation for Sweden's very low unemployment is, as Webber suggests, likely to rest on a range of factors including increased part-time working and increased public sector employment (see Webber, 1983). He does, however, cite the extensive labour market policy measures as the most important factor contributing to Sweden's low level of unemployment – an area in which Sweden has traditionally been very active. More recently, the Swedes have been developing a range of *local* responses to the unemployment crises, in part encouraged by the central government's desire to devolve some responsibility for industry and employment to these levels. These local responses can be grouped within three broad categories.

Firstly, local authorities are encouraging the setting up of new companies, from within their locality, by such policies as analysing project ideas, providing resources for product development, and providing premises, loans and subsidies (Henning, 1984b:5). Secondly, local authorities are encouraging inward investment, again via cheap tailor-made premises, loans, allowances, guarantees, free consultancy advice and services. Thirdly, support is being given to existing companies. An interesting aspect of this activity is the way in which local authorities are assisting companies to formulate applications for subsidies provided by central government agencies – which Henning describes as public officials taking over corporate tasks (1984b:6). Local authorities are also directly subsidising investment and production and are using local purchasing to assist local companies. These local initiatives (in essence further extending the degree of state intervention in the workings of the market) reflect a very significant shift in Swedish attitudes – in particular, a resistance to structural change and to increased mobility. Henning reaches pessimistic conclusions regarding the *real* employment effects of these local measures, notwithstanding the increased involvement of public authorities in the affairs of companies (1984b:15).

Sweden is also an interesting case at the macroeconomic level. For example, the Social Democrats, led by Olaf Palme, devalued the Swedish crown by 16 per cent on taking office (Sweden had devalued several times since 1974), and have expanded expenditure on traditional labour market policy and subsidies to industry (see Industri och Industripolitik 1982–3:15). For the present, that policy seems to have produced spectacular results – for example, industrial production rose by approximately 5 per cent in 1983 and in the first quarter of 1984, was up 8 per cent on the equivalent period in 1983. The growth is particularly strong in export-led companies. Indeed, the Swedish engineering industry has more than doubled its exports since 1969, having increased its exports by 6 per cent (in value) since 1983. The volume of investment in engineering rose by 20 per cent between 1983 and 1984.

Yet, Sweden is also seeing rising inflation, approximately 8 per cent at June 1984, a huge public debt (£45 billion) and a forecasted public sector deficit of £7.2 billion. Thus the OECD has warned Sweden of the desirability of achieving a phased reduction in the budget deficit over the next few years and of the need for a tighter monetary stance. Moreover, it suggests that the brunt of fiscal adjustment will have to be borne by public expenditure (OECD, Feb. 1984). Sweden is very anxious that Western European governments should take steps to increase demand. Finance minister Kjell-Olof Feldt has argued that it is simplistic to think that the labour market can absorb the jobless if only real wages fall sufficiently; demand would have to be allowed to increase substantially in Europe if unemployment were to be reduced (Speech to OECD, Spring 1984). This view was no doubt influenced by the fact that Swedish wage settlements have been running at approximately 10 per cent during 1984 (compared with a UK rate – which is causing worry to Mr Lawson – of just over 7 per cent).

The big question for Sweden is whether they are living in a fool's paradise (see *Sunday Times*, 24.6.84, 'Sweden's welfare bonanza dubbed a fool's paradise'). Certainly, the Swedish employers' organisation is extremely concerned at the pressures which are building up in the Swedish economy. They believe that the devaluation and the current economic upturn have not solved the structural problems of the Swedish economy. They see the large government deficit as likely to prevent necessary increases in private investment and as creating latent inflationary pressures (see *Viewpoint*, Federation of Swedish Industries, No. 3, 1984). If, as critics – and indeed the finance minister – believe, inflation kills the Swedish boom, then Sweden too will be faced with the difficult task of trying to reduce public expenditure, reduce inflation, and restructure its economy whilst trying to maintain its traditionally low unemployment levels. Sweden's gamble is whether its rejection of the current conventional wisdom of economic thinking will work in the context of a world which has turned its face against conventional Keynesian responses.

Should the unhappy scenario materialise, then Sweden will be a good test of the thesis (referred to earlier) that corporatist structures and processes can best handle the unemployment crisis. If the corporatist thesis is correct, Sweden will find a consensual way through its difficulties and will be able to make necessary adjustments without the kind of industrial unrest seen within the British coalmining industry. Moreover, it should be able to ensure moderate wage increases, in contrast to those that followed the breakdown of Labour's social contract. If the thesis is incorrect, then Sweden's corporatist structures will produce what Mancur Olson has termed an 'institutional sclerosis', preventing necessary radical change in its economic and industrial system (Olson, 1982).

6.4 West Germany

Two other cases, West Germany and France, may be particularly instructive for the UK, as societies which have similar industrial and economic infrastructures and attitudes to our own. (Japan – so often seen as the country for the UK to copy – is of course, a very different culture, making policy comparisons very difficult.) West Germany has implemented a range of policies designed to combat unemployment, which by 1982 had reached 7.6 per cent and is currently at 9.1 per cent. These have

included traditional labour market policies (training and retraining programmes, employment subsidies and job creation schemes), personnel
policies in the public sector, policies towards foreign workers and policies
affecting working time. (For a detailed review see Webber and Nass, 1984.)

The most surprising fact about West German responses, under the
coalition, is that not only did economic constraints – predictably – limit
what could be done, but the coalition's retreat from the full employment
goal was in part due to its own change in philosophy (Webber and Nass,
1984:187). The Liberal Party leaders were very influential in getting the
government to pursue a rather restrictive policy, but the Social Democrats
were ready to pursue a 'no alternative' policy. This policy was, of course,
opposed (as it was in the British Labour Party when implemented by the
Callaghan Government) by the trade unions and by the left of the party.
Thus, although the Social Democrats were part of the coalition government for most of the crisis period, West Germany has pursued what
Webber and Nass describe as a neo-liberal crisis management philosophy
(with important changes of emphasis during the 1974 – 82 period) rather
than the social democratic path pursued by Sweden.

West Germany has, it should be noted, demonstrated the phenomenon
remarked in the UK – that governments could survive historically high
levels of unemployment. Thus the Social – Liberal coalition was returned
to office in 1976 and 1980, despite the high salience (as in the UK) of unemployment as a political issue. Part of the explanation for this electoral
success was that the coalition was still seen as being better able to cope
with unemployment. Also, its record, by international comparison, was
reasonably good.

A very special factor in the West German case is that the government
finds it much more difficult than do British governments to influence or
control domestic interest rates. This is because of the special position of
the Bundesbank, which can act quite independently of the government. In
fact, the Bundesbank has operated a tight monetary policy which has
provided the 'backdrop' against which other economic and political actors
have had to play. In this sense, West Germany has been following a policy
much nearer to that of the UK than to Sweden.

Within this broad economic strategy, other particular policy initiatives
have had some effect on the level of unemployment. For example, the
number of foreign workers fell by 730,000 (more than one quarter) over
the period 1973 – 8, although the number of foreign workers began to
grow again after 1978 as the children of foreign workers began to enter the
labour market (Webber and Nass, 1984:178). (Switzerland too, has
managed to maintain low levels of unemployment, in part by 'exporting'
its foreign workers. In the Swiss case, 26 per cent of the foreign workers
present in 1973 had left by 1978 and the labour supply decreased by 7.2
per cent over the same period. By 1978, the level of unemployment in

Table 6.2   *Estimated reduction of unemployment by vocational retraining and work creation programmes in West Germany, 1975–1982 (thousands)*

	1975	1976	1977	1978	1979	1980	1981	1982
Work creation programmes	30	58	61	77	75	59	55	36
Full-time vocational retraining programmes	93	76	54	52	60	73	90	71
Total	123	134	115	129	135	132	145	107

SOURCE: Autorengemeinschaft, 'Der Arbeitsmarkt in der Bundesrepublik Deutschland im Jahre 1982', in *Mitteilungen aus der Arbeitsmarkt-und Berufsforschung*, no. 1, 1982:4

As quoted in Webber and Nass, 1984:171.

Switzerland was a mere 0.4 per cent.) Vocational training and work creation programmes in Germany have had a significant, though declining, impact on unemployment levels, as indicated in Table 6.2.

The total number of persons registered as unemployed in West Germany has risen since the change of federal government on 1 October 1982, by between 300,000 and 400,000. The total for the month of May 1984 was 2,133,200 (8.6 per cent of the workforce), compared with a total in May 1982 of 1,646,000. This rise took place almost wholly, however, within the first six months during which the new government was in office. Between May 1983 and May 1984, for example, registered unemployment declined – but only very slightly – from 2,149,000 to 2,133,000. The economic upswing since early 1983 has not yet had any strong positive impact on the labour market. Indeed, seasonally-adjusted, unemployment rose in the successive months March, April and May 1984. Any upswing in the economy seems to be heavily dependent on increased exports.

In general, there has been a high degree of continuity between the employment policies of the old and the new federal coalition governments, although the Christian – Liberal coalition has cut a range of welfare benefits (such as the primary unemployment benefit for single people, from 68 to 63 per cent of the former net income, and the secondary unemployment benefit by a lesser amount) which an SPD-led coalition would have been unlikely to do. The 'change of direction' in federal economic policy which was ushered in by the Social – Liberal coalition has possibly been accentuated by the new administration.

The new government has continued to pursue a restrictive overall budgetary policy. A range of cuts in public spending was made immediately after the government took office, amounting to between DM 5 and 6 billion, to be followed by another, larger package of cuts implemented after its election victory in March 1983. It is striking that, despite the growth in 'average' registered unemployment, from 1,833,000 in 1982 to over 2.2 million in 1983, the federal budget deficit could be lowered from around DM 37 billion to DM 31.5 billion; and that, despite increased unemployment, the BA (federal labour market administration) is forecast to achieve a surplus of DM 3 – 5 billion in 1984, compared with, in 1982, a deficit of DM 7.1 billion. This latter figure, in particular, reflects the powerful impact of cuts in unemployment benefits, other measures making unemployed persons ineligible for benefits, and increases in unemployment insurance contributions.

Among the benefits cut by the new coalition has been the maintenance grant for persons taking part in vocational retraining programmes (cut by the same amount as the primary unemployment benefit). It has also been made harder to obtain a grant for any retraining which is not regarded as strictly necessary. However, in September 1983, the number of persons participating on retraining programmes was, at 184,000, some 5,000 higher than in September 1982. Furthermore, publicly funded job-creation programmes have been expanded and will employ an average of 70,000 persons in 1984, compared with about 23,000 at the end of 1982. However, the first steps to reverse the cutbacks which first took effect in 1982 were actually taken while the old government was still in office.

No new kinds of employment subsidies have been introduced and there have been no temporary programmes to try to stimulate the economy, save one programme aimed at boosting the house-construction industry that was agreed on the government's accession to office. (Conditions for the granting of employment subsidies, etc., have, in fact, been further tightened.) In real terms, public investment has continued to fall, although more as a consequence of cutbacks in local, than federal, government expenditure.

For the first time in almost thirty years, employment in the public sector will stagnate in 1984. Public sector employment increased by 15 per cent between 1970 and 1974, and by 9 per cent between 1974 and 1979. This increase was mostly at the state and local levels, with employment at the federal level actually decreasing. The current stagnation of public sector employment, and the development of public expenditure and investment volumes, indicate that the state and local governments are also pursuing restrictive budgetary policies.

The government has introduced a temporary scheme offering financial incentives to non-EEC foreign workers who decide to return to their countries of origin, and reports suggest that over 50,000 of them might take advantage of the scheme. This is, however, a very small proportion of the 1,808,000 foreigners employed in West Germany (June 1982 figures).

The federal government has vigorously opposed the trade unions' push for a shorter working week. The Chancellor described the demand for a

35-hour working week, before the beginning of the May/June 1984 industrial conflict, as 'dumb and stupid' (a description often applied to himself), although he later remarked that cuts in working-time would not be 'taboo'. In order to try to strengthen the hand of the few rather conservative unions who are more interested in an earlier retirement age, the government, in 1983, passed a 'framework' law permitting collective agreements on retirement at the age of 58. The terms of this legislation have not proved very attractive for the unions, however, and its usage up until now does not seem to have been very widespread.

Other government policies – such as a reduction in company taxation and the relaxation of legislative curbs on the hours which apprentices can be compelled to work or start work – bear the trademark of neo-liberal crisis management. Some government propaganda also puts heavy emphasis on the accelerated introduction of new technologies such as cable television, as a major source of new jobs.

6.5 France

France has proved to be perhaps the most interesting Western European case, because of the reversal of the Socialist Government's attempt to implement a truly Keynesian (and socialist) policy after its election in 1982.

Registered unemployment in France totalled 1,645,000 when Mitterrand won the presidential election in May 1981, and carried on rising to top the two million mark in the last couple of months of that year. Between December 1981 and December 1983, the Socialist – Communist coalition government succeeded in almost stabilising the level of unemployment, which, seasonally-adjusted, totalled 2,119,000 in December 1983, 2,025,000 in December 1982 and about 1,880,000 in December 1981 – a much less rapid growth of unemployment than in West Germany over the same period. The government began, however, to abandon its initially expansionary demand-management policy during 1982 and adopted a major package of retrenchment measures in March 1983. The number of registered unemployed increased in the first three months of 1984 by more than it had done in the entire previous year. The seasonally-adjusted total at the end of April 1984 was 2,296,000 (an unemployment rate of 10 per cent). The French prime minister has forecast that the level of unemployment will reach 2,450,000 by the end of the year. Another minister has expressed the fear that, by then, the total will have reached 2,600,000. Having done more than most other Western states to withstand, or postpone the impact of the 1980 – 2 recession, France is now emerging from the recession more slowly than most other states. The OECD forecasts that the French economy will grow in 1984 by 1.2 per cent, compared with an average for the EEC of 2.2, and for the OECD world as a whole, of 4.2 per cent.

Faced with a large and growing deficit in the unemployment insurance funds, the government carried out a range of cutbacks affecting unemployment benefits and pensions for early retirers. The most generous of a range of unemployment benefits was cut from 90 to 80 per cent of the person's former income. The period for which benefits are paid was shortened for numerous benefits and, for others, the period for which contributions have to have been paid before benefits can be drawn was increased. The government has laid great weight on curbing the rise in the tax burden and containing the growth, or reducing the size, of the budget deficit (which is, in any case, as a proportion of GNP, low in France).

After introducing a 39-hour working week (with no loss of pay) in 1982, the government left further initiatives to the parties to collective-bargaining, who have reached no fresh agreement on this issue. Prime Minister Mauroy – after a very long silence – has renewed (in Spring 1984) his belief in the necessity of further cuts in working-time. This probably has to be interpreted as a gesture in the direction of the trade unions on account of their dissatisfaction with the consequences of the government's policy of industrial restructuring. This dissatisfaction had begun to increase considerably by mid-1984, and there was violence at the Talbot car plant at Poissy resulting in concessions over the size of proposed job losses and improved redundancy payments. This was followed by open attacks on the government from the head of the pro-socialist CFDT union because of the lack of consultation over the government's restructuring programme. The Communist CGT, in its statements, has been equally hostile to the government.

After having initially given foreigners living and/or working illegally in France the opportunity to 'legalise' their residence or employment, the government has now adopted a tougher stance towards foreign workers (who, with their families, make up about 8 per cent of the French population). This must be seen as a response, in turn, to the anti-foreign workers rhetoric of the Gaullists and the growth of the National Front. (A poll in September 1983 found that 51 per cent of the French thought that sending foreign workers 'home' was the best way of combating unemployment.) Following the Poissy conflict, the government proposed a new scheme offering financial incentives for foreign workers who wanted to return 'home'. An earlier, similar scheme did not, however, prove very appealing.

Most of the recent measures announced to try to curb the growth of French unemployment appear to amount to only slight variations on the old themes of French employment policy (encouragement of earlier retirement, vocational training courses for young unemployed, etc.). From the beginning of 1984, employees have the possibility of taking a sabbatical between six and eleven months long to try to set up their own businesses – and of returning to their old jobs, if they wish, at the end of the period if their venture does not succeed. Possibilities have also been created for employers to hire unemployed persons temporarily. Special measures have been announced offering tax and other incentives for investments in firms in the regions, such as Lorraine, worst hit by the accelerating decline of the traditional industries. There is also to be a 'retraining holiday' (for up to two years) for — probably quite a small minority of — workers made redundant in such industries. This latter measure may also be understood as an attempt to reduce opposition to mass redundancies in the coal, steel and other industries.

As always, France appears to be a country of contradictions. As Marie-Françoise and René Mauriaux suggest, on the basis of their survey of unemployment policy in France 1976 – 82, 'the combination of innovations and continuity, the juxtaposition of contradictory measures, and changes of intention make real change difficult to identify' (1984:164). Moreover, there have been changes in the *measurement* of unemployment, with a proliferation of indices of unemployment, creating considerable confusion. The French have found that economic and industrial reality is a hard task master. At the end of the day, the process of restructuring the economy — reducing subsidies for the mining industry, reducing subsidies to the steel and motor industries and reducing the size of the labour force in those industries, etc. — is as painful in France as it is in the UK. Thus, the Socialist Government's coal policy (often quoted by Mr Scargill in the 1984 miners' strike as a policy which Britain should copy) in fact plans for a real reduction in support for the industry over the next five years. Similarly, the government has announced steel job losses of 20,000 by 1987, one-fifth of the total labour force.

6.6 Conclusion

The late Michael Shanks, writing in 1982, drew attention to the possibility that the present economic crisis, leading to high unemployment, might have been inevitable. Thus, the Western capitalist nations may be going through a long-term fluctuation, lasting twenty or twenty-five years and known as the Kondratieff cycle (Shanks, 1982:8). According to Kondratieff, capitalist development takes place in 'bursts', driven by technical change, after which the world is in a situation of captial saturation. If this thesis is correct, then it will not be until the 1990s that the world will begin to enter a new 'burst' of economic activity. There is a danger, in what Shanks terms the post-manufacturing economy, that there will be a substantial minority which just cannot find employment in the new economy that will eventually emerge.

So one very disagreeable feature of post-manufacturing society could well be the existence of a sub-class of excluded men and women, more or less permanently unemployed ... The risk that they would become permanently disaffected, a focus for increasing crime and violence is a real one . . . This is perhaps the biggest danger for the West from the present recession. (Shanks, 1982:30)

Touleman and Vandamme have also warned of the likely problems of re-structuring the economies of Western Europe, pointing out that any policies which are likely to retard industrial change will exacerbate the crisis. They quote the statement, by the Economic and Social Committee of the European Community in 1977:

The Community will lose out in the forthcoming adjustment process if it pursues an industrial policy which seeks to preserve the status quo, rather than adjust the industrial sector to a changing world; if this happens, the plight of the Community's unemployed will be even worse and the prospects of those who have jobs will be still more uncertain. (Quoted Touleman and Vandamme, 1982:20)

It is clear that all Western governments recognise that this process of structural change has its own dynamic. In practice, the 'politics of unemployment' has represented an attempt to manage the social and economic, and political effects of this powerful process. Typically, the policy responses have been through some measures to stimulate the demand for labour, measures to reduce the supply of labour, and measures to assist the matching of supply and demand. In practice each country has devised its own 'package' of responses and in each case unemployment has undoubtedly been less high than it might otherwise have been. In almost every country, governments have eventually paid the political price of high unemployment, although – surprisingly – governments have, for periods, won elections in the face of high unemployment (notably, but not exclusively Mrs Thatcher's Government).

It is possible that, in each country, governments of both right and left must be seen to preside over high unemployment before governments are re-elected. There is always a huge gap between the size of policy response and the actual job-creation effects, such that we might be forgiven for seeing policy responses as more akin to placebos than a cure for the disease. Policies may be ineffective in significantly reducing unemployment (or may, by reducing unemployment, be temporarily holding back necessary and inevitable structural change), but may be very effective in bringing the patient to come to terms with an incurable disease. Governments, by relatively pragmatic responses – despite their ideological rhetoric – may be guiding us through a Kondratieff cycle until we reach more favourable times. So far, Western societies seem to have exhibited that skill and maturity necessary to manage societies in this difficult transition phase.

In the British case, it might be reasonable to argue that the adjustment process is proving particularly painful because of a reluctance on the part of all governments in the past to see the process of adjustment take place. For example, by being prepared to prop up smokestack industries rather than radically reinvest or restructure we have merely postponed our 'exit' from these industries. The exit process is taking place in all Western democracies, at varying rates. In our concluding chapter, we consider the prospects for the UK, beyond the restructuring phase.

7 Conclusion

7.1 The prospects for unemployment

In earlier chapters, we discussed some of the factors which have affected the level of unemployment in the UK – for example, the international economic situation, government policies, the relative lack of British competitiveness, and the basic structural problems of British industry. These (and many other) factors interact against a cultural background which may not be fully understood and which seems likely to restrict the range and effectiveness of responses available.

Thus, to take a particularly controversial example, Britain is, in 1984, having tremendous difficulty in effecting a relatively small reduction in its planned output of coal, with the attendant shedding of 20,000 coal-mining jobs, with no management threat of enforced redundancy. Whatever the rights and wrongs of the handling of the dispute between the National Coal Board and the National Union of Mineworkers, the dispute does illustrate the importance of the restructuring process in British industry and the importance of deeply held values in limiting the rate of change. The coal-mining industry is in many respects a typical example of the difficult process through which the UK is passing. Thus employment in coal mining was 602,100 in 1960, but had fallen to 287,200 in 1970/1 and to 207,600 by 1982/3. This massive fall in employment in this traditional 'smokestack' industry was bound eventually to produce bitter resistance on the part of the workers and their families who were the victims of what is probably an inevitable process.

Whilst many were shocked by the violence of the 1984 dispute, it did illustrate the depth of feeling which could result from the restructuring process. Quite why, in 1984, the proposed job losses should provoke such a violent reaction when massive job losses had taken place peacefully in the 1960s is difficult to explain. One important fact is, undoubtedly, the existence of already high levels of unemployment in Britain. Quite simply, the need to restructure and to increase competitiveness has arisen – because of the international economic situation – just at the time when there are few alternative employment opportunities open to those who might lose their jobs. In this sense, it might be argued that Britain was very badly served by its politicians and civil servants in the relatively good years of the 1950s and 1960s, when it might have been easier to facilitate the restructuring process and to increase our competitiveness, and when resources and opportunities were available to cater for the 'victims' of the process.

The UK is now faced with every prospect of a continuation – or indeed an increase – in its level of unemployment. As one commentator noted, 'jobs in manufacturing are still melting like snow in summer', despite a gradual recovery in output in the UK since 1981 (*The Economist*, 23.7.84). In mid-1984 there were 1.2 million people who had been out of work for over a year, out of a total of more than 3 million unemployed. Moreover, the *supply* of labour, because of demographic trends, is continuing to grow at a rate little short of the rate of creation of *new* jobs in the economy. Thus Britain is running very hard in order to stand still.

Like other Western economies, the service sector is growing, but relatively slowly (approximately 0.9 per cent per annum since 1973). Further, there is evidence that we have seen a de-coupling of the relationship between economic growth and increased employment. Surveys conducted on behalf of the CBI Special Programmes Unit suggest that the majority of firms in the UK can expand their output quite considerably without taking on extra labour. If this proves to be true in practice, then Britain could be quite successful in achieving faster economic growth (given an improved international economic situation), yet this would pass the 3 million unemployed by, as the vast majority who have jobs grew richer. The government's own publication, *Social Trends,* reveals that the gap between the haves and the have-nots is in fact widening (Social Trends, 14, 1983). The problem is, of course, not unique to Britain. For example, the OECD has estimated that the Western nations will need to create 20,000 jobs *per day* over the five years up to 1989 if they are to reduce the level of unemployment to 1979 level (OECD Employment Outlook, September 1983).

These astronomical figures begin to lose all meaning in terms of individuals caught up in these trends. In practice, for governments, it means trying to find solutions to specific examples of job losses. For example, the proposed closure of the Leyland truck plant at Bathgate in Scotland will make 1,700 workers redundant by 1986. Just how many new small firms would need to be created (bearing in mind the very high failure rate of new small firms) in order to absorb the workforce of even one truck plant is difficult to imagine. Any realistic assessment would suggest that only a tiny fraction of redundant workers will be absorbed in this way – yet, the fact remains that the national and international truck market has collapsed and it was, therefore, perfectly rational (in economic and financial terms) for Leyland to propose closing the plant. Although the small firm is seen by all governments as one of the main solutions to the unemployment crisis, it can only be so in the very long term as the few really successful small firms become the big employers of the future.

Neither is 'new technology' likely to be a particularly successful solution. Significantly, government ministers have begun to express some doubts as to whether new technology really will be a sufficiently large source of new jobs to absorb the continual shedding of traditional manufacturing jobs in Britain. Thus, in June 1984, in a speech to the British Footwear Manufacturers' Association, the Secretary of State for Employment is reported as saying that '. . . there has been too much talk recently about sunrise and sunset industries'. Similarly, the Parliamentary Under-Secretary of State for Industry is reported as saying that 'high tech' was not an alternative to 'low tech' and that we should not neglect the prospect of our traditional industries (see Congden, 1984).

The Scottish example is particularly significant, in terms of the scope for shifting the nature of employment from being based on traditional manufacturing to an economy based on 'new tech' and service industries, as Scotland has made particularly vigorous efforts to encourage new technology. In the Scottish case there has been a loss of 123,000 manufacturing jobs since 1980, but a five-fold increase in employment in the electronics industry. Despite this tremendous achievement in electronics, some 200,000 fewer people are employed in Scotland in 1984 than was the case in 1979. This is, of course, not an argument against governmental intervention to encourage 'new tech', though intervention has its costs – both in terms of finance and in terms of fewer public resources for existing industries. Without the intervention, it is probable that the net loss of jobs would have been even greater – and the consequent political unrest too.

It could be that, at a certain point, the new technological revolution really will begin to take off. Certainly, the Scottish Development Agency believes that the electronics industry in Scotland has reached what it describes as 'critical mass' (see SDA Annual Report for 1984) and that, as a result, Scotland is high on the list of 'high tech' companies wishing to invest in Europe. A more cautious note has been expressed by the OECD, warning that microelectronics might have a greater impact on the levels and nature of skills required and on organisational structures than on the aggregate demand for labour (OECD, 1982). Britain, like other Western European nations, might be in a 'catch 22' situation where 'new tech' does not generate sufficient employment to mop up the loss of jobs in manufacturing (and our service sector is growing much slower than, say, that of the USA), but if we do not invest in new technology our competitiveness will decline still further. In short, 'new tech' may not be the cure, but without it the disease will worsen.

An added problem for Britain is that we will eventually have to cope with declining oil production and will therefore face what the Chancellor of the Exchequer has described as the 're-entry' problem (*The Times*, 10.4.84). He is optimistic that the economy will be in a position to cope with this process, which will in any case be partly cushioned by interest and profits from Britain's acquisition of overseas assets during its oil boom, but, as he conceded, other factors will need to be right for Britain to be successful in this 're-entry' phase – such as exchange rates. Our struggle for increased competitiveness is far from won. As the CBI's Director of Social Affairs argued in early 1984, Britain's competitiveness is on a 'knife edge' (see *The Times Business News*, 23.3.84).

The drive to increase our competitiveness is far more complex than adjusting exchange rates or lowering unit wage costs. It involves cultural factors. Does our 'national character', for example, encourage competitiveness and entrepreneurship? (see Weiner, 1981) and certainly raises questions about the 'stock of human capital'. In the long run, we need a more effectively trained labour force if we are to compete, yet to achieve this requires not only money, but a willingness to change on the part of deeply entrenched interests in society, such as the professions, as well as the trade unions. Education in scientific subjects is a good example. In addition to the relatively poorer teaching in mathematics, sciences generally are not valued as highly in the UK as, for example, in West German or Japanese schools. A government report indicated that 90 per cent of UK primary school teachers have no science training and that science resources in secondary schools are grossly inadequate (DES, 1982).

Further evidence of this British disease was provided in a report to a conference of the Association for Science Education, suggesting that the 'O' level and CSE physics examination papers included no questions on developments since 1930; and that only 14 per cent of boys and 9 per cent of girls study the three main branches of science: physics, chemistry and biology (DES (1982) *Science in Schools;* see *The Times*, 5.1.84).

For Britain to raise the standard of scientific attainment of its population probably requires a fundamental change in our attitude to the subject, and to the way we organise its teaching in schools, starting in primary schools. If it is possible to raise the general standard of attainment (as indeed Sir Keith Joseph believes it is for general numeracy), then the actual benefits – in terms of better levels of technical and scientific ability in the labour force – will take at least a generation to become apparent. Similarly, 'more and better engineers' (a current buzz slogan in the UK) may or may not improve our competitiveness, but will in any case be very difficult to achieve quickly.

All governments have seen fit to try to address these very broad issues in the hope that somehow their combined effects will produce relative success. The present so-called non-interventionist Conservative Government is heavily involved in job-creation programmes, via the MSC, intervening to stimulate new technology, trying to change attitudes to engineering in society, and generally trying to raise the level of skills and training through education and training reforms. One very considerable difficulty is that all of our main competitors have exactly the same ideas and policies. They are not standing still while Britain catches up – in that sense the finishing line is moving all the time!

An added problem is that we may, as a society, decide either that it is impossible to compete with certain countries or that the price of successful competition is just too high in terms of the sacrifices needed in our basic cultural values. Thus Japan – which has done so much to harm the fortunes of UK and Western European industries – may be impossible to compete against unless we become like the Japanese, in their attitudes towards work, leisure, education, and so on. We may decide that Britain does not want, say, to have its children studying mathematics to the same intensity as Japanese children, or to organise our working lives to the same degree of 'order' as the Japanese do.

In total, successfully competing with the Japanese could radically change the way of life in Western Europe, and we may collectively, through the EEC, decide that such competition is 'unfair'. The cry 'copy the Japanese' may yet produce a more fundamental debate on how we want to live and work in modern British society. But there are, of course, other possibilities for trying to cope with mass unemployment. Just as there is no real agreement on the causes of unemployment, so there is no agreement on its solution – hence a flourishing debate on policy options.

7.2 Changing the balance of policies?

If current predictions are correct – that unemployment in the UK will remain at its very high level, or rise, over the next few years – then there is no doubt that the intensity of debate over practical policy responses, irrespective of the broader issue such as life-style, will intensify. At its most stark, the debate can be summarised by two quotations from a recent House of Lords debate. Lord Cockfield, Chancellor of the Duchy of Lancaster, while admitting that the burden of the recession had been carried by those out of work, claimed that, 'The unions, and particularly their leaders, must bear a major share of the responsibility for this. Excessive pay increases extracted by the union leaders have left employers no alternative but to reduce employment, in order to remain competitive and stay in business.' In contrast, Lord Wells-Pestell, for the Opposition, argued that, 'the Government's belief that mass unemployment must be suffered by the poor as the price of wealth creation could only lead to disaster and physical violence. Violence was the language of the hopeless, the frustrated and the depressed' (House of Lords Debates, 4 July 1984). Similarly, an ex-Conservative MP, Sir David Lane, has urged that it is time, not only for a change of style, but in the direction and emphasis of policy in order to restore hope to the many sufferers of the recession (*The Times*, 30 June 1984).

The present government may find it increasingly difficult to resist a change in direction, especially as powerful pressure seems to be building up for more selective action. Thus, the CBI has further emphasised its desire to see more public spending on 'infrastructure', which it believes will increase Britain's competitiveness, and has called for an extra £1 billion a year to be spent over the next decade on road, rail, water and other public works (see CBI, June 1984). In part this expenditure, the CBI argued, would be offset by reductions in other areas of public spending, in a proposed £6 billion programme for reducing employment in the civil service, local government and the health service, and for increasing efficiency of the public sector. Such a shift in national priorities would be difficult politically, although there appears to be developing a coalition of interests pressing for selective increases in public expenditure. (In practice, the CBI and TUC are not that far apart on demanding selective measures, e.g., in construction.)

Indeed, the government is itself committed to changing the allocation of resources – for instance in its proposals, announced in December 1983, for a complete redesign of Britain's regional industrial policy (Regional Industrial Development Cmnd 9111, December 1983). Britain, having spent some £20 billion (at 1982 prices) on regional aid over a period of twenty years, seems set to try to shift the direction of this aid, away from capital developments towards those developments which look like producing the most jobs. Whilst, in principle, this seems a sensible objective (essentially the government hopes to create more jobs per pound under the proposed new system) the political problems of achieving that objective seem daunting, as those interests who benefit from the existing arrangements gather their forces to try to prevent radical policy changes. No doubt, concessions will have to be made (to Scotland and Wales, for example), as the final policy emerges from the extensive consultations which were held on the White Paper.

The 'selective reflation' argument is likely to gather momentum, pressurising the government to do more. Similarly, the argument for a more general reflation will continue to be pressed (by both the government's supporters and by its critics). However, the practical difficulty in such a policy might be that, as in the past, Britain will merely suck in more foreign imports of consumer goods, with UK manufacturers failing to exploit the opportunities presented by a general reflation. This again illustrates the extreme difficulty of governments (of whatever political party) trying to balance competing and conflicting objectives. A general reflationary response would also have the obvious implications for public expenditure. In a document leaked to *The Times*, the Treasury, in one of its scenarios, warned that public expenditure could be 6 per cent higher as a percentage of GDP, by 1990 – 1, than it was in 1979 – 80, if economic growth and productivity growth were sluggish. In any case, there is likely to be extreme pressure on public resources because of projected increases in welfare spending (due to demographic changes) and because of the difficulty of managing the defence budget (assuming no big changes in stated defence policy).

This conflict is as apparent at the micro-level of the economy as it is at the macro-level. For example, it would be in the interests of British consumers if the EEC policy of trying to force car manufacturers to bring European prices into line could succeed, as it would reduce the price of cars in the UK. On the other hand, it is very doubtful if British Leyland (and other car manufacturers located in the UK) could withstand the increased competition (which is why BL has tried to block the import of right-hand drive Leyland cars purchased elsewhere in Europe). Yet again, the problem of our lack of competitiveness emerges as a key issue, constraining policy choice. A protectionist policy (for some sectors) would also run the risk that the British consumer would end up paying more for his goods and that there would then be no real incentive for UK manufacturers to produce the right products for the international market. Protectionism, for it to work, would need other public policies (more government intervention) in order to prevent British industry becoming used to 'feather-bedding'. Policies in response to unemployment will, therefore, continue to evolve by a process of 'muddling through', in the hope that something will turn up, either in terms of a world economic recovery, or that, in total, the various UK measures will begin to have a positive impact.

7.3 The changing nature of work and attitudes to work

Whilst we may succeed in muddling through the unemployment problem (as we have done since 1974), other changes may be taking place which, if they do not actually solve the problem, may assist in redefining it. It is often suggested that we are seeing 'changing working attitudes'. This usually implies that, not only does the population *wish* to work less – preferring early retirement, working fewer hours per week, and having longer holidays – but also that this would implicitly relieve the unemployment problem. This is because more employees would be needed to achieve existing levels of output, and because, in exercising their leisure, workers would create job opportunities in the service and consumer products sector.

The country which has been foremost in achieving reductions in working hours is Sweden, where there has been a clear societal shift in preference towards more leisure time during the 1970s (Webber, 1983). Indeed, in 1984, a survey of Swedish employees conducted by the Ministry of Labour indicated that 51 per cent would prefer shorter working hours at current wages to higher wages at current working hours. Only just over one-in-five part-time workers wanted increased hours (SIP, *Newsletter from Sweden*, 6.6.84). In the UK, considerably more hours per employee are worked in the year than in her main European competitors (see Eurostat, various). Interestingly, it was the German trade union movement that was in the forefront of the battle for shorter hours in the West German engineering industries, in order to protect jobs. This is unlike most British trade unions, with the notable exception of ASTMS and some TUC committees, who see overtime working as an essential supplement to the basic wage.

The EEC has recently recommended that all member states should work towards a 35-hour week. This, however, has been resisted by the British government, who believe that where shorter working weeks have been achieved, employees simply do more overtime, so cancelling out any overall employment benefits. The main obstacle to the achievement of shorter working weeks in the UK is, of course, that trade unions do not wish to see corresponding reductions in pay, whilst employers will resist any threat of increased production costs. Another point is that marginal reductions in working time are absorbed by productivity agreements, and thus no employment benefits accrue. Employers are understandably wary of reducing working hours when the most successful industrial nations – USA and Japan – both have long working weeks.

The government has attempted to meet any demand for a shorter working week by means of the Job Splitting Scheme. However, as indicated earlier, this has initially been met with a rather low response, though it should be added that this is a more radical attempt by government at reducing working time than has been made elsewhere in Europe, where smaller reductions in individual working time have been achieved more widely.

Most recently, the retiring TUC General Secretary, Len Murray, expressed sympathy for a trade-off between lower wage rises and more jobs. The TUC has raised the example set in France, Belgium and Holland of 'solidarity contracts', such that additional workers will be hired as hours, and in some cases, wages, are cut by the existing workforce. Whether the TUC can secure the confidence of the mass of individual unions over this principle remains to be seen.

Early retirement is the other main element in the 'reduced working time to reduce unemployment' argument. Although Britain's statutory maximum retirement age is in line with that of most of her competitors, there are considerably fewer opportunities for early retirement, due either to long service, disability, or flexible pension arrangements. The termination of the requirement of unemployed men who receive no benefit to register as unemployed, and the treatment of those unemployed men over 60 as retired persons by immediately granting them long-term rates of supplementary benefits, provide at least a cosmetic change in policy in order to reduce the numbers in the labour market. The government's other main response to this has been first the Job Release Scheme, which was especially sophisticated in that it was designed simultaneously to create jobs for the unemployed (Chapter 3). This has had a good response, though its part-time variant has hitherto attracted only a small number of participants.

A more comprehensive policy of early retirement is, of course, much more difficult to achieve, requiring upheaval in public and private pension schemes. It is possible that if the current proposals for 'transferable pensions' were achieved, early-leaving pension provisions might fall in their wake. The broader problem is, of course, that like most Western societies, the UK is facing in addition to mass unemployment, an increase in the proportion of old people. This threatens a future whereby a diminishing workforce is expected to provide – in the form of tax payments – for a growing retired cohort. Thus, there is a policy rationale for not increasing early retirement too quickly, as well as one for increasing it.

In addition to making some changes in the working time to absorb unemployment, the government is also seeking to change broader attitudes to work in order to improve the country's competitiveness, and thus create jobs. These have been summed up in the recommendations of the Treasury to the NEDC debate, 'Where will the new jobs be?', held in December 1983. It suggested that employees should be more willing to move to jobs from the high unemployment areas, and that they should accept more flexible work contracts, permitting either variation in hours per week worked, or annual hour contracts, or seven-day working or multi-shift working. Here again is a superficially good proposal which, in practice, may entail strong opposition from trade unions and resistance to change on an even larger scale than that witnessed in the miners' strike. Conversely, it is possible that many unions will accede to such changes simply *because* of the current levels of unemployment.

One of the possible future solutions to unemployment may thus be in the linking of the unemployment problem with a contemporary potential 'silent revolution' detected in post-industrial societies: the change to an emphasis on non-material values (Inglehart, 1977). If it is the case that citizens demand different kinds of 'goods' which require more leisure, then part-time working, job-sharing and early retirement policies may find fertile soil in many Western systems. Other European powers are certainly attempting to exploit this convergence, but the record of the British Job Splitting Scheme to date suggests that greater political impetus is required in this country to develop it as a contribution to easing unemployment. Whilst exploring these possibilities might be a fruitful avenue for Britain, we have tried to show that there would be accompanying adverse policy effects which would also have to be taken account of.

7.4 The political consequences of high unemployment

If our thesis is correct – namely, that unemployment will continue at a very high level, that it is extremely difficult to devise effective solutions, and that a general Keynesian reflation is fraught with difficulties – then are we not sitting on a political time bomb, if only because Britain is so clearly two nations, consisting of those who have a job and those who cannot get one?

The evidence, so far, suggests that if it is a time bomb, governments have been rather effective in preventing it from exploding. Much of this 'success' is due to the fact that governments have been rather pragmatic about it. Despite the strictures from Mr Pym, Mrs Thatcher has often behaved like a traditional Conservative when faced with the political reality. In practice, the Conservative Government, just like its Labour and Conservative predecessors, has been very active indeed in trying to respond to the unemployment crisis. The Government has managed to perform the very difficult feat of, on the one hand, driving home the message that Britain really must become more competitive and that this was not really within the power of *governments* to achieve, and, on the other hand, being active in introducing policies, such as YTS, various 'high tech' support schemes, and inward investment policies, so that it could be seen to be at least trying to solve the problem.

In this sense, the direct responses to unemployment are rather like placebos, possibly having no long-term curative properties but performing the essential function of enabling the patient to come to terms with what could turn out to be an incurable disease. We use the term placebo, not in any perjorative sense, but merely to indicate that, though genuinely meant to help the unemployed, the policies do not have the capacity to effect a cure. These policies have been backed up by use of the 'numbers game' and by certain changes in attitudes to unemployment (which cannot directly be linked to government policies), and have produced a great political success for the present government: public expectations have been lowered, and unemployment is more widely accepted as being here to stay.

All this has enabled the government to pursue its broader objective of increasing Britain's international competitiveness, where considerable improvements in productivity were long overdue. The government can thus claim some success in combating what many see as Britain's most serious disease: overmanning. Demanning (or 'shakeout' as Sir Harold Wilson called it when he was at No. 10) has been achieved, albeit causing many personal setbacks and public expenditure costs. (We are not of course arguing that *all* current unemployment is a function of demanning.) It remains to be seen whether emphasis on improving Britain's international competitiveness will in fact stimulate economic growth, and whether enough is being achieved in this respect.

It also remains to be seen whether the Conservative Government can continue to avoid the full obloquy that would normally accrue to a government with 3,084,000 people (at June 1984) on the dole. Its chances of doing so will depend as much on the effectiveness of the opposition parties as it does on the government's own actions. The issue will continue to retain its political salience and therefore its potential for being exploited. Moreover, all of the evidence suggests that the British electorate is now extremely volatile in its voting habits – and far more prone to issue-voting than, say, in the 1950s. As Särlvik and Crewe suggest, the erosion of party loyalties continues to soften the Conservatives' as well as Labour's electoral base. They argue that, '. . . the February 1974 election signalled a crisis in confidence in the established party system from which it has not recovered' (Särlvik and Crewe 1983:333). The combination of a 'de-aligned' electorate and the very high salience of unemployment as an issue is an unpredictable amalgam in terms of electoral fortunes.

The political effects of the unemployment issue are also difficult to predict in other respects. Being out of work does not itself produce political radicalism and social unrest. The fact that Britain is a democratic country with a long-established system of welfare support, and that there are few long-standing unattended grievances, means that unemployment can be managed as a single (though complex) issue rather than as a reflection of other deep-seated social grievances. (The exception is, perhaps, the ethnic minorities in the UK who may link the two issues of unemployment and racial discrimination and become more militant, as in the Toxteth and Bristol urban riots.) Britain in general does not present a fertile soil for the type of radicalism caused by an authoritarian regime exploiting the masses. (The line of the song that goes 'As soon as this pub closes the revolution starts' may be not only a joke, but an accurate reflection of British attitudes to revolutionary change!) We do not have a radical working class movement capable of being mobilised against the state.

Neither are the unemployed themselves organised as an effective pressure group. Although unemployment policy is characterised by a considerable degree of pressure-group activity (the unemployment industry, as we termed it) those groups acting on behalf of the unemployed are not run by the unemployed themselves. The unemployed could perhaps be regarded as a latent pressure group, but have yet effectively to be mobilised as a political force. If anything, the unemployed are almost underground, as 'interests' go. For example, in Scotland there appears to be a 'samizdat' press in operation, with a rash of underground newspapers emerging in the last two years.

One such paper, *Beat the Dole Drum,* published by Grampian Unemployment Union, claims to have 6,000 readers. In one issue, it advised them all to turn up at the local DHSS office for the arrival of visiting Inspectors from the government's Specialist Claims Control Unit, so as to give them a rough welcome. Its specific advice was nothing if not unusual in terms of the history and development of pressure group activity in

Britain, namely 'Just turn up at Elbury House, 10.30 a.m. and bite their bums'! Other papers in Scotland include *The Lothian Unemployed Worker*, the *B'roo News: the Voice of the Unemployed in Stirling* (B'roo being the Scottish word for dole), and *The Newsletter of the Motherwell Unemployment Club*. Much of their concern appears to be with unemployment benefit (and with 'snoopers' from the DHSS), rather like the Claimants' Union, but they also give tips on reduced-price leisure activities for the unemployed – such as cheap entry to cinemas, leisure centres, etc.

What evidence there is suggests that the hard core permanently unemployed are far more likely to opt out of society – and to create their own sub-cultures with, for instance, underground newspapers, etc. – rather than become politically active. This containment of the problem is assisted by the fact that the majority of the unemployed manage to find a job in less than a year, and possibly accept a period of unemployment as inevitable nowadays – rather like actors who have traditionally expected to be out of work for significant periods. The potential explosiveness of unemployment will also be reduced, to some degree, by resorting to the black economy and by the fact that in many cases *someone* in the household has a job.

Thus, ironically, the political problems are more likely to come from those sections of society already well integrated into the political process, such as established Tories. To quote another Scottish example, the Conservative Convenor (Chairman) of Lothian Regional Council publicly criticised his party in May 1984 for not having a conscience over unemployment. He argued that the problem of unemployment was 'stirring up tremendous social problems in the long run' (*The Scotsman*, 30.4.84).

The irony of some of the specific policy responses referred to earlier is that they may themselves unwittingly increase resentment if they are seen not to work. The Youth Training Scheme could yet prove to be such an example, if 'graduates' of the scheme fail to find work on the open labour market. Their disenchantment with 'the system' could be all the greater if they feel that they have been duped into believing that the acquisition of more skills and more experience would improve their employability. It is safe to predict, as we come to the end of the first year of YTS, that there will be an overriding political imperative to develop 'YTS plus' in order to take these youths off the streets. The alternative would be to see opposition parties exploit the issue of a 'lost generation' who spend their lives taking drugs and vandalising our inner cities. In such circumstances, political rhetoric will be brushed aside by political expediency (and quite justifiably so).

Such a depressing scenario also raises the question of the funding of further anti-unemployment, or 'mopping up' schemes. Conventional wisdom has it that we are already over-taxed and that further taxation, to fund further increases in public expenditure, is not possible (hence the beginnings of a debate, in Britain, on how we can fund the increasing costs of an ageing population in the decades ahead).

Yet, a recent survey suggests that we are *not* near or at the limits of our capacity to squeeze more money out of taxpayers. Fewer than ten per cent of respondents wanted a tax cut if this meant lower spending on health, education, and social benefits (Jowell and Airey, 1984). If we were to conclude that the only short-to-medium-term solution to the unemployment crisis, should it begin to get out of hand in political or social terms, is more publicly funded job-creation and training schemes, then this survey evidence suggests that those who are in work might be willing to pay higher taxes for those out of work. As Hibbs and Madsen suggest, the composition of the tax burden is of central importance. 'The long-run cause of welfare state backlash is the expansion of the system based on rapidly rising, highly visible general revenue taxes . . . from the political point of view the optimal tax system thus relies heavily on indirect and programmatic (earmarked) taxes' (Hibbs and Madsen, 1981:434). Similarly, Hemming and Kay have argued that ' . . . the evidence runs strongly against the argument that tax rates in Britain, or any other country, are at levels such that the maximum available tax revenue is close to being obtained . . . if we ask the question "would it be possible, if it were thought desirable, to raise substantially more tax revenue than is at present derived in the UK?" then we believe that the answer is "yes" ' (Hemming and Kay, 1980, 86–7). Moreover, it could be argued that ultimately citizens will come to realise the benefits of taxations, as well as the obvious costs (Tufte, 1980:568). Thus, provided that considerable political skill – and will – is used, it might be possible to devise specially earmarked taxes in order to fund carefully designed anti-unemployment measures.

It is also true that the government has the option of saving money on other public policies (e.g., on its nuclear defence policy) if it so decides. Part of the political skill would be in devising schemes which both participants and taxpayers regarded as worthwhile. Counting lamp posts, and such like, would, naturally diminish the public esteem of such programmes (just as the Arts Council diminishes its public support by funding piles of bricks or old motor tyres as 'art') and would increase hostility to higher taxes.

But the exact opposite reaction can, of course, occur. For example, the Countryside Commission has recently complained that the MSC's decision to cut back its support for environmental schemes will hit the Glamorgan Heritage Coast Project in a severe way. The officer in charge of the scheme commented that 'countryside management successfully tackles many jobs which otherwise get neglected. Job creation has provided massive impetus but this new policy is going to affect it very badly indeed' (Countryside Commission News, May 1984). In the USA, the early CETA programmes became notorious for supporting 'non-jobs', and Senator Proxmire instituted the 'fleece of the year award' for the worst example of nonsense funded under CETA! A delicate path has to be trodden between leaving the unemployed as third-class citizens, ignored by those of us who have jobs, and creating the impression amongst the employed that 'make work' schemes are a soft option, providing a very comfortable life for the unemployed while the rest of us have to work harder and harder in the new entrepreneurial competitive Britain. Indeed, the more we succeed in developing an American-style entrepreneurial and competitive spirit, the more likely it is that the majority could slip into thinking that those who fall by the wayside do so because they lack the right spirit and have not helped themselves.

We can conclude by suggesting that, from the political perspective, unemployment in Britain has been managed surprisingly successfully. The future pattern is extremely difficult to predict, but there is no reason to assume that our political system cannot cope. If social unrest on a significant scale does occur, then the system is likely to respond with new schemes and new money. Such a process might see Britain through to an economy which is more productive, and has been restructured, with a better-trained and more efficient workforce. On the other hand, the finely tuned political system might merely manage to ensure that our decline continues to be relatively graceful.

Bibliography

Allen, Rod, Anwer Bati and Jean-Claude Bragard (1981), *The Shattered Dream: Employment in the Eighties*, London, Arrow.

Ashford, Nigel (1984), 'Consensus and Conflict Within NeoLiberalism', *Strathclyde Papers on Government and Politics*, No. 34.

Auletta, Ken (1982), *The Underclass*, New York, Random House.

Barnett, Joel (1982), *Inside the Treasury*, London, André Deutsch.

Booth, Simon and Douglas Pitt (1983), 'A Paradox of Freedom: Conservative Interventionism in the Scottish Economy', *Strathclyde Papers on Government and Politics*, No. 23.

Brown, R.G.S. (1974), *The Administrative Process as Incrementalism*, Open University Press.

Butler, David and Dennis Kavanagh (1974), *The British General Election of February 1974*, London, Macmillan.

Butler, David and Dennis Kavanagh (1975), *The British General Election of October 1974*, London, Macmillan.

Campbell, Mike and Douglas Jones (1982), 'Racial Discrimination against Asian School Leavers', Unemployment Unit Bulletin, No. 5.

Casey, Bernard (1983), *The Development of Labour Market Policy: A comparison of trends and volume of interventions in Austria, France, The Netherlands and the U.S.A., in the period since the world recession of 1974/75*, Berlin, Wissenschaftszentrum.

CBI (1981), *Company Responses to Unemployment, a Report by the Social Affairs Directorate*.

CBI (1984), *Fabric of the Nation*.

CBI SPU (1983), *Record of Achievement and Programme for 1983*.

CBI SPU (1983) *Community Action Programmes 1981–83*.

Central Statistical Office (1983), *Social Trends*, HMSO.

Central Statistical Office (various) *Monthly Digest of Statistics*, HMSO.

Cmnd 8455 (1981), *A New Training Initiative: an Agenda for Action*.

Commission for Racial Equality (1982), *Young People and the Job Market – A Survey*.

Commission for Racial Equality (1983), *Annual Report 1982–1983*.

Community of St Helen's Trust (1984), *Director's Report to Trust Supporters July/December 1983*, No. 2.

Community Service Volunteers (1982), *CSV Reports 1981–82*.

Congden, T. (1984), 'A Case for Ending High Technology Incentives that Penalise Traditional Industry', *The Times Business News*, July 4, 1984.

Conservative Central Office (1976), *The Right Approach*.

Conservative Party (1970), *A Better Tomorrow*.

Conservative Party (1971), *National Union of Conservative and Unionist Associations Conference Verbatim Report*.

Conservative Party (1972), *National Union of Conservative and Unionist Associations Conference Verbatim Report.*

Conservative Party (1974), *Putting Britain First* (October).

Conservative Party (1979), *The Conservative Manifesto.*

Crewe, Ivor (1981), 'Why the Conservatives Won', in Howard R. Penniman (ed), *Britain at the Polls* (1979), Washington, American Enterprise Institute for Public Policy Research.

Crewe, Ivor (1983), 'Why Labour lost the British election', *Public Opinion,* July 1983.

Daniel W.W. (1981), 'Why is high unemployment still somehow acceptable?', *New Society,* 19.3.81.

Deacon, Alan (1981), 'Unemployment and Politics in Britain since 1945', in Brian Showler and Adrian Sinfield (eds), *The Workless State,* Oxford, Martin Robertson.

Deakin, B.M. and C.F. Prattern (1982), *Effects of the Temporary Employment Subsidy,* Cambridge, CUP.

de la Cour, Michael (1983), 'MSC Report on the Long Term Unemployed', *Unemployment Unit Bulletin,* No. 8.

Department of Employment (various) *Employment Gazette.*

DES (1982), *Science in Schools,* HMSO.

Downs, Anthony (1972), 'Up and Down with Ecology – The Issue Attention Cycle', *Public Interest,* pp 38 – 9.

Economist Intelligence Unit (1982), *Coping with Unemployment: The Effects on the Unemployed Themselves.*

Finer, S.E. (1956), *Anonymous Empire,* London, Pall Mall.

Food and Drink Manufacturing EDC (1983), *Review of the food and drink manufacturing industry,* NEDC.

Foot, Michael (1984), *Another Heart and Other Pulses,* London, Collins.

Frey, B.S. and H. Garbers (1971), 'Politico-Econometrics – On Estimation in Political Economy', *Political Studies,* Vol. XIX, No. 3.

Frey, Bruno S. and Friedrich Schneider (1978), 'A politico-economic model of the UK', *The Economic Journal,* Vol. 88, June.

Friedman, Milton (1976), *Inflation and Unemployment: The New Dimension of Politics,* (The 1976 Alfred Nobel Memorial Lecture), Institute of Economic Affairs, Occasional Paper 51.

Gilmour, Sir Ian (1983a), 'Policies fading, prospects grave', *The Times,* 13.10.83.

Gilmour, Sir Ian (1983b), *Britain Can Work,* Oxford, Martin Robertson.

Glasgow Council for Voluntary Service (1982), *Annual Report 1981 – 82.*

GLC (1983), *Jobs for a change.*

Goodhart, C.A.E. and R.J. Bhansali (1970), 'Political Economy, *Political Studies,* Vol. XVIII, No. 1.

Grayson, David (1983), 'Sheffield's Employment Department', *Initiatives,* No. 4.

Gregory, Roy (1984), 'The Local Government Response to Unemployment in the UK', in Jeremy Richardson and Roger Henning (eds), *Unemployment: Policy Responses of Western Democracies,* London, Sage.

Harris, Jose (1972), *Unemployment and Politics: A study in English Social Policy, 1886 – 1914,* Oxford, Oxford University Press.

Harrison, Martin (1982), 'Television News Coverage of the 1979 General Election', in Robert M. Worcester and Martin Harrop (eds) *Political Communications: The General Election Campaign of 1979*, London, George Allen & Unwin.

Hayward, J.E.S. (1974), 'National Aptitudes for Planning in Britain, France and Italy', *Government and Opposition*, Vol. 9, No. 4, Autumn 1974.

Heald, David (1983), *Public Expenditure*, Oxford, Martin Robertson.

Hemming, R. and J.A. Kay, (1980), 'The Laffer Curve', *Fiscal Studies*, Vol. 1, No. 2, 83–90.

Henning, Roger (1984a), 'Industrial Policy or Employment Policy? Sweden's Response to Unemployment', in Jeremy Richardson and Roger Henning (eds), *Unemployment: Policy Responses of Western Democracies*, London, Sage.

Henning, Roger (1984b), *Local Industrial and Employment Policy – An Element in the Swedish Bargaining Economy*, Stockholm, F.A. Radet.

Hibbs, D.A. Jr, and H.J. Madsen, (1981), 'Public Reactions to the Growth of Taxation and Government Expenditure', *World Politics*, Vol. XXXIII, No. 3, 413–35.

House of Commons (1983), *Committee of Public Accounts, 4th Report*, 104.

Howells, David J. (1980), 'The Manpower Services Commission: The First Five Years', *Public Administration*, Vol. 58, No. 3.

Incomes Data Services Ltd. (1984) *YTS: A Review* Study 311.

An Independent Sector Assessment of the Jobs Training Partnership Act. Phase 1. The Initial Transition (1984), Washington, D.C. National Employment Commission.

Industri och Industripolitik 1982–3 (1983), Stockholm.

Inglehart, R. (1977), 'Political Dissatisfaction and Mass Support for Social Change in Advanced Industrial Society', *Comparative Political Studies*, Vol. 10, No. 3, October 1977.

Johnston, Janet Wegner (1984), 'An Overview of U.S. Federal Employment and Training Programmes', in Jeremy Richardson and Roger Henning (eds), *Unemployment: Policy Responses of Western Democracies*, London, Sage.

Jordan, A.G. and Jeremy Richardson (1982), 'The British Policy Style or the Logic of Negotiation?' in Jeremy Richardson (ed) *Policy Styles in Western Europe*, London, George Allen & Unwin.

Jordan, Bill (1982), *Mass Unemployment and the Future of Britain*, Oxford, Basil Blackwell.

Jordan, Grant (1984), 'Enterprise Zones in the UK and USA: Ideologically Acceptable Job Creation?' in Jeremy Richardson and Roger Henning (eds), *Unemployment: Policy Responses of Western Democracies*, London, Sage.

Joseph, Sir Keith (1978), *Conditions for Fuller Employment*, Centre for Policy Studies.

Jowell, Roger and Colin Airey, (eds) (1984), *British Social Attitudes. The 1984 Report*, Gower, Aldershot.

Keegan, William and R. Pennant-Rea (1979), *Who Runs the Economy?: Control and Influence in British Economic Policy*, London, Maurice Temple Smith.

Keogh, G. T. and Peter Elias (1980), 'Regional Employment Prospects' in Robert M. Lindley (ed), *Economic Change and Employment Policy*, London, Macmillan.

Kogan, Maurice (1971), *The Politics of Education. Edward Boyle and Anthony Crosland in Conversation with Maurice Kogan*, London, Penguin.

Labour Party (1970), *Now Britain's Strong – Let's Make It Great to Live In.*

Labour Party (1971), *Labour Party Conference, Verbatim Report.*

Labour Party (1972), *Labour Party Conference, Verbatim Report.*

Labour Party (1974), *Britain Will Win With Labour,* (October).

Labour Party (1979), *The Labour Way is the Better Way.*

Labour Party (1982a), *Economic Review*, No. 14.

Labour Party (1982b), *Programme for Recovery.*

Labour Party (1982c), *Britain on the dole: Unemployment and the Socialist Alternative.*

Layard Richard (1982), *More Jobs, Less Inflation: The Case for a Counter-Inflation Tax*, London, Grant McIntyre.

Liberal/SDP Alliance (1982), *Back to Work*, Interim Report of the Liberal/SDP Alliance Commission on Employment and Industrial Recovery.

Liberal/SDP Alliance (1983), *Back to Work – The Alliance Plan for Creating Jobs*, (Press Release).

Lundberg, L. (1979), 'Subventionerna till industrin', quoted in Henning (1984a).

Lundgren, N. and I. Stahl, 'Industripolitikens spelregler', Stockholm, Industriforbundets forlag.

Makeham, Peter (1980), *Youth Unemployment*, Research Paper No. 10, Department of Employment.

McGrath, Pam (1983), 'Community Task Force Rose to YTS Challenge', *Youth Training News*, No. 3.

Miller, W. L. and M. Mackie (1973), 'The Electoral Cycle and the Asymmetry of Government and Opposition Popularity: an alternative model of the relationship between economic conditions and political popularity', *Political Studies*, Vol. XXI, No. 3.

Miller, W. L. (1984), 'There Was No Alternative: The British General Election 1983', *Strathclyde Papers on Government and Politics*, No. 19.

Minford, Patrick (1983), *Unemployment: Cause and Cure*, Oxford, Martin Robertson.

Moon, Jeremy (1983a), 'Policy Change in Direct Government Responses to UK Unemployment', *Journal of Public Policy*, Vol. 3, No. 3.

Moon, Jeremy (1983b), 'The Spectrum of Issue Salience: Britain and European Economic Integration 1950 – 1963', *Strathclyde Papers on Government and Politics*, No. 14.

Moon, Jeremy and J. J. Richardson (1984a), 'Policy-making with a Difference? The Technical and Vocational Education Initiative', *Public Administration*, Vol. 62, No. 1.

Moon, Jeremy and J. J. Richardson (1984b), 'The Unemployment Industry', *Policy and Politics*, Vol. 12, No. 4.

Moon, Jeremy, Chris Moore, and J.J. Richardson (forthcoming), *Local Partnership and the Employment Crisis.*

MSC (1975), *Annual Report 1974 – 75.*

MSC (1976), *Annual Report 1975 – 76.*
MSC (1977), *Annual Report 1976 – 77.*
MSC (1978), *Annual Report 1977 – 78.*
MSC (1980), *Annual Report 1979 – 80.*
MSC (1981a), *Review of Services for the Unemployed.*
MSC (1981b), *A New Training Initiative: A Consultative Document.*
MSC (1981c), *A New Training Initiative: An Agenda for Action.*
MSC (1982a), *Annual Report 1981 – 82.*
MSC (1982b), *Labour Market Quarterly Report.*
MSC (1982c), *Manpower Review 1982.*
MSC (1982d), *CEP is Working: The Report of a study of the Community Enterprise Programme*, Research and Development Series No. 7.
MSC (1982e), *Voluntary Organisations and Manpower Services Commission Special Programmes.*
MSC (1982f), *Youth Task Group Report.*
MSC (1983a), *MSC Corporate Plan, 1983 – 1987.*
MSC (1983b), *Towards an adult training strategy.*
MSC (1983c), *Annual Report 1982 – 83.*

National Commission for Employment Policy, *Eighth Annual Report*, No. 15, Dec. 1982, Washington, D.C.
Northern Ireland Development Agency (1980), *Annual Report 1979 – 80.*

OECD (1982), *Microelectronics, Robotics and Jobs*, Paris.
OECD (1983a), *Historical Statistics 1960 – 81*, Paris.
OECD (1983b), *Employment Outlook.*
OECD (1984), *Economic Surveys 1983 – 84*, Sweden.
Olson, Mancur (1982), *The Rise and Decline of Nations – Economic Growth, Stagflation and Social Rigidities*, Newhaven, Yale University Press.

Parkinson, Michael and James Duffy (1984), 'Government's Response to inner-city riots: the Minister for Merseyside and the Task Force', *Parliamentary Affairs*, Vol. XXXVII, No. 1.
The People and Work Unit (1984), *Young People in Gwent: A Report.*
Pinto-Duschinsky, Shelley (1981), 'Manifestoes, Speeches and the Doctrine of the Mandate' in Howard R. Penniman (ed), *Britain at the Polls, 1979*, Washington, American Enterprise Institute for Public Policy Research.
Pissarides, Christopher A. (1980), 'British Government Popularity and Performance', *The Economic Journal*, Vol. 90, September.
Platt, Steve (1983), 'Unemployment and Parasuicide ("Attempted Suicide") in Edinburgh 1968 – 1982', *Unemployment Unit Bulletin*, No. 10.
Pliatzky, Leo (1982), *Getting and Spending: Public Expenditure, Employment and Inflation*, Oxford, Basil Blackwell.
Peston, Maurice (1981), 'Economic Aspects of Unemployment', in Bernard Crick (ed), *Unemployment*, London, Methuen.
Pym, Francis (1983), 'Jobs: the case for compassion', *The Times*, 1.12.83.

Regional Industrial Development, Cmnd 9111, December 1983.
Richardson, J. J. (1982), 'Political Problems in Reducing Public Expenditure: The Experience of the Thatcher Government in Britain', *Politica*, No. 1.

Richardson, J. J. (1983), 'The Development of Corporate Responsibility in the UK', *Strathclyde Papers on Government and Politics*, No. 1.

Richardson, J. J. and W. Lawther, (1981), 'Problems of Steering and Control in Decentralised Public Programmes: U.S. Manpower Policy', *Policy and Politics*, Vol. 9, No. 1, 1981, 72–103.

Richardson, J. J. and Joan Stringer (1981), 'The Politics of Change: With Reference to the Politics of Industrial Training Policy 1964–1980', *Industrial and Commercial Training*, February 1981.

Riddell, Peter (1983), *The Thatcher Government*, Oxford, Martin Robertson.

Robertson, David (1971), 'Content of Election Addresses and Leaders' Speeches', in David Butler and Michael Pinto-Duschinsky, *The British General Election of 1970*, London, Macmillan.

Rodgers, William (1984), 'A Winter's Tale of Discontent', *The Guardian*, 7.1.84.

Rose, Richard (1964), 'Parties, Factions and Tendencies in Britain', *Political Studies*, Vol. 12, No. 1.

Rothschild, Lord (1976), 'The Best Laid Plans...', Israrel Seiff Memorial Lecture, London.

Rouse, Lynda and Dominic Hobson (1981), 'The Causes of Unemployment', *Politics Today*, No. 19, 26.10.81.

Särlvik, B. and I. Crewe, (1983), *Decade of Dealignment. The Conservative Victory of 1979 and Electoral Trends in the 1970s*, Cambridge University Press, Cambridge.

Schmidt, Manfred G. (1981), 'Economic crisis, politics and rates of unemployment in capitalist democracies in the seventies', Paper presented to the European Consortium for Political Research Workshop. Unemployment and Selective Labour Market Policies in Advanced Industrial Societies, Lancaster, 1981.

Scottish Business in the Community (1983), *Chairman's Statement for the year 1982–83*.

Scottish Development Agency (1980), *Annual Report, 1980*, Glasgow.

Scottish Development Agency (1981), *Annual Report 1981*, Glasgow.

Scottish Development Agency (1984), *Annual Report 1984*, Glasgow.

Shanks, Michael (1982), *Work and Employment on Post-Manufacturing Society*, European Centre for Work and Society, Maastricht.

Sheffield City Council (1982), *Employment Department: An Initial Outline*.

Showler, Brian (1980), 'The Political Economy of Unemployment', in Brian Showler and Adrian Sinfield (eds), (1980), *The Workless State*, Oxford, Martin Robertson.

Sinfield, Adrian and Brian Showler (1980), 'Unemployment and the Unemployed in 1980' in Brian Showler and Adrian Sinfield (eds), (1980).

Sked, Alan and Chris Cook (1979), *Post-war Britain: A political history*, Harmondsworth, Penguin.

Social Trends, **14**, 1983.

Stewart, Michael (1977), *The Jekyll and Hyde Years: Politics and Economic Policy since 1964*, London, Dent.

Strathclyde Regional Council (1983), *Social Strategy for the Eighties*.

Taylor, Marilyn (1983), 'Growing up without work: a study of young unemployed people in the West Midlands', in *Growing Up Without Work*, European Centre for Work and Society, Maastricht.

Todd, Graham (1984), *Creating New Jobs in Europe: How Local Initiatives Work*, Economist Intelligence Unit, Special Report No. 165.

Touleman, Robert and Jacques Vandamme, (1982), *Industrial Change and Employment Policy in the European Community*, European Centre for Work and Society, Maastricht.

Treasury (various), *Economic Progress Report*, London, HMSO.

TUC (1983a), Economic Review, *The Battle for Jobs*.

TUC (1983b), *Youth Training: A TUC Guide and Checklist for Trade Union Negotiators*.

Tufte, E. R. (1980), book review, *American Political Science Review*, Vol. 74, No. 2, 567–8.

Tym Roger and Partners (1984), *Monitoring Enterprise Zones: Year Three Report*.

Webber, Douglas (1983), 'Combating and Acquiescing in Unemployment? Economic Crisis Management in Sweden and West Germany', *West European Politics*, Vol. 6, No. 1.

Webber, Douglas (1984), 'Social Democracy and the Re-emergence of Mass Unemployment in Western Europe', in William E. Paterson and Alastair H. Thomas (eds), *The Future of Social Democracy*, London, OUP.

Webber, Douglas and Gabriele Nass (1984), 'Employment Policy in West Germany', in Jeremy Richardson and Roger Henning (eds), *Unemployment: Policy Responses of Western Democracies*, London, Sage.

Weiner, M. J. (1981), *English Culture and the Decline of the Industrial Spirit 1850–1980*, Cambridge University Press, Cambridge.

Welsh Development Agency (1981), *The First Five Years*.

White, Tony (1983), 'Voluntary Organisations in YTS', *Youth Training News*, No. 4.

White Paper on Employment Policy (1944), Cmnd 6527.

Wilson, Harold (1979), *Final Term: The Labour Government 1974–1976*, London, Weidenfeld & Nicolson.

Yuill, Douglas (1980), 'Regional Incentives in the United Kingdom', in Douglas Yuill, Kevin Allen and Chris Hull (eds), *Regional Policy in the European Community*, London, Croom Helm.

Index